YEAR
of the COW

YEAR
of the COW

How 420 Pounds of Beef
Built a Better Life for One
American Family

JARED STONE

FLATIRON
BOOKS
NEW YORK

www.flatironbooks.com

Designed by Kathryn Parise

LIBRARY OF CONGRESS CATALOGING-IN-PUBLICATION DATA

Stone, Jared.
　　Year of the cow : how 420 pounds of beef built a better life for one American family / Jared Stone.
　　　　pages cm
　　ISBN 978-1-250-05258-2 (hardcover)
　　ISBN 978-1-250-05379-4 (e-book)
　　1. Cooking (Beef)　2. Meat cuts.　I. Title.
　　TX749.5.B43S76 2015
　　641.6'62—dc23

2014042130

Flatiron books may be purchased for educational, business, or promotional use. For information on bulk purchases, please contact the Macmillan Corporate and Premium Sales Department at 1-800-221-7945 extension 5442 or write to specialmarkets@macmillan.com.

First Edition: April 2015

10 9 8 7 6 5 4 3 2 1

For Summer

"Tell me what you eat, and I will tell you what you are."

—Jean Anthelme Brillat-Savarin

Contents

Acknowledgments

I'm disproportionately blessed to be surrounded by such wonderful, talented, and charming people—without any number of whom, this book would not exist.

First and foremost, I'd like to thank my wife, Summer, for saying yes to yet another ridiculous adventure. And my kids, Declan and Nora, for being such bundles of wonderful wrapped up into two compact packages.

Enormous thanks to my fantastic agent, Laurie Fox at Linda Chester Literary Agency, for her endless patience and sage counsel.

Huge appreciation goes to Frank DePalma and Darlene Chan for believing in this project before they had any reason to.

My utmost gratitude to Bob Miller, Jasmine Faustino, Whitney Frick, and everyone at the brand-spanking-new Flatiron Books for taking me into the fold and letting me be a part of their very first offering.

Deepest appreciation to Eben Copple for always giving me the lowdown on culinary matters both great and small. And, perhaps most vitally, for first showing me the power and joy of a beautiful meal, one night in college many years ago.

Thank you to my parents, Ray and Judy Stone, for always encouraging me in whatever asinine insanity I happened to dream up that day.

Thanks to Billy Mernit, Steve Mazur, Sarah Adina Smith, Barbara Stepansky, and the rest of the writers I've workshopped with for many high fives and well-deserved punches in the gut.

Thanks to Chris Kerston, formerly of Chaffin Family Orchards, for taking so much time to show a city kid the ropes.

Finally, to Ben Krout, Zac and Katie Alexander, Rich and Natalie Courtney, Uriah Bueller, Andy Loos, Jen Hooker, Allan Holt, Chris Martin, Roo Krout, Mike Odishoo, and anyone else I've broken bread with since this beast landed in the box in my backyard: Thank you so much for your kind words and encouragement, through good meals and bad. Let's do it again sometime.

YEAR
of the COW

Prologue

I work in television. I know television. I studied it in college, read about it in books, and spent a considerable chunk of my adult life deciphering the arcane machinations through which an image moves from life to lens to living rooms across America.

However, for much of that time, I knew next to nothing about the food I ate. The little pieces of the world around me that eventually become my physical body. The stuff that, quite literally, becomes me.

Meat, for example. Meat does not originate shrink-wrapped to Styrofoam in a supermarket. When we eat meat, an animal dies.

This transaction with death is a Rorschach for the soul. How you feel about it says a lot about you—how you feel about animals, how you view your relationship with the natural world and humanity's unique place within it. In today's hyperpolarized environment, it possibly even speaks of where you come from and what your political beliefs are.

Set apart from that discussion is the fact that many Americans don't feel anything at all about their meat. For them, it may as well originate in their local supermarket. It's like flypaper, Frosted Flakes, and fluorescent lighting. It just is.

I grew up in Kansas in a family of hunters. Every autumn, my father and brother would take a deer, and it would feed us through the High Plains winter. I never participated in their hunts—just wasn't my thing—but the origin of the contents of our freezer was never in question. Its head was literally on the wall.

As life went on, however, I lost the connection that I once had to the source of my meals. I think it's spectacularly irresponsible to assume that the rest of the ecosphere exists solely for the nourishment and comfort of humans. When an animal dies so that we can eat, that's a big deal. That's important.

Yet as an adult, I was eating from the same Styrofoam trough as most of America.

One spring day, I reflected on my prairie youth from the comfort of my West Coast home and asked myself a question: Am I doing this right—am I feeding my family in the best way that I possibly can?

I like asking questions. I ask a lot of them. I tend to research more than is probably wise, and definitely more than is prudent. Ask me about dogs, midcentury jazz, or the martial arts of southern China and I will gleefully ruin your cocktail party.

And so I found myself asking more and more questions about the food that kept me upright: What is good food? What makes it so? I talk a good locavore game, but walking it is tough. How can I feed my family in the most ethically and environmentally responsible way? And how can I get really damn good at it?

So, naturally, I decided to buy a cow and cook the entire thing, little by little, over the course of a year.

I'm a decent cook. You won't find me in the kitchen of the French Laundry, but I don't cook out of a box either. To paraphrase comic artist Jeph Jacques: Cooking is science for hungry people. I love science, and I love delicious things. Cooking is a skill I've honed simply by virtue of years of repetition and intermittent hunger. I'm no pro, but I know a thing or two about technique, watch a lot of Alton Brown, and have a lot of friends in the industry.

Hell, I used to work in the industry, if you count getting yelled at by drunken cowboys in a pancake house at three in the morning while you're bringing them waffles as working in the industry. But I digress.

To rectify my food chain ignorance, I had to start somewhere. So I decided to focus my attention on beef, partly because it seems like such a quintessentially American food and partly as a salute to my childhood near the cattle trails of the High Plains. I asked myself, how is beef raised? What is the animal's life like? Which beef option is the best for a consumer? Or is any? And how can I maximize both sides of the beef production/consumption equation? Finally, would I still be a carnivore at the end of this project?

I was also morbidly curious about how my beef experiment would affect me physically. I've always been relatively fit, though not outrageously so. However, at the beginning of this project, I'm pretty sure that my friends started taking out life insurance policies on me. That can't be a good sign. Frankly, though, my curiosity was dramatically greater than my fear. I was ready for adventure. A new project. The chance to shake up a daily routine that had become too, well . . . routine. The promise of great meals and great experiences shared with friends.

I began to research.

Most cattle raised in the United States are raised on grain. That is, the majority of their diet is corn, which is cheap and highly caloric and bulks up the cattle quickly. Envision, if you will, a herd of cattle romping gaily through a cornfield, nibbling all the while. Can't imagine it? That's because it doesn't happen. In this scenario, the corn is shipped in to feedlots, combined with a protein source, ground into gruel, and fed to the cattle. Hence the term *corn-fed*—meaning "huge"—which is immediately familiar to anyone who's ever seen the University of Nebraska football team.

This grain-fed production model also allows a lot of animals to be raised while remaining confined to a relatively small space; they don't need to forage for food. Thanks to heavy corn subsidies, it's also cheap.

The other option for consumers is grass-fed beef. Here, the cattle graze on pasture, like in *City Slickers* or any other movie you've ever seen where a guy wears a nonironic bandanna. It takes longer for cattle to grow to market weight on a diet of grass—and ranchers need more room to do it because the animals need to wander around and eat the lawn. However, cattle raised this way are generally healthier than those raised on corn. As a result, they don't need the heavy doses of antibiotics that corn-fed animals usually require. Antibiotics, as any kid will tell you, are not delicious.

In addition, grass-fed beef are generally raised without growth hormones and steroids, which frequently help grain-fed beef reach their Herculean proportions. Personally, I prefer to avoid chowing down on 'roided-out Anger Cattle.

There is also evidence that grass-fed beef has higher levels of omega-3 fatty acids (the good ones) and lower overall fat content. People who enjoy grass-fed beef tend to be passionate about it, trumpeting its more intense "beefy" flavor and sparking near-oenophilic discussions of *terroir*.

I decided on grass-fed beef for my family. Better for the cow. Better for the environment. And better for us.

My research quickly led me from the whys of grass-fed cattle to the wheres of grass-fed cattle. When buying an entire beast, the simplest and most cost-effective method is to go directly to the rancher. I discovered Eatwild.com, which is something like eHarmony for people seeking humanely raised produce and livestock. And from there, I discovered Chaffin Family Orchards—they like cooking, meeting new people, and long walks on the beach.

The more questions I asked, however, the more I discovered lying in wait. How did we come to depend on feedlot beef, anyway? And what other changes were wrought by our disengagement from the mechanisms of our food supply?

Most people aren't farmers—less than a third of households even have gardens. For most of us, our only participation in the food supply is as consumers: We buy it. The decision to purchase an entire cow may seem batshit crazy for a city dweller like me, but it's relatively common for someone in a more rural setting who's closer to the guts of the food supply infrastructure. I think that Chris, my rancher, actually had to suppress a smile a few times while hearing me discuss this project. "I got kids," some of his other customers reported. "Gimme three sides."

Buying an entire grass-fed steer led me to the investigation of ancestral foodways—the ways that people used to eat for hundreds or thousands of years. And these ancestral foodways led me to a novel place. Beyond Slow Food and locavore street cred. Beyond offal epiphanies and lazy afternoon braises.

I realized that what I was really seeking through this project was a doorway to a more soulful life. I yearned for some sort of yeoman platonic ideal where I wasn't penned in an office building through the entire Southern California summer, where the toil of my days would yield the feasts of my evenings, where I'd get home before dark and see my family before bedtime.

What I came to understand is that this doorway doesn't exist. It's a road. And it's long. And like so many other trips, the journey is just as important as the destination.

And so one sunny Saturday afternoon, I set off. The project would grow well beyond a year, well beyond food, well beyond me, and well beyond anything I ever expected.

1

Meet the Meat

O ne cow is approximately one Prius-full of meat.

This is the latest fact I've learned in the past twenty-four hours. It's also the most pressing, as the aforementioned cow has been frozen, packed into eight neat boxes, and stacked into the back of my jet-black Prius. I'm behind the wheel, hell-bent for leather, racing against the cold pouring off the boxes in palpable waves. Due south. Los Angeles by sundown.

"Ben, do we have another blanket we can toss on top of the cow?"

"Yep. On it."

Ben is my partner in a multitude of crimes. He's a spark plug of a man with forearms like footballs, thanks to his work as a film grip. If you're wondering what a film grip does, it's largely this: Grips solve problems. Ben's able to MacGyver his way out of nearly anything. He's also one of my oldest friends. If you need help with a project, but you don't know what you don't know—you need Ben.

Ben shifts in his seat and throws another blanket over the boxes in the back.

Outside the car, it's eighty-five degrees. Inside, it's about sixty. Regardless, I crank the air conditioner to MAX COLD. Foot on the gas.

Twenty-four hours earlier, Ben and I had headed in the opposite direction. Straight up the I-5, toward a small town about an hour and a half north of Sacramento. I needed to see a man about a cow.

The decision to buy this particular animal was the result of months of research. I had decided that I didn't know enough about where my food comes from and that I needed to address this ignorance head-on. Since, like many Americans, my go-to protein is beef, I started there.

As we zip north, we pass another of my potential beef supplier options: the largest beef facility on the West Coast. Harris Ranch, located along the I-5, is a textbook example of what most people think of when they consider beef production. Feedlots sprawling like agricultural suburbs—their soil a darker black than the soil outside due to the hooves and dung of countless cattle. They process up to a quarter-million cattle annually—handling every aspect from feeding to slaughter, packaging, and shipping.

Harris Ranch is a leading purveyor of corn-fed beef, the type to which most Americans are accustomed. If you've had a hamburger in a restaurant or bought beef at a supermarket and it wasn't otherwise labeled, it was fed on some mixture of corn and other grains. Beef fed on cheap corn can reach market weight in a little over a year. The result: lots of beef at low prices.

However, there are other costs. First, cattle aren't really built to eat corn—they're built to eat grass. The first of their four stomachs is called a rumen (hence, "ruminant"). It's like a gigantic beer keg in the animal's chest. The rumen holds beneficial bacteria that ferment the chewed grasses the cattle eat. These bacteria in turn become a major source of protein for the animal. That's how cattle are able to derive protein from a protein-free grass—they're eating the bacteria that feed on it.

When cattle eat corn, fermentation in the rumen stops. The rumen becomes more acidic in order to break down this suboptimal food. Effects are manifold: First, cattle stomachs become more like our stomachs. As a result, any potentially harmful bacteria in the rumen adapt to their new environment and become in turn more able to make humans sick. Bacteria like *E. coli.*

An acidic rumen can also give cattle something roughly analogous to bovine heartburn, called *acidosis.* This disease keeps them from eating, defeating the purpose of feeding them corn. As a result, heavy preventative doses of antibiotics are introduced to keep acidosis at bay. An estimated 80 percent of all antibiotics used in the United States are administered to livestock.

Remember the *E. coli* breeding in their rumen? The aforementioned antibiotics can make the bacteria antibiotic-resistant.

Further, corn-fed beef lose their source of protein as the beneficial grass-digesting bacteria in their rumen vanish, requiring their diet to be supplemented with other forms of protein. In industrial times, that protein has come from the ground-up carcasses of other animals, including other cattle. This bovine cannibalism turned out to be a spectacular way to spread mad cow disease (aka bovine spongiform encephalopathy, or BSE)—which is transmitted by contact with infected brain or spinal tissue. Consumption of mad cow–tainted beef has been linked with Creutzfeldt-Jakob disease in humans—a degenerative and fatal brain disorder, symptoms of which include rapidly progressing dementia, loss of muscular coordination, personality changes, impaired vision, and a raft of other neurological impairments. Eating mad cow–tainted beef is a tremendously bad idea.

Because of fears over mad cow disease, in 1997 the U.S. Food and Drug Administration (FDA) prohibited the use of ruminant protein in cattle feed. Now, cattle protein is frequently fed to poultry and poultry protein is fed back to cattle. It isn't cannibalism, but cattle eating chickens isn't exactly natural, either.

Corn-fed beef also requires, well, corn, which is one of the most energy-intensive crops produced. Gigantic petroleum-dependent combines plant the corn and harvest it, petroleum-derived pesticides and fertilizers ensure a prodigious crop, and petroleum-driven vehicles transport it to feedlots. Some sources estimate that a single corn-fed beef steer is the product of 284 gallons of petroleum over the course of his life.

When you hear people say that beef production is energy-intensive—this is why.

I don't fault beef producers such as Harris Ranch for trying to make a living. Like any agricultural pursuit, ranching is a wildly risky proposal. The debt to get started can be tremendous, the competition intense. Nobody—no matter how altruistic—wants to go bankrupt.

Industrial beef producers are responding to market forces, and in a minuscule way I am a part of that market. With my food dollars, however, I'd like to vote for a different process.

Ben and I pull into Chaffin Family Orchards, a working ranch and farm just outside Oroville, California, after nine hours of driving. Chris Kerston, the ranch's chief marketing guy, has agreed to show us around.

The ranch looks like many small-scale farms. Though the landscape is picturesque, the farm buildings themselves are weather-beaten and worn—the effort put into building this place has clearly gone into function over aesthetics. A small house sits by an enormous barn. Dirty pickups crowd a gravel driveway. A road leads up a grassy slope to parts unknown.

I walk toward the barn. A small lean-to in front houses their farm stand, offering nectarines, fresh eggs, chickens, olive oil, and a few other items. Notably, there is no one here. There is, however, a box with a slit in the top.

I point at the cash box. Despite the fact that we're alone, I whisper to Ben, "Dude, I think this place works on the honor system."

"That's awesome. I don't think you could do that in LA."

"Isn't that how we pay for the subway in LA?"

"Who pays for the subway in LA?"

"Touché."

The front door of the house opens and a tall, thin man walks out. I wave as I approach, as one only does in the country. "Morning. . . . Chris around?"

"I'll get him."

The thin man disappears back into the house. I shove my hands in my pockets and take in the view. Across the road, rows of fat, gnarled trees stretch all the way to the horizon. There is no sound but the wind.

The door to the house clangs open and Chris ambles out. He's probably thirtyish but looks younger in a red button-down shirt and jeans. He sports the dirty ball cap of a man who works outside, but he rocks a soul patch like he might have followed Phish once upon a time. At his age, that couldn't have been too long ago.

When he sees us, he grins like it's his default response to the world. "Hey, I'm Chris."

"Hey, man. Jared. This is Ben."

"Great to meet you guys. Ready to go for a ride?"

The three of us jump onto a carryall, and Chris shows us around the ranch, very little of which is dedicated to raising cattle. It turns out they don't raise cattle for their own sake; they do it to produce better fruit.

Chaffin Family Orchards started about a hundred years ago when its founder, Del Chaffin, bought the land from UC Berkeley, which had an agricultural research station there. The research station grew olive trees, and those trees still stand—I spotted them from the barn.

Olive trees have needs. They need fertilizer and pruning. The area between them must be kept mown, otherwise grass and shrubbery will grow and choke out the trees. And once every three months, the trees like to be petted and told that they're pretty. Because they are.

Most commercial farms handle these needs through chemical or mechanical means. They plant gigantic fields with a single crop—say, peaches. They spray their crop with chemical fertilizers to help the plants grow and hire a guy to mow between the trees to keep out competing plants. The result? A broad expanse of bare dirt growing exactly one species of plant. That's called a monoculture. (And monocultures are never told they're pretty.)

Because from an ecological perspective, monocultures aren't especially efficient. The system to create them requires huge energy inputs from the grower: for the tractor, the guy who drives the tractor, the fuel for the tractor, and the fertilizer for the trees. It isn't just an environmental burden on the grower—it's an economic burden.

Chaffin Family Orchards does things differently. Rather than hire a guy to mow between the trees, they send in goats. One of the main threats to orchard trees is shrubbery. The goats roam through the field and clear out any shrubbery that would otherwise choke out the trees. They also climb through the lower branches—yes, they're tree-climbing goats—and keep the lower six feet of branches pruned of green shoots, which would, if they were allowed to bloom, decrease the yield of the tree. Further, the goats fertilize the soil, eliminating much of the need for chemical fertilizer.

"But," you may ask, "what about predators?" As was the custom long ago, the shepherds at Chaffin raise and socialize livestock guardian dogs that live with the herd and protect them from coyotes and whatever else might go bump in the night.

As a result, rather than paying for a tractor, fuel, and extra manpower, the farmers produce an additional crop—chevon, or goat meat. This is in addition to the services the goats provide trimming the trees and fertilizing the soil.

After the goats, the ranchers send a herd of cattle through the orchard to mow down the grass that the goats leave behind. These cattle further fertilize the orchard while providing another crop: grass-fed beef.

The steer that I will be taking home once grazed here. Chris takes us to see the current herd—a group of about thirty, reddish-brown, eleven-hundred-pound steers cavorting through century-old olive trees. I try to get closer, but they aren't having it. They canter off into the distance, weaving behind trees to get away from me. They're remarkably graceful. Like bovine ninjas.

The cattle will live on this land for most of their life. After sixteen months or so, they'll be moved to an adjacent pasture for finishing—eating their fill of bright green clover and grass until they come up to harvest weight. At that point, they'll be taken one at a time to a local processor, quickly stunned into unconsciousness with a bolt stunner, and then slaughtered. The processor—colloquially known as a "butcher"—is an Animal Welfare Approved (AWA) local businessman. And per the AWA standards, the animal should have absolutely no awareness of the event. Afterward, the butcher partitions and flash-freezes the carcass according to Chris's instructions.

We leave the herd and wander farther afield to the mobile hen-houses, newly arrived to this bit of acreage. After Chaffin sends the cattle through the orchard, they follow up a few days later with chickens. Chickens are omnivores, and they're at their best when they eat both grass and animal protein in the form of bugs—like the bugs that hatch from the cattle and goat manure. The chickens, in turn, lay eggs in the mobile henhouse that travels around the farm with them.

"We don't play Easter morning every day out here," says Chris.

Truly free-range eggs, another crop, and the chickens also further fertilize the trees.

This system of crop rotation means that Chaffin is able to produce each individual crop for less than it would cost if they tried to produce that crop in isolation.

From a beef-production perspective, this agricultural system has distinct advantages. Cattle raised on pasture evade most of the pitfalls of feedlot cattle—no acidosis, so far less need for antibiotics. No need for protein supplementation, so dramatically reduced risk of mad cow. The cattle eat the lawn, so no need to plant, grow, harvest, and ship corn.

For the most part, the steers aren't raised on dedicated, single-purpose pastures, so land use is more efficient as well. Rather than support one crop, each acre supports three or four.

Finally, and perhaps most important, the cattle are sold directly by the rancher—who keeps more of the sale price—and are sold at a premium, to boot. People will pay more for beef raised this way. I suppose I'm living proof.

We head back toward the barn, steering the carryall past our cars and up a winding road that crests a tall mesa behind the farm. This is Table Mountain, so named because it's a mountain that looks like a table. Funny, that.

Atop the mountain, Chris points the carryall at a small, rain-fed lake. A barbecue grill standing next to it is the tallest object for miles. In the west, the sun is just beginning to dip below the horizon.

"Damn. Great view. You guys grill up here a lot?"

Chris grins. "All the time. You guys should come back later in the summer."

"Might have to."

"You should get into farming, man. Don't do it for the money, 'cause there isn't any. But it sure is fun."

Los Angeles is nine hours from Oroville. The plan is to snag a hotel room for the night and head homeward first thing in the morning. Chris is keeping my steer in cold storage at the ranch overnight, so we'll pick it up from him right before we leave.

He suggested we crash at the Gold Country Hotel and Casino. I pull up, and Ben is immediately a fan.

"Dude! A bear that will eat your dreams."

I look to where he's pointing. Painted on the side of a building, twenty feet tall, is a grizzly bear charging through a dream catcher. The hotel logo, or a mascot, or something.

"Gold Country Hotel and Casino—Where Dreams Get Ravaged by Nocturnal Predators." Sometimes I speak in taglines. "You hungry?"

The top floor of the casino has a steakhouse that Chris raved about. Given the nature of our trip, steak is definitely the plan for the evening.

We walk in, doing our best not to look like we've been working on a farm all day. Management doesn't blink, and we score a Hollywood booth facing a massive window. After a beer and a lobster bisque, we survey our choices.

All their steaks are grain-fed, which is expected. Grain-fed steak has more intramuscular fat—in other words, marbling—than grass-fed, and offers the taste and texture to which Americans are accustomed.

The restaurant's steaks are also graded Prime by the U.S. Department of Agriculture (USDA). This grade is almost entirely determined by the degree of intramuscular fat, with Prime being the most desirable and the most marbled (i.e., fatty). Almost all the Prime in the United States goes to high-end restaurants—this intramuscular fat is why people generally find them so delicious. Fat is flavor. Below the Prime designation is Choice and Select, both of which you usually find in supermarkets. These are less fatty than their higher-end counterparts. The grades below Select are the stuff they feed to prisoners and college students.

The steaks at the restaurant are also dry-aged for thirty-one days, according to the menu. In dry aging, the beef is hung, uncovered, in a refrigerator for several weeks. This allows moisture to evaporate from the meat, concentrating its flavor, and also allows natural enzymes present within the beef partially to break down the muscle fibers, increasing tenderness. Dry aging is a very good thing.

In short, the Gold Country Hotel and Casino offers a textbook high-end steakhouse. It'll serve as an excellent control test for all my beef adventures to come.

With this comparison in mind, we decide on rib eyes. Medium rare, because we aren't Philistines. Show me a person who orders a steak cooked past medium, and I'll show you a person who doesn't actually like steak. And rib eye is the king of steaks. It's the steak that people who like steak like liking. Properly preparing a rib eye is frequently considered the pinnacle of the grilling arts.

Rib eye comes from the appropriately named rib primal. That primal sits on top of the animal and doesn't do a lot of work moving the animal around. As a result, it's quite tender and has a fair bit of marbling. The steaks arrive perfectly cooked. Nicely seared exterior, warm red center. Beautiful.

Here's the thing about grain-fed beef: It doesn't suck. The texture is very tender, made even more luscious by the abundant marbling. It tastes every bit like the indulgence that it is.

If this is a taste—no pun intended—of things to come, in the next year I am going to eat like a king.

After nine hours on the road back to Los Angeles, our beef-laden Prius wheels into the garage of my modest home in the suburbs. My wife, Summer, meets me at the door. She's tall and freckled just so, with fat rings of auburn hair that she can never quite tame. Right now, her face is trying to decide whether to display "wary" or "excited."

"Success?"

"You could say that."

Ben and I unload the car. Box after box, like it's a clown wagon full of cow flesh. My enormous Rhodesian Ridgeback, Basil (like the herb, not the Brit), sniffs each of them excitedly. She's a solid hundred pounds and the most food-motivated pooch I've ever seen. Even my toddler son knows to clutch his crackers to his chest and hit the deck when she starts sniffing around.

Ben and I drop the eight massive boxes on the patio in my backyard. I tear one open, revealing two dozen or so neat plastic packages, hard as rocks. Our ersatz meat wagon did the trick.

Summer surveys the haul. "So that's it?"

"That's it. Four hundred and twenty pounds of grass-fed beef. Dry-aged twenty-one days."

"And how much is this setting us back?"

"Twenty-five hundred bucks. Ish."

I see the wheels turning in her head. Doing the math. Mentally carrying the one. Finally, she responds. "Okay. Where did you put the key to the freezer?"

Our freezer is a 14.7-cubic-foot chest model we picked up at the hardware store with a gift certificate and all our Christmas money. It sits in one corner of our backyard. It's a beast. And it's been running for seventy-two hours in preparation for this moment.

"It's in the key drawer. With all the other keys," I reply.

Summer shakes her head. "I thought so, too. But it isn't there."

"What do you mean? It has to be."

"Try again."

I rush to the kitchen and throw open our aptly named key drawer. Keys of all shapes and sizes slosh forth in a brass wave. Door keys. Padlock keys. What I believe may be boat keys, for some reason. No freezer keys.

The freezer is locked and empty.

I rush back outside. My newly acquired cow is sitting in boxes in the Southern California sun. In June. In the afternoon. Quietly thawing.

"Shitty shit shit. Summer, Ben, can you guys help me throw some blankets back over these boxes? We have to find that key."

Everyone else is moving in slow motion. I zip to the car and grab the blankets. Back to the yard.

Somehow, the freezer is open.

Ben slips a flathead screwdriver back into his pocket. "I picked the lock."

Like I said, grips solve problems.

We tear open the boxes and begin to load the freezer. This project isn't theoretical anymore—it's as real as real gets. As I open case after case of premium beef, I am apprehensive.

This is way more beef than I expected.

❧

It doesn't fit.

I reassess. It's supposed to fit. Eight boxes, twenty inches by thirteen inches by eight inches, into a 14.7-cubic-foot freezer, using base twelve calculations. I did the math. Math is logical and reasonable. Math is what makes this not nuts. If I have math, then I haven't just made an enormous mistake.

The butcher that Chris hired to disassemble my steer broke it out into two halves, each partitioned differently. One half has been carved to optimize the cuts most suited for grilling and barbecue—steaks, ribs, and the like. The other half makes the most of the roasts and other cuts that need plenty of cooking time to reach their full potential. Both halves of the steer have been divided into dozens of packages of between approximately one and four pounds—though one package, a massive standing rib roast, tips the scales at just over six. And all of these packages, neatly labeled and ready for long-term storage, desperately need a temperature-controlled sanctuary from the Southern California sun.

I try again. I stack beef cut after beef cut after beef cut into the iron monster that is my freezer, and I still have two of the eight boxes left to go.

I may have math. But reality has the upper hand.

This is one of those things you don't consider when you decide you're going to buy an ungodly amount of meat. On paper, it's all so simple. "Oh, I'll need a big freezer for that. I should go get one." There, done.

The reality is that big freezers are just that—big. They operate at enormous scales. And if my math is off, the waste will be similarly enormous. Say, for example, one was to purchase 420 pounds of beef and miscalculate the space required to store it by a mere 10 percent. (Because the packages are irregularly shaped and vary tremendously in size, it's an easy mistake to make.) That's forty-two pounds of beef that doesn't have a home. That's stressful.

I glance from my two spare boxes to my still-open freezer and back.

"It doesn't fit," my wife says.

"It has to fit."

"Does it know that?"

Ben frowns. "We can make it fit."

"We have to. Let's pull it." I suggest. Ben and I start unloading the 350 pounds of meat that did fit. "We need a plan."

Ten minutes later, an entire exploded cow surrounds us on my patio, each piece swathed in shrink-wrap. Is that moisture on the outside of a couple of the pieces? Can't be. Shut up, brain.

Ben thinks. "Big stuff at the bottom?"

"Maybe. But big stuff is irregularly shaped," I say.

Summer frowns. "Little stuff at the bottom doesn't really make sense."

I have a revelation. "Ground beef comes in little one-pound rectangles. Let's line the floor and sides with it."

"We have those weird hanging drawers in the side," Summer notes.

"Even better. We can stack all the ground beef at the bottom, and fill those drawers with all the small stuff, and pile all the big stuff in the center."

We spend the next fifteen minutes reloading about four hundred pounds of beef. This time, it looks like it's going to fit.

It almost does. "Fiddlesticks," I say, glancing down at my son, Declan, who has wandered outside to watch the beef drama unfold.

The word in my head is not fiddlesticks—ordinarily I swear like a Tourette's-addled sailor. But as Declan has grown, the Kid Censor in my head has become well-oiled and Ferrari-smooth. At nearly two years old, Declan is just starting to learn the fun words.

"Honey, what's in the freezer inside the house?"

"It's full."

"Actually full? Or 'I need to set boundaries' full?"

"Both."

Ben squints. "We can make it fit."

I survey the remaining pieces. Maybe twenty pounds. "Okay. Beef Tetris."

Once again, we unload four-hundred-plus pounds of rock-hard, ice-cold, irregularly shaped beef bits back into their boxes. Quickly—as it's June, we're in Los Angeles, and I'm genuinely beginning to worry that I've just wasted Dec's college fund.

"Okay. First, all the ground along the sides. In the drawers. Everywhere. They're regularly shaped so we can pack everything in tight. No spaces, no air."

Ben nods. "Good plan." Which is like having James Bond tell you that you can hold your liquor and look good in a tux.

"All right, so . . . big stuff in next. Pack it tight. Don't just toss it—shove it in there. Pack it so tight this guy could walk around and moo if he felt like it."

At this point, between our unloading, loading, reloading, unloading, and reloading again, we've moved about 1,300 pounds of beef. But this—this try is our most promising yet.

Summer smiles. "I think we have a winner."

It gets dicey toward the end. I have particular trouble with a bag of marrow bones (I have marrow bones?) that just won't cooperate. After a few more minutes of jockeying for space and a couple of particularly M. C. Escheresque maneuvers with a hanging tender—we are good. The lid closes. The freezer hums. A green light on the front glows serenely.

"All right. Who's hungry?"

"I have an entire cow in an iron box in my backyard. I can cook, literally, any piece of beef the world has ever known. What do I do?"

Summer laughs. "If you don't cook a steak, you're doing it wrong."

She has a point. Americans eat, on average, fifty-two pounds of beef per person per year, and about a quarter of the carcass, give or take, comprises the primal muscle groups we associate with steak. Further, apart from burgers, steaks are the most popular single beef dish eaten in restaurants. No matter how you slice it, Americans eat a lot of steaks.

I had a steak the night before, but anything else seems sacrilegious. The question becomes, then—which steak? T-bone, porterhouse, filet, strip, rib eye, hanging tender, top round, round, sirloin—all steaks. I'm overwhelmed with options.

Rib eye? Had it last night.

Porterhouse? Huge. Those things look like they're out of a cartoon.

T-bone? Maybe.

Filet? No. I have plans for those.

Sirloin? That's like, "default beef," right?

Round steak? Looks oblong to me.

Tenderized round steak? The same, but in touch with its feelings?

London broil? Sounds like a steak. But is, in fact, a five-pound roast.

Hanging tender? What the hell is that?

Crosscut shank? Looks steaky, from the size of the package. But again, a mystery.

Further, a new conundrum presents itself. I'm trying to make the best use of each cut of this animal that I possibly can. Familiar or not, I have only a limited number of each cut. I mess up the wrong dish—I may not get a second chance.

Summer and Ben are looking at me like I'm about to raise my arms and make some sort of grand proclamation about dinner. They're hungry. "KC strip," I decide, keeping my arms firmly at my sides. A lovely steak—and a familiar one.

The Kansas City strip steak comes from the short loin of the animal. It's far from the head and the hoof, which means that it doesn't do a whole lot of work moving the animal around. As a result, it doesn't develop a lot of connective tissue the way, say, a chuck steak would. It's best treated simply, grilled hot and fast, and served medium rare.

I open my freezer to pull it, sifting through all the packages I just managed to close the lid on. The strip steaks are nowhere to be seen.

They must be on the bottom.

For the fourth time that day, I begin to unload beef from my freezer. Not all the way—I just stack the packages on the edge of the freezer, excavating a hole into which I delve for steaky goodness. "Smart," I think. "Less work loading and unloading the entire haul." I pile the other cuts around the edge of the hole, spelunking into a man-made cavern of rock-hard, irregular bricks at subzero temperatures, searching for a single elusive gustatory prize. Finally, I find a single package of strip steak at the bottom of the hole. I reach for it.

Beefalanche. All the stacked—and, it turns out, slippery—cuts balanced around the edge of the hole tumble everywhere. I manage to grab the steak, but a five-pound London broil clatters to the concrete, barely missing my toe. Filets skitter across the pavement like hockey pucks. It's pandemonium.

However, I am victorious. I hold in my hand a slim, plastic-wrapped brick of beef. And with this package's absence, I have ever so slightly more room in the freezer than I did previously.

And I have a dinner to cook.

Safe in the kitchen, I thaw and rinse the steaks, pat them dry, then take a good look. They're not the Technicolor-bright red of grocery store steaks—they're a deeper crimson. This could be due to aging, or it could be because they're grass-fed. I don't know. And while they do have some marbling, they pointedly do not have the copious fat streaks of grain-fed beef. I'm told they cook faster as a result, so I'll have to keep an eye on them. I'd prefer to not wreck my very first meal from this enormous beef stockpile. Especially with guests.

I slather a little canola oil on my hands and rub it on the steaks. The fat will serve as a heat conductor and contribute to a quality sear. A liberal dose of salt and pepper and the steaks are prepped.

Each steak is about an inch and a half thick, which translates (roughly) to three minutes a side at 450 for medium rare. With some minor fanfare, I slap them on the grill.

Night's coming on. Somewhere, a cricket chirps. Ben and I are bone-tired, in the way that driving nine hours and juggling nearly a quarter ton of beef can make you. We're also hungry.

Timer says ninety seconds have elapsed. On a lark, I peek at the steaks.

Oh, they're ready. So very ready—seared beautifully and cooked nearly to half their thickness. Hurriedly, I flip them. They hit medium rare in half the time suggested for grain-fed. I'm very lucky I checked. My inability to spend a moment without a task barely kept us from eating shoe leather. It's a win for self-diagnosed borderline obsessive-compulsives everywhere. Another ninety seconds and the steaks are done.

I set them aside to rest, throw some broccoli in a pan to broil, and turn to find Declan watching me. This is the hardest part of my day: "Bedtime, little man." My days are long and my evenings all too short. Usually, I'm only just arrived home from the office before it's time for him to sleep. We've barely seen each other this weekend.

Declan shares the blond mop and bright green eyes I had when I was his age, and to him everything is an adventure. He's a white-hot pulsar of enthusiasm and wonder, and I wish I got to spend more time with him. I give him the biggest hug in the history of affection, and he toddles toward his room. Summer reads him a story while I slice what looks to be a fantastic potato caraway bread she baked especially for tonight's meal.

A few minutes later, dinner is ready. Summer, Ben, and I sit down at the table in our backyard and survey the feast. Despite my kitchen ninjitsu, the steaks have nudged up toward medium. They're still gorgeous, however, with a deep-brown sear and a bright pink center. They're paired with just-picked sweet corn, roasted broccoli with Parmesan, and the aforementioned potato bread that Summer made, which couldn't have been easy or quick.

The table falls silent as we slice our steaks—the first sojourn into what will hopefully be a year of remarkable meals. My steak is unlike anything I've ever tasted. It blows the doors off the grain-fed steak I had the night before at the high-end steakhouse. But really, it's an apples-to-oranges comparison.

The grain-fed steak was a luscious, succulent thing. Heavily marbled with fat and practically falling apart, it had an exorbitant richness to it. A luxury, it was certainly delicious—and exactly as I expected it to be. It tasted like a well-prepared steak.

This steak, both because it is a different cut and because it's grass-fed, is less marbled. Also well-prepared (if I do say so)—it tastes nothing like I expected. It tastes *far* richer. Not gamier per se, but beefier. More like itself. It tastes like everything a person would like about a steak—cranked to eleven. And then shot into space. And then kissed by angels.

Grass-fed beef, unlike grain-fed beef, is the product of a specific time and place. It has qualities usually considered only when discussing fine wine. To eat a grass-fed steer is on some level to taste the land and the *terroir* the animal came from, lived in, and experienced.

I've read about *terroir*, but I've never really been privileged enough to experience it firsthand. I've taken the word of wine labels—the brief stories on the labels designed to conjure an image of some half-invented idyll that you too can supposedly experience if you will only buy a bottle—but I've rarely visited a location, then sampled its wares elsewhere and had my impressions of the place come rushing back. It's a heady experience.

The three of us pop open a bottle of Pinot Noir as the sun first glows orange, then fades to the deep crimson of our steak, before finally vanishing. I swirl the wine in my glass. The way this cow lived—its *terroir*—is reflected quite dramatically in this steak. In its very flesh. These steaks taste like fresh air, lazy afternoons among fruit trees, and a life lived at a slower pace. I'll be cooking this meat for the coming year—I wonder what will be reflected in me. I hope that, a year from now, I will find myself somehow improved. Somehow better. Perhaps, through some act of sympathetic magic, somehow more at peace with the world and my place in it.

It should be a very interesting year.

The Simplest Strip Steak

Time: About 30 minutes

Serves 2 to 4 people, depending on what you serve it with

The strip steak is a major muscle off the short loin primal. It has almost no connective tissue, so it can be cooked hot and fast. It's also relatively lean and cooks quickly. Be sure not to overcook or you'll lose what makes this cut great. (Be especially careful if it's grass-fed, as it'll cook even faster.)

It's a simple cut to cook for dinner parties. Just don't be an idiot and overdo it; let the meat speak for itself.

2 Kansas City strip steaks (or New York strip steaks, depending), about 1½ inches thick

2 tablespoons canola oil (or peanut, sunflower, or vegetable oil, or clarified butter)

Kosher salt and freshly ground black pepper

1. Thaw the steaks and bring them to room temperature. If you're short on time, you can thaw the steaks in about an hour by placing the still-packaged meat in a bowl in your sink with a thin stream of cold (not warm!) water running into it. The cold water is warmer than the frozen meat, and the constant stream will gently thaw it.

❦

Don't do this during a drought. Also, don't do it if you have an enormous dog who will make your dinner her own. Not that this has ever happened to me.

Be sure to bring the meat fully to room temperature or it won't cook evenly. Don't worry about food-borne pathogens here—they live on the surface of the meat, and you're going to sear that to oblivion.

2. Bring your grill to 450°F. Use an independent oven thermometer on the grill grate if at all possible. Lid thermometers lie. If you don't have access to a grill, a cast-iron griddle or skillet works as well. Place it over your biggest burner and heat it until it smokes.

3. Rub the entire surface of the meat with the high-heat-tolerant fat of your choice, and shake off excess.

4. Season the steaks with salt and pepper. Use more than you think you need, and use more salt than pepper. Pepper can burn, while salt can't—it's a rock. Also, a lot of your seasoning will fall off, so don't be shy.

5. Grill the steaks to medium rare, with an internal temp of about 130°F. (If grain-fed: about 3 minutes per side, flipped twice, for a total of 12 minutes. If grass-fed: about 90 seconds per side, flipped twice, for a total of 6 minutes.)

❦

To check for doneness, you can (a) use an instant-read thermometer or (b) use the finger test: Touch your middle finger to the tip of your thumb, then feel the fleshy part of your hand at the base of your thumb. That's what medium rare feels like. Or you can (c) cut into the steak to check.

6. Remove the steaks to a plate and cover loosely with aluminum foil; let rest for 10 minutes.

7. Plate and serve.

You know that bottle of Pinot Noir you've been saving for a special occasion? Now's a good time to break it out.

2

Grid

Monday morning, I'm back at my workaday life.

     At 9:00 a.m., full of optimism and the promise of a new day, I wheel onto the 101 Freeway on-ramp, point my car at the broad blue horizon—and stop.

I move another ten feet. Stop again.

This is how I spend the first hour of the day outside my house and the last before I return to it. Ten feet. Stop. Ten more. This is my commute.

By Los Angeles standards, I don't have *that* bad a commute. But that's like saying that by Kenyan standards, I don't get *that* mauled by lions. Oh, I still get mauled, mind you. Mauled horribly—just mauled less. But in order to do my job, I have to perform this daily ritual. This temporal sacrifice to whatever gods of commerce oversee the network promotion of primetime dramas.

My phone chirps, and I glance at the screen. It's an e-mail about work; I can answer it when I get in. Ten more feet. Stop. Eh, I can answer it now. I type a quick response and hit send. Ten more feet. Stop. Repeat.

I have a hard time disengaging from my phone. I compulsively check boxes, fix problems, and answer e-mails. I can resolve this issue now, here, in the car—so-and-so prefers HDCAM over D5 tapes, *send*—and then I won't have to deal with it later. I can get ahead! I can make a dent in my day's workload. I can get shit done, out of the way, and off my plate. I can make room for the stuff that really matters.

Oddly, though, it never really seems to work out that way. It's like bailing water from a boat in a rainstorm. Bucket after bucket— I can bail like crazy, but the rain still falls.

Today, however, is different. Today, on this bright, beautiful Monday morning, I feel like I have a secret. I have an entire cow in an iron box in my backyard. I am poised on the precipice of a fantastic adventure. Epic, even. The possibilities, though not quite endless, are close enough for jazz.

I'm a creative director at a marketing agency that specializes in the promotion of network and cable television programs. That blank look on your face right now is the normal reaction people give me when I tell them what I do. To put it a different way, think of your favorite show. Think of the commercials you see on television that tell you when that show is on and why you should watch. I make those.

I'm a small cog in a very large machine. This Machine is the sprawling complex of devices that converts desires into dollars and does so at a breakneck pace. Look, want, buy, rinse, and repeat. The Machine creates new appetites and provides endless ways to sate them. Desire begets consumption begets new desire, played out—in my world—in twenty-two-minute increments.

I do it because I love stories. On my best days, I'm a multi-media cheerleader for television shows that really deserve someone to cheer for them. And those shows are out there. Little neglected pieces of heartfelt entertainment that some writer poured their everything into because they had no other choice. The writer had to tell this story, and if no one listened—if no one in the entire world cared in the slightest—the writer had to tell it anyway. Because it'd burn a hole in that writer's soul if they kept that little bit of narrative imperative trapped inside. And my job is to say: Here it is. Here's why it's good. You should watch it.

The rest of the time, I pimp shows about famous people falling in mud.

I'm not trying to disparage those simpler shows. If people didn't watch them—or if television execs somewhere didn't think people would watch them—they wouldn't get made. Believe it or not, television is something of a meritocracy. What bothers me on this particular morning—on most mornings—is the structure of my day, such as it is.

I finally pull into the parking garage of a nondescript office building in the shadow of a major studio. Four floors up, I settle into a thirdhand office chair to make quality television for eight hours. Or ten. Or twelve. Maybe fourteen. That's part of the problem: I can never tell for sure. I've seen the sun rise in this building more than once. I work with lovely, talented people, and issues like this are by no means limited to the entertainment industry, but because of the nature of the process, my time is not my own. We stay until the project is done.

Television, for all its thrill and magic, is largely a function of meetings. And the people in those meetings got there through various ministrations of intelligence, creativity, bluster, accident, and nepotism. The people who actually make the stuff that goes on your television—the end result, really; the reason people watch—have to sluice their work through the fine mesh of those meetings so that the people who write the checks feel reassured that those checks they're writing aren't written in vain. If five MBAs signed off on a pilot script, it must be good. Right?

Those meetings are where my work lives and dies. A roomful of people who couldn't agree on lunch need to agree that an ad or a promo is "good." If it's deemed acceptable—great. If not, if we're lucky, we'll be told why—assuming the person actually conveying that information is one of the people who actually participated in said meeting. Or, if not, assuming the person knows what the people who were in the meeting actually said. Or, barring that, assuming that person is a relatively perceptive individual, with a solid educated guess why it flopped in the room and is willing to work with us. Or, barring that, has a prophesying dead grandmother who comes to them in their sleep and lays bare to them the hearts and minds of television executives. Or, barring that, simply isn't looking to throw the agency under a bus to look good while really having no idea what's going on. If nothing else, we're convenient scapegoats.

Such is agency life. In a way, I'm like an animist priest, offering up a video sacrifice. If the gods are kind and the sacrifice is accepted, I am released. If the gods are cruel, I am handed the boulder of Sisyphus and pointed back toward the hill.

Sometime after dark, I clamber out of the Hollywood trenches and make my way back toward home. I'm not done yet; we still have a spot in play, but I can review it and give notes from home. The best thing about working late is that the traffic is less intense—everyone else has already returned to their loved ones. My shoulders hurt, but that's normal. They always hurt after a day at work because my job is tremendously stressful. I can almost tell time by what aches.

Even though it's wildly illegal, I check my phone a few times on the ride home. Something could go wrong. Something frequently does. And when it does, my team and I are the last line of defense against dead air on television. Rest assured, America, you shall not lose access to your beloved wannabe actors performing ridiculous tasks on my watch. Tonight, all is well. For now, at least.

At home, however, something is different. A scent greets me before I even make it inside the house. My wife is cooking.

Summer's commute is even longer than mine, and she's usually every bit as tired as I am when she walks through the door. As a result, my wife cooking is an event. I mean that not only in the "this is special" sense of the word, but also in the experimental physics sense. When my wife is at the helm, Heisenberg's Uncertainty Principle is at play. From observing the current position of the culinary process, one can divine nothing of the project's velocity. The room is an explosion of flour and knives and probably something wet. I call it Schrödinger's Kitchen. The meal is both perfect and ruined, simultaneously. Only when the meal is served does the wave function collapse, and we discover the final outcome.

Tonight, Summer's making an heirloom recipe passed down from her mother and passed to her mother from some mythic figure lost in the depths of time. She is making taco pie. It is, essentially, ground beef, cheddar cheese, and sour cream on top of a crust built from premade crescent-roll dough—all topped with crushed Fritos corn chips on top. Dinner.

Taco pie is the sort of dish that's tremendously common in the particular corner of the Midwest where I grew up. Like green bean casserole made from cream of mushroom soup, canned green beans, and canned fried onions. Or Rice Krispies treats. It's food made from other processed foods. It's much faster than making each of the component ingredients separately, and it doesn't taste half-bad. It isn't haute cuisine, but when you're too tired to cook, it's an easy one-dish meal.

By the time I arrive, Summer has already fed Declan a sliver of the pie, which he's nibbled on and picked at, birdlike. I sit down across from him to talk about his day for a few minutes. He made a lot of art at day care today. He loves art. After showing me a couple of watercolor paintings, it's time for bed. I wish I had more time with him in the evenings, but these few scant minutes are all that remain between my return and his bedtime. I tuck him in, sing him a song originally warbled by sock puppets, and ten minutes later he's out cold.

Finally, Summer and I sit for our own meal. Exhausted. "Thanks for making dinner," I say. "We haven't had taco pie in a while."

Summer nods. "I know. We have the world's largest stockpile of ground beef, now. . . . I figured Dec might like it. It's so hard to get him to eat protein."

"What's not to like? Pie. Corn chips. Cheese. It's like the toddler trifecta."

She chuckles and picks at her plate.

"Good day?" I ask.

"Long day," she replies. "There was a wreck on the 405." Translation: longer commute. "I almost didn't make it home to get D. in time." Our day care closes at 6:00 p.m. We arrive at 5:59 on the best of days. If we were late, I don't *think* they'd keep our child overnight to prove a point, but it's probably best not to press the issue.

"Did they seem mad about it?" I ask.

"No. But he was the last one to be picked up, again. I don't like doing that to him."

"I know," I mumble, idly fingering my phone. No new e-mails.

"Do you have to do that?" she asks.

"Do what?"

"You're checking your e-mail."

"We're finishing a piece tonight. I'm expecting a link to proof the final version."

"Do you have to check while we're eating?"

"The guys are still working. They're waiting on me to look. If I don't check, they have to stick around the office staring off into middle distance while they wait for stupid me to say nice things."

"I'm waiting for you to say nice things. And I'm your wife. Talking about our son." Then, a beat later, she adds, "And don't call yourself stupid."

I demur, thumbing the lock button on my phone to blank the screen.

I take another bite of this pie that my wife made for us to share together. It's crunchy from the corn chip topping. There, munching on my Fritos-covered grass-fed beef, I pause. I feel guilty. I know what high-quality beef this is. I know how much hard work went into raising the animal humanely, harvesting it quickly and painlessly, and getting it into my backyard. It does not deserve to be covered in Fritos dust. Suddenly, I am not hungry.

But I don't want to be rude. Quietly, I lay down my fork and turn back to Summer. "So he was the last one?"

"The very last." She pokes at her food, silent. Finally, "I feel like I'm missing his childhood."

"You aren't missing his childhood."

She counts on her fingers. "I don't see him in the morning at all. I leave before he gets up. You take him to day care, and I pick him up at six. Drive home, hang out for an hour, then it's time to get ready for bed. I see him for a little over an hour a day."

"It's hard, I know."

"Hard? It's not hard. I'm just missing out."

I sigh heavily, not really sure what to say. "What if—"

Klaxons sound from my phone—a special "Oh, shit!" ringtone I've assigned to the office. I glance from the phone to my wife. "I need to get this."

She shrugs, dismissing me. I thumb the talk button and listen for a few moments. The Machine is down. Something's broken and something's lost and it all has to be fixed tonight. I turn back to Summer.

"I have to go."

She knows. She always knows.

A few days later, I'm standing in Declan's room in the dark. Early morning dark, with the sky just starting to nudge toward purple and indigo before really getting to the business of rising. Summer and I watch over Dec as he sleeps for the first time tonight.

He's sick. But not sick like adults get: [*cough cough*] *I don't feel so good.* He's sick like very small children get. The world-shattering, *my life is pain*, cataclysmic horror show of an illness. The kind of sick kids get that when the coughing starts you don't know which orifice some bodily substance is going to erupt from or what it'll be. And it's been going all night.

Summer and I back out of his room with as much grace as we can muster, terrified of knocking over or kicking or looking sideways at anything that could wake Declan from his hard-fought slumber.

Safe in the living room, I collapse onto a couch while Summer slumps in a chair.

"You or me?" she asks.

"You or me what?"

"Do you want to stay home or should I?"

I take a long, deep breath as I rub my eyes. "I don't know. Whaddaya got?"

"I can't really afford to be out. I'm the only one in the office, and we're finishing credits on a film this week."

"If you stayed home you could get some sleep."

"I can't take calls and take care of Declan at the same time."

"Right." She has a point. At times like this, I wish we lived near family. We're two thousand miles from the nearest person either of us shares a chromosome with. Besides Declan, that is.

"You guys busy?"

"Sure. Three projects and a sales tape. Trying to knock them out before the trip."

"Can anyone cover?"

"Not really." I crack my neck. It's gonna be me, and I know it. "I can handle it from here, though. I have mostly scripts and e-mail today."

"You sure?"

"Yeah. I'm sure. It'll be alright." I am in fact sure of no such thing. But it's our only option. "Let's get some sleep while we can."

Dec is intermittently awake throughout the morning. After firing a quick e-mail to the office, I split my time between petting his back and doing what I can to put things in order around the house. Basil needs to eat. There are dishes to do. Sheets to be changed, washed, sterilized—and maybe burned, depending.

The day is calming, in a way. Despite the situation, there is a serenity in these domestic tasks and in putting the house in order. Sometime after noon, with Dec finally down for something like a nap, I turn my attention to dinner that night. If not for Declan, then at least for Summer and me.

Braising is the order of the day. I'm tired, Dec's exhausted, and I'm sure that Summer will be wiped out when she gets home. We need something homey and satisfying, and braises are food for the soul. There's something about meat cooked low and forever that offers fortitude for the journey, whatever that journey may be.

Braising is the act of cooking a piece of meat in a liquid at low temperature for a very long time. If this project is about making the most out of every cut, braising a pot roast is a reasonable first step. I've done a pot roast before—simple fire-and-forgets in a crock pot with whatever vegetables I had at the time—but today, with nothing but time on my hands, I'm going to do it right. I pour a big cup of coffee and set to work.

The cut in question is a chuck roast. A cut off the shoulder of the cow, it has a lot of beefy flavor but also a lot of connective tissue that has to be dealt with in some way. In this case, braising will melt the connective tissue and thicken the braising liquid into a sauce. If cooked too hot or too fast, that tissue will remain intact and will not be delicious. The road to Nasty is paved with messed-up braises.

My chuck roast is a little over two pounds. It's a rich, vibrant pink oblong, streaked with white fat and a few crevasses across the surface of the meat. I lay it on a cutting board and pat it as dry as I can with paper towels.

First things first: I put a couple of cups of all-purpose flour in a pie pan, along with a couple of heavy pinches of salt and some solid grinds of black pepper. I nestle the roast in the pan, turning it to coat the meat. I go heavy on the seasonings because most will fall off anyway. When coated, it looks like a fluffy white pillow.

I set a casserole dish on my stove's biggest burner, pour in some canola oil, and gun the heat. When the oil dances like a Rockette, I gently lay the roast in the dish, turning the meat to sear all sides into golden-brown loveliness.

Suitably seared, I move the meat to a plate and add a quick mirepoix (diced onion, celery, and carrot in a 2:1:1 ratio) back into the casserole dish, along with some whole garlic cloves and an entire bottle of Shiraz. I also knock the heat back down to medium and preheat the oven. When the wine reaches the barest of simmers, I gently nestle the meat back into the pot. About three-quarters of the meat is covered by the deep-maroon liquid, like a meaty iceberg in a nighttime sea. I turn off the burner, cover the pot, and slide it into the oven.

That done, and the boy still sleeping, I pause for a moment. I have to wait for this pot roast now. In the meantime, I seem to have a moment to myself. It's weird. I sit down on the couch with my laptop to sort my inbox, really out of habit more than anything else.

"Daddy?" I turn. Declan stands in the doorway, rubbing eyes still half-closed from sleep.

"What's up, little man?"

"I want Mommy." The universal proclamation of sick kids everywhere.

"I know, buddy. I miss her, too. How's your tummy?"

"Hurts." He fights against a lower lip quiver and almost wins. "Where's Mommy?"

"She's at work, buddy. But she'll be home real soon." Tears begin to well up in his eyes, so I continue. "Wanna come sit on my lap?"

I set my laptop aside and he clambers into my arms, head resting on my chest. We sit there for a long moment. If there is a silver lining to this particular dark cloud of childhood contagion, it is in moments like these. I haven't gotten to spend this much weekday time with Declan in months. Though I certainly wish he felt better, this time together is quietly lovely. "Do you want me to sing a song, D.?"

"No," he replies. "I want an imagination story." A story I make up.

"You got it." I pet his back and continue. "Once upon a time, there was a ladybug."

"A ladybug?"

"Not just any ladybug. A *giant* ladybug."

"What was his name?"

"His name was Murray."

Three hours later, the boy is asleep and the house smells amazing. Savory and earthy and slightly acrid from the wine. I check the meat, and it disintegrates at a touch. Dinner is near.

I start some polenta with Parmesan and remove the meat to a foil-tented plate. My dog, Basil, will disappear this meat like a spy in Smolensk if I turn my back, so I stash the plate in the microwave to keep it safe. I strain the braising liquid into a bowl, then add the liquid back to the casserole dish, put a fire under it, and reduce it to build a sauce. When it coats the back of a spoon, I add in a little butter. In classic French cuisine, this is called *monter au beurre* and gives the sauce a glossy finish. I like glossy finishes.

When Summer returns home, I dish her a bowl of cheesy polenta, topped with chunks of tender, melt-in-your-mouth beef and a Shiraz-reduction pan sauce.

"I want our house to always smell this way," Summer says over dinner. The meat is rich and gently sweet, mixed with the dry nuttiness of the polenta.

That is to say: This is good. Real good.

I'm kind of amazed. *I* made this?

"Thanks." I smile. "I'm glad you're digging it."

"How'd it go today?" she asks.

"It was okay. He slept a lot," I answer. "You?"

"Good. Productive. Hard to be away, though."

"I know. We missed you. Dec especially."

"Dec especially?" she teases.

"You know what I meant. It's nice having the band back together. I mean, when we aren't running higgledy-piggledy all over the place."

"I bet. I don't like that Declan's sick today, or anything. But I can see how it'd be nice to spend a whole day with him. Without a whole weekend to-do list to worry about, I mean."

I take another bite of my dinner. Pensive. "Is it weird that two moderately capable people barely have the time to manage their household, keep up with their careers, and also parent a little boy?"

"I don't know." Summer shrugs. "The question of our time, I suppose."

"Man, we're busy."

She nods. "That we are."

Red Wine–Braised Chuck Roast

Time: 3 to 5 hours

Serves 4 to 6

Braising transforms tougher cuts into gorgeous, tender dishes that will make your whole house smell amazing. Cooking in a moist environment over low heat changes a connective tissue called collagen into a different substance, gelatin. The result: incredibly tender meat and a beautiful, naturally thickened sauce.

Perfect cuts for this will come off the chuck—chuck roast, arm roast, chuck eye roast, blade roast—but cuts off the round can work, too.

2 cups all-purpose flour

2 tablespoons kosher salt

2 teaspoons freshly ground black pepper

1 (2- to 3-pound) chuck roast

Canola oil (or coconut oil, ghee, bacon fat, or lard)

1 white onion, diced

2 carrots, diced

1 rib celery, diced

2 cloves garlic, sliced

1 (750-milliliter) bottle red wine

2 tablespoons unsalted butter, cut into cubes

1. Preheat the oven to 300°F.

2. Combine the flour, salt, and pepper. Dredge the meat in the mixture until well covered. (Alternatively, you can omit the flour and simply season liberally with salt and pepper.)

3. In a Dutch oven a little larger than the roast, sear the meat on all sides over high heat in just enough oil to cover the bottom of the pan. Remove the meat and set it aside.

4. Add a little more oil to the pot, add the onion, carrots, celery, and garlic, and cook over medium heat for a few minutes, until they're aromatic and slightly translucent. Scrape the bottom of the pot to release any stuck-on browned bits.

5. Pour in the wine and bring to a simmer.

6. Add the meat; the liquid should cover at least two-thirds of the roast. (If it doesn't, add a little water.) Cover the pot and transfer to the oven.

7. Cook, covered, for several hours, until the meat falls apart at the slightest touch or whisper of its name. The liquid should be simmering—bubbling every second or two—not boiling. If it's bubbling too vigorously, turn down the heat. Check the level of the liquid every 45 minutes or so. If the level drops to cover less than half the meat, add hot water to bring the level back up to two-thirds. Total braising time will vary. The dish is done when the meat is very, very tender.

Everything up to this point can be done up to a day in advance, if you wish. If preparing in advance, let the meat cool in the braising liquid. Then, when preparing the actual meal, reheat the dish over low heat and proceed as directed.

8. Remove the pot from the oven. Stash the meat on a plate and loosely tent with foil.

9. Time to make a sauce. Strain the braising liquid, discarding the solids, and return the liquid to the Dutch oven. Boil the liquid, uncovered, for 10 to 15 minutes over medium-high heat until the liquid is reduced and coats the back of a spoon.

10. Remove from the heat, add the butter, and stir until the butter melts.

11. Slice the roast and serve over a starch of your choice, topped with a few spoonfuls of the sauce. Wild rice, polenta, and mashed potatoes are all excellent starch options.

If you have an extra bottle of the wine you braised in, serve it at the table. It's classy.

3

Heritage

You bought a what?"

"No, you heard right. I bought a cow." It's noonish. I'm in a diner too hip for its zip code, sitting across the table from my friend Mike. He's a television editor I used to work with, a paragon of dry wit and keen intellect. Los Angeles by way of Chicago. We do lunch from time to time.

"Well, what are you going to do with it?"

"Eat it."

"You're gonna die."

"I'm not gonna eat it all at once," I counter. "Nobody's trying to reenact a Monty Python scene here."

"You're gonna get so sick of beef."

"Maybe. I'm gonna try not to repeat myself, though. Try and make the most of the beast. Branch out. See what I can learn."

"Well, good luck to you, man. It's honest, at least. That's a hell of a thing." He raises a glass. "Here's to your cardiovascular health," he toasts with a wry gallows grin.

I raise my own glass. "To a hell of a thing."

Our glasses tap, and he continues. "So, this cow. Is it a heifer, then? What are you working with here?"

First things first: I should really stop calling this beast a cow. Technically speaking, a cow is a girl of the species, specifically one that's had a calf. (Girl cattle that haven't had a calf are indeed called heifers.) The beast in my backyard is actually a steer. A boy cattle, if you will. Boy cattle that have been—ahem—"fixed" are steers, and steers that have been trained as draft animals are oxen. Boy cattle left unaltered are bulls.

That's a lot of terms for different ages and sexes of what is essentially one species—but cattle have been with us a long time. It stands to reason that we'd have a huge number of very specific terms to describe them. Similar highly specific language has cropped up around sheep and chickens, for example—themselves agricultural staples we've long relied on.

This steer came to my house in the back of a Prius from Oroville, and as a species, it's come even further. Yet in our imaginations, beef is the quintessential American food, associated with wide-open spaces, the Wild Wild West, and backyard barbecues everywhere.

How precisely this happened can't be completely definitively answered. But we know of some key moments—sort of a *This Is Your Life* review of American beef cattle.

Ten thousand years ago, what we think of as modern beef cattle didn't exist. Instead, a species of massive horned ungulate dominated the landscape from Spain, all across Europe and North Africa, and through large swaths of Asia. This was the aurochs (like "deer," the plural and singular version of the word is the same). And by any measure, aurochs were terrifying.

A complete aurochs skeleton can be seen on display in the National Museum of Denmark. The animal stood six feet tall at the shoulder and weighed in the neighborhood of 2,200 pounds. That's about twice as heavy as my steer weighed when it was alive and somewhere around ten inches taller, give or take. (My animal provided me with 420 pounds of beef, but the steer on the hoof weighed much more.) Aurochs were more comparable in size to American buffalo (or bison, if you prefer) than beef cattle.

The aurochs on display in Denmark was found along with three stone arrowheads fired by Mesolithic hunters. The arrows didn't bring the beast down, though—he fled and drowned in a bog. The hunters were denied a meal, but they were also spared what could have been the fight of their lives. Even wounded, the aurochs were more than capable of killing a human.

Aurochs are depicted in the famous Paleolithic cave paintings of Lascaux as fearsome beasts. They share wall space with rhinos and bears—animals firmly at the other end of the kill-or-be-killed spectrum. In a Lascaux chamber called the Hall of the Bulls, two tremendous black aurochs dominate the walls. The largest of the two animals is a whopping seventeen feet long, drawn so that the natural curvature and undulation of the water-carved walls accent the musculature of the beast. Clearly, these animals were revered, even in prehistory.

Nobody knows precisely *how* the first cattle were domesticated from aurochs—Neolithic hunter-gatherers didn't keep written accounts. All we have to go on are the archaeological record, a timeline of genetic changes coaxed from cattle DNA, and a rough history gleaned from those pictures daubed on the walls of caves. From these, we can tell that the first cattle were likely domesticated in the Fertile Crescent, approximately 8,800 years ago. These cattle would eventually become *Bos taurus*, or the taurine cattle breeds. Then, fifteen hundred years later, in the Indus Valley along what is now the India/Pakistan border, a second domestication event occurred, giving rise to the cattle that would become *Bos indicus*, or the modern zebu.

Two domestication events, giving rise to all the cattle in the world. Domestication is rare, and domestication of a bad-tempered herd animal the size of a Volkswagen is rarer still. Then, as Neolithic humans spread out from the cradles of civilization, they took their cattle with them. Very generally, the taurine cattle breeds went west, and the zebu went east.

These new bovine allies conferred tremendous benefits on human populations. Cows eat grass. Suddenly, grassland could be converted into a reliable protein source without the risk associated with hunting game. Cattle could provide enough milk to feed both their own offspring and their human herders, allowing humans to incorporate dairy into their diets on a regular basis. Hides could be converted into any number of leather goods, and—though over time they became generally smaller than aurochs—domesticated cattle were the best source of draft power available.

Aurochs didn't immediately vanish, however. They still roamed Europe during the time of the Romans, where they were popular antagonists in the arenas of the empire. Julius Caesar himself noted in his *Commentaries on the Gallic War* that aurochs were "a little below the elephant in size, and of the appearance, color, and shape of a bull. Their strength and speed are extraordinary; they spare neither man nor wild beast. . . . But not even when they are taken very young can they be rendered familiar to men and tamed." The last true aurochs died in 1627 in a forest in Poland.

Meanwhile, the taurine cattle multiplied and diversified into animals of all shapes and sizes: huge white cattle in France, mousy-brown cattle in Switzerland, short-horned red cattle in England, shaggy brown cattle in the highlands of Scotland. Then in the late 1800s, cattlemen began actually recording their pairings, leading to the formalization of many of today's cattle breeds: France's Charolais, Switzerland's Braunvieh, England's Shorthorn, Scotland's Highland cattle.

Speaking of Scotland, the beef in my backyard came from a Red Angus/Black Angus cross—named for County Angus on the northeast coast of Scotland, where the breed began in the eighteenth century. There, in the counties of Aberdeen and Angus, the native cattle were a unique strain of hornless, or polled, cattle. These cattle came to be called *humbles*, for their lack of horns, or *doddies*, because names are more fun when they sound utterly ridiculous.

These cattle were something of a curiosity, until a breeder named Hugh Watson began assembling a herd of doddies in County Angus. Watson came from a family of cattle breeders and had a knack for breeding the animals to bring out the traits he was looking for. In Angus, he developed a herd of polled cattle of exceptionally high quality—strong, symmetrical animals with gentle dispositions. Besides breeding exceptional animals, however, Watson had two notable insights. First, he showed them off, taking the animals to livestock shows to tout their quality far more than was common at the time. And second—he selected only for animals that were entirely jet black.

Hugh Watson was branding. Not in the *Ponderosa*, iron-in-a-fire sense, but in the modern marketing sense. He was forging a brand identity.

At a time when most steers were multicolored, Watson's jet-black animals stood out. And they were naturally hornless, which also stood out. And because he was an excellent breeder, they were big, beautiful examples of the species, which definitely stood out. As a result, Watson's distinctive beasts started winning livestock competitions. And they won a lot.

Watson's herd was the foundation of what would become known as the Aberdeen-Angus breed. Other breeders in those counties started breeding for similar characteristics. Then in 1867, Queen Victoria herself accepted a gift of beef from an Aberdeen-Angus steer for her Christmas dinner, and the Aberdeen-Angus was famous.

The first Aberdeen-Angus cattle arrived in the United States in 1873, when George Grant, a Scottish expat, transported four bulls to Kansas with a mind toward starting an empire. He called his new town Victoria, after the monarch who enjoyed Aberdeen-Angus beef. That fall, two of the bulls were shown at the Kansas City Livestock Exhibition. American cattlemen, however, weren't used to seeing polled cattle and considered them freakish. Grant's venture failed, and he died penniless a few years later.

The Aberdeen-Angus cattle, however, had arrived. They proved adaptable and hardy on the High Plains, and an American breeders association opened ten years later. In 1917, the association forbade the registration of any nonblack cattle, in accordance with Watson's desire for a solid black breed (hence, *Black Angus*). Then in the 1950s, the name was shortened to the American Angus

Association. Today, Angus cattle are the most prevalent beef cattle breed in the United States.

My steer, however, isn't a Black Angus. It's a Red Angus/Black Angus cross. As one might surmise, the difference is a matter of coloration. Black is a dominant genetic trait in Angus; red is recessive. (Really, it's more of a reddish brown, but who am I to quibble?) Watson, back in the 1800s, kept only the black individuals, and other breeders followed his lead to capitalize on the marketing campaign that Watson had set in motion.

In the United States, however, savvy ranchers quickly realized that quality animals were being eliminated from Black Angus herds simply because of their color. Some ranchers began buying up these otherwise excellent *Red Angus*. In 1954, the Red Angus Association of America was founded.

My Red Angus/Black Angus cross, then, is an Angus steer, without regard to coloration. I like that. I like that my rancher valued form and function over fashion. Seeing *Angus beef* in restaurants or supermarkets is a branding statement—just as it was for Hugh Watson's herd in the early 1800s. It isn't necessarily an indicator of quality in the same way that, say, Prime, Choice, or Select is. It's an indicator of the breed of steer that the beef came from.

Because Angus beef reaches full size so quickly, everyone raises them. They're an impressive breed of cattle, if not a unique one. Even if beef isn't specifically labeled Angus beef, it probably is anyway.

Burgers. I should really do burgers.

Summer and I are tiptoeing between the cars in our garage,

arms loaded with bags from the supermarket, as our son walks ahead of us at a brisk two-year-old pace. Of course, this pace is painstakingly slow from a fully grown human perspective. Even more so when those humans have each arm loaded with forty pounds of groceries. But with both cars parked in our two-car garage, there's no room for us to pass him.

"Do you have anything in mind for dinner, Sum?"

"No, I haven't thought about it." Then, to Dec, "Keep going, honey. These bags are heavy."

"I thought I'd make burgers."

Dec spies a particularly interesting pebble on the floor of the garage. Or maybe it's a mote of dust. He pauses to examine it, and the Grocery Train stops.

Summer sighs. "Honey, why didn't you tell me? I would have bought hamburger buns while we were at the store."

"I wasn't thinking about making burgers when we were at the store. Do I need to go back?"

The Grocery Train starts moving again. "No, it's fine. I'll figure something out."

"Sorry, Sum."

"Don't worry about it."

Declan reaches the back of the garage and the person-sized steel door that leads to the backyard. It doesn't shut all the way—I should fix that, maybe tomorrow—so he grabs the edge of the door and pulls. It swings open with a creak. Then it begins to swing shut.

"Honey, could you hold the door for Mom—"

"Buddy, the door . . . Don't let it—"

It slams back against the door frame with a loud clang, leaving Summer and me standing in a cramped garage, overburdened with two armfuls of groceries.

A few hours later, I'm standing in front of a small grill while two double handfuls of lump charcoal glow fiercely from beneath a coating of snowy-white ash. Lump charcoal is nothing more than pieces of hardwood heated to high temperatures without oxygen so they don't combust. The result is a wood-shaped block of almost pure carbon, which burns at temperatures much higher than the original wood. (Charcoal briquettes are made from sawdust by the same process and use chemical binders to form them into blocks.)

My charcoal is ready for cooking, so I slip back into the house. I've already divided one pound of ground beef into eight patties. On another counter, I cut some very sharp cheddar into slices about an eighth inch thick and an inch square.

I season the meat with kosher salt and freshly ground black pepper. Then I place a square of cheese on top of four patties, then place another patty on top of those, crimping the edges of the meat. These quarter-pound burgers will be cheesed from the inside. Cheesed *sneakily.*

"Those look good," Summer says, drifting through the kitchen.

"Thanks. You get the bun situation figured out?"

"Yep! Look at the oven." I turn and see a timer is set with only a few minutes left. Summer has been baking.

"Oh, nice! You made hamburger buns."

"I made sharp cheddar hamburger buns."

I look in the oven and see that she's shredded cheddar onto the top of the buns. It's turned a lovely golden brown. "Impressive."

"Glad you think so." She winks, then turns on her heel to leave.

Twenty minutes later, Summer and I bite into our burgers, while Declan noshes on their component parts. The burgers are simply seasoned, cooked medium, and earthy from the sharp cheddar both within the patty and atop the bun. It's an excellent, if simple, variation on this most American of dishes.

"These buns are silly good," I tell Summer between mouthfuls. "Really lovely."

"Burgers are nice, too," she says. "The cheese inside is a nice touch."

"Stealth cheese," I offer. "Glad you like it."

America, from Colonial times, inherited Britain's fondness for beef. No less a personage than Shakespeare commented on the British love of beef around 1599 on the plains of Agincourt in *Henry V.* In Victorian times, vegetables were incorrectly considered nutritionally deficient (it was thought that they would ferment in the stomach, as grass does in a cow's rumen), whereas grains were associated with the poor. Poultry and game were expensive, but beef was both accessible and retained a cultural history of vitality and yeoman pride.

When the first Aberdeen-Angus cattle arrived in the United States in 1873, they happened to arrive at a particularly formative time in U.S. history—the heyday of the cowboy and the romanticization of the West. At the time, America had a lot of open rangeland, most of it having been recently vacated by the nearly eradicated American buffalo. This landscape is an excellent habitat for large ungulates (e.g., hoofed mammals, such as buffalo), and cattle could thrive with minimal human intervention. The grass ocean of the Great Plains, then, provided a gigantic expanse of terrain ideal for raising cattle—and Americans raised a lot of them.

In Texas in the 1870s, longhorn cattle were the dominant breed.

Semiferal holdovers of spectacularly horned taurine cattle brought to the New World during Spanish colonization, they roamed in enormous herds across the prairies. They were so numerous that cattlemen could just ride out onto the range and take them. There in rural Texas, however, a steer sold for three dollars. In the meat markets of Chicago, the same animal sold for forty.

This brings us to another major factor in Americans' love of beef—democratic meat distribution. In Europe at the time, because they lacked America's wide-open spaces, beef was largely funneled to and consumed by the aristocracy. In America, however, it could be purchased by anyone, regardless of class. All anyone needed was the opportunity.

This demand for beef in the city led to the development of the epic cattle drive. Getting those cattle from the frontier to city markets was a tremendous undertaking. Cowboys would guide enormous herds along the Chisholm Trail from the wilds of Texas to the nearest railway terminals in Abilene and Dodge City, Kansas. From there, they would be shipped to meat markets in Chicago and elsewhere.

These cowboys—romantic figures, alone on the prairie, pitting their wile and guts against an ambivalent yet savage nature—captured the imagination of a nation still reeling from the Civil War. Cowboy dime novels flew off the shelves. In 1883, the same year that the American Aberdeen-Angus Breeders' Association was founded, Buffalo Bill Cody first staged his Wild West show. It depicted an exotic, untamed West where a man could start anew. Where it didn't matter what kind of family he was born into or where he was during the still-recent Civil War. Cowboys lived by their own code and by their own rules—largely free of hierarchy, intrusive government, a moralizing church, or the limitations imposed by large cities. In this, they came to represent a new and uniquely American vision of what it means to be free.

In 1893, twenty years after George Grant arrived on the High Plains with his black Scottish bulls, historian Frederick Jackson Turner presented a paper at a meeting of the American Historical Association in Chicago, entitled "The Significance of the Frontier in American History." In it, he argued that the unique situation of the American frontier was the crucible in which the essence of our democracy was forged. In adapting to the difficult and varied challenges of frontier life, Turner argued, useless or outdated European customs and thought patterns were burned away. Adaptation to the frontier transformed immigrants into Americans. The frontier was the scene of a democratizing process that enabled our unique experiment in government to thrive.

Turner presented his hypothesis at a significant time—census data published in 1890 had officially noted that scattered settlements throughout the West had erased any true geographic line denoting an end to U.S. occupation. Put another way, by the time Turner published his paper, the frontier had already vanished.

The West—and cowboys especially—carried a mystique. By some cultural osmosis, beef acquired some of this mystique itself: The cowboy can't exist without the cow. And to partake of a thick steak was to partake of a cultural experience both wild—as in Wild West—and celebratory of the unique abundance associated with the conquering of a "new" continent. To eat a steak was a reaffirmation of patriotism. Of Manifest Destiny—which revealed the High Plains upon which the new cattle empires thrived. Of America.

I grew up on those High Plains. The memory of those times is still palpable in the air there. It blows in with the dust, across the still-visible ruts the wagons made in the dirt of the Oregon Trail. You can feel it in Abilene, where the cattle climbed into boxcars bound for the great cities of the East.

The fate of cattle in those cities first came to light in Upton Sinclair's novel *The Jungle*. Published in 1906, it attempted to shed light on the plight of exploited immigrant labor working in Chicago's meatpacking industry. It described in grisly detail the most egregious of slaughterhouse abuses—dead rats poisoned by plant workers and swept into the pork sausage–making apparatus along with the poison that killed them, for example. Instead of focusing on the exploited immigrant laborers, however, the public focused on the revolting food safety practices. The uproar that the book caused led to the Pure Food and Drug and Meat Inspection Act, passed by Congress later that year. Sinclair would write in a 1906 article, "I aimed at the public's heart, and by accident I hit it in the stomach."

But the immigrants living in the great American cities, perhaps working in those meatpacking plants, and possibly eating beef for the first time in their lives, weren't necessarily eating steak as we know it today. If they were poor, they probably were eating something that we would consider more akin to a meatball: chopped beef odds and ends, likely served with caramelized onions or other filler and eaten with a knife and fork. They were likely eating something called the Hamburg steak.

Of uncertain provenance—some claim it came from Hamburg, Germany, others say it has an English origin—the Hamburg steak appeared in New York restaurants as far back as 1837. Regardless of where it originated, the Hamburg steak found a welcome home in the United States. It was a cheap, filling meal for workers on the go, and because the cuts it utilized were so inexpensive, it could sustain a reasonable profit margin for restaurants. At this point, however, it still required a knife, a fork, and a plate.

There are conflicting accounts regarding the first person to serve this meatball between two slices of bread. Various restaurants and culinary entrepreneurs all claim to have been the first to toast some bread or a bun and slide something like a Hamburg steak between them. Regardless of who had the initial idea, there's no debate about who first took the idea wide.

White Castle was founded in Wichita, Kansas, in 1921. We have them to thank for several innovations crucial to the transformation of the Hamburg steak into the hamburger that we know today. Among them: flattening the hamburger into a patty from a spherical shape and serving it on a special bun intended to showcase it. The first innovation allowed the Maillard reaction (aka "browning") to take place along a greater surface area of the meat, resulting in a golden-brown and delicious crust paired with a rarer, juicy interior. The latter invention, the bun, was toasted on the griddle alongside the patty, developing its own layer of golden-brown deliciousness—a layer that the meat juices would not soak through as quickly as they would a plain slice of bread. These developments together made the hamburger portable and largely gave rise to the sandwich we're familiar with today.

White Castle expanded rapidly, establishing 116 restaurants by 1930. They did so by relying on standardization and uniformity to mollify a nation still spooked by the revelations of *The Jungle*. White Castle's restaurants were white and airy, to reassure patrons of the facility's cleanliness. The company implemented (and extensively advertised) a set of protocols called "the White Castle System" to assure the public that every White Castle was absolutely identical to every other White Castle on the planet. Restaurant operators received specific instruction in every aspect of daily business, from building construction (prefab, to ensure uniformity), to cooking procedures, menus, napkins, and the smallest detail of employee dress.

White Castle enjoyed moderate success, and its formula for clean, identical hamburgers was widely copied. In 1948, however, the hamburger business would change forever.

It is upon White Castle's foundation that Richard and Maurice McDonald built their hamburger restaurant in San Bernardino, California. They co-opted the atmosphere of cleanliness and dependability but streamlined the operation to eliminate every process that made the business of moving hamburgers out the door less efficient. They slimmed down the menu to seven items. Eliminated all flatware and dishes—everything became disposable. No carhops or waitstaff; everyone ordered at a counter or a drive-through window. They mechanized every aspect of the operation, down to holding the hamburgers at service temperature under a heat lamp, so that they would be ready the instant a customer ordered them. It is this process that so impressed Ray Kroc that he joined the organization in 1954 with an eye toward founding an empire.

Entire books can and have been written about the McDonald's story. But the meat of the matter is this: Kroc was able to take a process that was already largely mechanized and standardized—namely, the making and selling of hamburgers—and spread it with a genius and an aggression that would make Napoleon blush. The result? Visit any highway off-ramp in the country. Odds are there's a McDonald's very close by.

White Castle, and then McDonald's, was able to take something unique to the American experience—plentiful, readily available beef—and make it ubiquitous. Cheaper, faster, and—notable for an era of primarily mom-and-pop restaurants—of a uniform, dependable quality.

Far from the horrors of *The Jungle*, the fast food hamburger became merely another product of American innovation in the atomic age. Another modern convenience, rather than something base and dirty like an actual animal.

Though fast food titans had plenty of animals to work with, thanks to developments in chemical engineering. At the conclusion of World War II, the United States found itself in possession of enormous quantities of surplus ammonium nitrate, with plenty of capacity to make more. This chemical has two major uses: as an oxidizer for explosives (it was built for the war effort) and as a precursor of nitrogen fertilizer. Corn is one of the most nitrogen-hungry crops on the planet, and nitrogen fertilizer can boost per-acre yield tremendously. As a result of munitions manufacture for the war, America now found itself awash in cheap corn. By and large, this surplus corn was fed to cattle. The feedlot system, originally developed in Chicago in the 1870s, meshed seamlessly with this postwar agricultural boom.

Because of the feedlot system, by the 1950s Americans had a nearly unlimited supply of beef. However, instead of being raised entirely or mostly on grass, cattle were being shipped to feedlots and quickly brought to market weight on cheap corn.

The entire process, however, begins with the manufacture of nitrogen fertilizer. To do that, one needs petroleum—the raw material needed to sustain the reaction that produces ammonium nitrate. This reaction, through the manufacture of fertilizer, turns petroleum into produce, specifically corn. And then feedlots turn that corn into beef.

The result of all this innovation is a cheap, uniform product, available anywhere, sold at a low, low price, and distributed through a business model that is almost infinitely scalable. McDonald's alone operates in 119 countries nationwide, with billions and billions of hamburgers sold.

Regardless of its long-ago origin in the Fertile Crescent, beef has become an American icon because, perhaps more than any other country, America literally made beef what it is today. For better or worse, we are largely responsible for its means of production and its means of distribution. Our doctrine of Manifest Destiny gave us the wide-open plains to produce it. We built our national myths around it, rode it hard in the cattle drives, and created a system around it to feed a growing and hungry nation.

In a way, we've succeeded beyond our wildest dreams. The flipside of this system, of course, is that if something is cheap and ubiquitous, we don't value it as much. Behind the mechanization and the drive-through windows, that product was once an animal.

I wanted to unpack the myth of beef and the cultural accoutrements that accompany it. That's why I bought an entire cow. I wanted to really wrap my mind around the idea of this animal that feeds my family, known to me only in its death. I wanted to rescue it from anonymous commodification and see why we eat the way we do. And, perhaps, find out if there's a better alternative.

To some extent, grass-fed beef producers are now rebelling against the mass production of beef—but as a result, grass-fed beef demands a higher price. Similarly, the locavore, farm-to-table, and Slow Food movements are trying to take back mealtime from mass production. In Los Angeles alone, scores of new restaurants are providing information on how and from where they source their food. As consumers, we vote with our dollars for the production methods we prefer.

The Best Burger on the Face of the Earth (Seriously)

Time: About 4 hours

Serves 4

Umami Burger, a restaurant that originated in Los Angeles, makes what is in my opinion one of the best burgers on the planet. This is an approximation of their signature sandwich. It isn't the same, but it's close.

To make a good burger, you need good ground beef. You have several options:

    (a) Use ground beef from the supermarket. Get 80/20 ground chuck if they have it.

    (b) Grind your own. Run 85 percent chuck and 15 percent sirloin through a hand grinder or the grinder attachment on your stand mixer.

    (c) Use already ground beef from your meat share or grass-fed steer. This is what I did.

If you'd like to prove yourself a true badass, you can brand the buns. See instructions below.

UMAMI KETCHUP

1 (28-ounce) can whole peeled tomatoes

2 tablespoons olive oil

1 large white onion, diced

½ cup cider vinegar

⅓ cup packed dark brown sugar

2 tablespoons tomato paste

1 teaspoon kosher salt, plus more to taste

2 teaspoons oyster sauce

2 teaspoons tamari

2 teaspoons Worcestershire sauce

5 anchovy fillets, finely chopped and mashed to a paste

CARAMELIZED ONION

1 tablespoon unsalted butter

1 large white onion, sliced

ROASTED TOMATOES

6 plum tomatoes

2 tablespoons olive oil

SHIITAKE MUSHROOMS

2 tablespoons unsalted butter

1 pound shiitake mushrooms, stems removed, finely diced

PARMESAN DISKS

4 ounces Parmesan cheese, shredded

THE BURGER

1 pound ground beef

Kosher salt

4 tablespoons unsalted butter, softened

4 good-quality hamburger buns

TOOLS

Wire coat hanger (optional)

Needle-nose pliers (optional)

The patience of a saint

1. To make the umami ketchup, begin by pureeing the tomatoes in a blender until smooth.
2. Heat the oil in a medium saucepan until shimmery, then add the onion. Cook over medium heat until the onion is soft and slightly translucent but not browned. If you hear sizzling, lower the heat.
3. Pour the pureed tomatoes into the saucepan, along with the vinegar, brown sugar, tomato paste, and salt. Slide this pan to a back burner, uncovered, and leave it alone to simmer gently over low heat for 1 hour. We'll come back to this later to add the rest of the ingredients. Don't let it boil vigorously—it can watch you cook, but it shouldn't comment.
4. To make the caramelized onion, begin by melting the butter over low heat in another skillet (cast iron is nice), then add the onion. Let it cook over low heat, stirring occasionally, for 45 to 60 minutes, until brown, sexy, and wildly caramelized. (Again, if they make noise, turn down the heat.)
5. While the onions are caramelizing, make the roasted tomatoes: Preheat the oven to 325°F.
6. Slice the tomatoes in half lengthwise and lay them cut side up on a baking sheet. Drizzle them with the oil and roast in the oven for 30 to 45 minutes, until they've shriveled and are beginning to caramelize. Be prepared for smoke.

7. Pull the roasted tomatoes from your oven and stash them somewhere out of the way to cool.

8. Knock your oven temp down to 300°F.

9. After 1 hour, remove the pureed tomatoes from the heat of your back burner. Add the oyster sauce, tamari, Worcestershire sauce, and anchovies to the tomato mixture. Puree with an immersion blender until smooth.

10. Fill a large steel bowl (or sink, or something similar) with icy water to create an ice bath. Stash the ketchup saucepan in the ice bath to cool, making sure the water from the bath remains below the lip of the pan so water doesn't flood in and wreck the ketchup. When the ketchup is at about room temperature, move it to the fridge until ready to serve. (How are those onions from step 4 doing? Don't forget about them.)

11. To make the shiitake mushrooms, begin by melting the butter in a skillet over low heat (it can be the same one used for the onions if they're done already), then add the mushrooms. Cook over medium heat for about 7 minutes, until the mushrooms are tender. Set aside.

12. To make the Parmesan disks, begin by folding a piece of aluminum foil into a sturdy strip and wrapping it around the circumference of a hamburger bun. Fold the ends over each other to make a bun-sized circular mold. Line a half sheet pan with parchment paper and drop your aluminum mold on top. Sprinkle the Parmesan into your mold, forming a disk of grated Parmesan the exact diameter of your hamburger bun and about ⅛ inch thick. Repeat three more times—creating four disks total.

13. Slip the sheet pan (making sure to keep it level!) into your

oven, which should now be at about 300°F. Bake these little disks for about 10 minutes, until just golden and transformed into tiny cheese Frisbees. Set aside. They should still be pliable when you pull them from the oven and will harden as they cool. If your onions are done, pull them from the heat and set aside.

14. Finally! The beef! Season the meat with a heavy pinch of salt and divide it into four patties, using the same mold you used for your Parmesan crisps for size.

15. Cook the burgers on (preferably) a cast-iron griddle or a grill over high heat for about 4 minutes per side for medium rare. Under no circumstances should you press down on the burgers with a spatula while they're cooking. It's bad for your soul. When the burgers have finished cooking, set them aside to rest.

16. Butter the hamburger buns. Don't be shy: Spread the butter to the very edge of the bun—it'll help them brown evenly. Drop the buns, butter side down, onto the griddle or grill for a few minutes, until they've reached the appropriate level of toasted Maillard-y glory.

Badass move: Brand your buns. Straighten out a plain wire coat hanger. Remove any and all nonmetal pieces from the hanger and fold the end into either the shape of your initial or that of your guest. Then bend the wire 90 degrees (needle-nose pliers help), so that the letter is perpendicular to the rest of the wire's length. You've just created a branding iron. Stash it in a 400°F oven for 20 minutes, or until hot. Be careful. Using oven gloves (duh), remove your branding iron and brand the top half of each bun.

17. Take a deep breath. You're about to eat. Bring out all the toppings and accoutrements from hiding and get ready to assemble the burger.

18. First place the bottom half of a bun in the center of a large plate. On top of this bun, smear some umami ketchup and then place a beef patty. Next comes the Parmesan crisp, a few mushrooms, a few tomato halves, and some onion. Place the top half of the bun on top, being careful not to press down.

19. Serve, enjoy, and bask in richly deserved adulation.

4

New Heights

When the weekend rolls around, I have a project. I'm prepping for an ascent up Mount Whitney, the highest peak in the contiguous forty-eight states. I can't wait. It's easily the most extensive expedition I've ever participated in. We'll start at the trailhead, Whitney Portal, at elevation 8,500 feet. Then we simply have to walk uphill for ten miles, until we hit elevation 14,505 feet, and there's no more uphill to walk. I need to be ready.

In this case, ready means well provisioned. To that end, I'm making jerky. I've never done it before, but I have a recipe that seems dummy-proof, and dummy-proof is key. This isn't food I'm eating at home; this is food I'm taking up a mountain. If I mess it up, there's no supermarket at elevation to fall back on, so I'd rather not mess it up.

Beef jerky is essentially nothing more than beef, dried and

seasoned to make it both lightweight and inhospitable to bacteria. Lightweight is good, because I'm going to be carrying it on my back a very long way. Inhospitable to bacteria means it won't go bad quickly, and I won't become explosively ill when I eat it. I've been explosively ill, and I can't say I recommend it.

In the jerky approach I'm using, the beef is first marinated in an acidic, salty liquid that hopefully tastes good. As you may recall from biology class, cells bring liquid through the cell membrane through a process of osmosis. Weirdly enough, that process is a passive one—it doesn't depend on blood flow or respiration or any other biological activity. When cells are immersed in liquid, cell membranes want to equalize the salinity of the liquid on either side of the membrane. So if one were to slice beef ridiculously thin, exposing a lot of cell membranes, and then submerge that beef in a delicious salty liquid, the cell membranes would draw said liquid into the meat, in essence seasoning the meat from the inside.

One great cut for jerky is flank steak. It's about the right size, is low in fat, and has a big, pronounced grain structure for easy slicing. That's clutch. Muscles are basically bundles of extremely thin cord that shrink as they dry. If I slice this piece laterally across those cords, the meat will fall apart as the meat dries into jerky. Like lace. The reason flank steak is so good for jerky is that you can slice *along* those long cords, keeping them intact. This will result in a long stick of relatively intact jerky, rather than a crusty meat doily.

Flank steak primarily comprises the abdominal muscles of the cow, off the belly, in front of the back legs. The problem is, I have a single cow. And that cow has only so much flank steak, which is good for lots and lots of preparations. Due to its scarcity, I'm not entirely sure I want to sacrifice any of it to make jerky.

Most butchers use top round for jerky. It's similarly low-fat, can be cut to the right size, and, if I slice with the grain, can be cut molecule-thin. I decide that this is the cut for me. Top round comes off the back leg of the animal, and since there are two back legs, I have scads and scads of top round.

The low-fat content of this cut is also key. Fat can go rancid at room temperature simply from exposure to oxygen, which would defeat the main point of making jerky: preservation. The lack of fat also makes cuts from the round primal prone to drying out easily, which is good for me, as drying out some meat is exactly what I'm trying to do.

First things first. I find a top round steak in the two-pound range. As jerky, it'll weigh considerably less, but I figure it should be enough to get me up and down the hill. I pull it from the freezer but don't thaw it all the way. If it's still a little frozen, it will stay firm and slice more easily.

I cut the top round along the grain, slicing it as thin as humanly possible. If a stiff breeze came through, these slices would flutter away. I could read an eye chart through these things.

That done, I prep my marinade. It may be possible to botch a marinade from a flavor standpoint, but from a chemical standpoint they're pretty straightforward. I need to build a salty, acidic liquid that tastes good. Soy sauce, Worcestershire, and red pepper feature prominently. I like the heat.

I stash all the meat in a Ziploc bag and stow it in the fridge. It needs to relax overnight so that the marinade has time to penetrate the meat. It won't penetrate far—despite what you've read, say, everywhere, marinade does not reach deep into the meat. It penetrates the surface of the meat a few millimeters, but no farther. Lucky then that my meat is only the thickness of a sheet of graphene.

So—cool. I have to let the beef marinate overnight, and the rest of my day is unscheduled. Summer has the little man, and they've set out on the town to run some errands. I'm all alone, with time on my hands.

Yep. Nothing on the list.

Nothing at all.

I have a hard time doing nothing. I'm done, now, with the task set before me, and any sane being would rest. But I'm pretty thoroughly conditioned to seek out the next bit of stimulus—the next box to check, the next bullet for boredom, the next activity to slot into my schedule to free me from the impending panic of not being productive.

I fire up the laptop. I'm the nerdiest guy in most rooms, and I've been a gamer since the deep dark wayback of the proto-Internet. So I take this opportunity to rid a fictional sleepy little town of a horde of the slavering undead. This is in no way relaxing, though it does provide the task-oriented part of my cerebral cortex with the illusion of productivity. My sense of accomplishment is real enough, though. However unearned it may be.

The next morning, back in the real world, it's time to get weird. I said this jerky was dummy-proof, and I meant it. The fastest and most efficient way that I could screw this up would be to burn it. I've had burned jerky—it's like chewing a charcoal briquette. Since the jerky is so thin, it'll burn if you so much as give it a come-hither look. Unless you don't use heat.

The approach I'm using comes from culinary guru and *Weird Science* party-scene extra Alton Brown. It involves drying the meat without any heat. Furnace filters. Strapped to a box fan. Set on high. And left alone.

Yeah, let's get weird.

After a quick trip to the hardware store, I'm getting ready to lay tiny slices of beef into the grooves on twenty-by-twenty furnace filters and trying not to wonder if the filters are fiberglass. Let's say they aren't. For safety, these filters should really be made of paper. Their packaging is unclear on the matter.

I'm sure they're paper. They must be paper. Why wouldn't they be paper?

But they really look like fiberglass. I'd prefer not to eat fiberglass.

Finally, caution gets the best of me, and I sandwich paper towels in between the furnace filters so that the beef isn't directly touching the material-that-may-or-may-not-be-fiberglass. I turn the fan on high and walk away.

Eight hours later, I check the protojerky. Still moist.

Ten hours. Still moist.

Twelve. Moist. Also, did I mention that for some reason I did this inside? I did. That was perhaps a mistake. My entire home smells like a smokehouse. I move the box fan outside and plug it back in, wafting meat fumes across the lawn.

Thirteen hours in, there are cats in the yard. The fan comes back inside.

Finally, fifteen hours later, the beef is dry. The furnace filters are beyond ruined, stained brown with marinade and meat juices. But the jerky is done.

I examine a piece of jerky. It's mostly dry and pencil-thin. It didn't maintain a rectangular shape—each piece contracted into a cylinder. They look like little beef ballpoint pens.

I taste a piece. It's lovely. Chewy and spicy, with just a subtle sweetness in the finish. I try another. I could definitely see myself eating this for a long period of time—on a climb up a very tall mountain.

I'll soon get my chance.

I've never climbed a mountain before.

I love the outdoors, and I clamber around in the mountains near my house whenever I have the opportunity, which isn't as often as I'd like. And I love to camp—in the same vague, but-I-never-do-it way that I love attending the symphony or painting with water-colors. Summer, on the other hand, makes no pretense about the woods—she'd rather wander through a downtown than the back-country and sleep on high thread-count sheets than under the stars.

When the opportunity to climb Mount Whitney presented itself, however, I couldn't say no. It came in an e-mail from my friend Zac. He and his wife, Katie, have been my close friends since high school, and as we've moved around the country in the intervening years, we've weirdly always managed to stay within a two-hour drive of each other. Our families plan vacations together. And somehow, Zac manages to get out into the wilderness a little more than I do. For both of us, this is a tremendous adventure. For me, this is a rare treat.

I'm going in a party of five—an assembly of friends and friends of friends, all hale and hearty and ready for the challenge. I'm by far the weakest link. Zac is the nucleus of the group and the only one who knows everyone. He's a navy physician and the kind of guy who files down the plastic nubs of the playing pieces of board games. He measures the weight of his pack down to the milligram, and he's one of my oldest friends. His buddy Uriah, in addition to having the best name on the planet, is a friend of Zac's from way back. Uriah's a gnome. Five feet six on his tippy toes, with the forearms of someone who both free climbs cliff faces near his Colorado home and also happens to be a recreational blacksmith. Rich is another navy doctor—a genial bear of a man—and an excellent general outdoorsman. He's been up the mountain a half a dozen times, and he knows it well. He's the closest thing we have to a guide. His wife, Natalie, is the only woman on the trip. She's a yoga instructor and prone to breaking into spontaneous handstands. Then there's me. My expertise is mainly limited to bad jokes and trivia questions.

Of the five of us, two are practicing military physicians with experience in emergency medicine; one is a skilled technical climber, acclimatized to high altitude; one is a fitness professional in peak physical condition; and one has an unproduced screenplay about fairies.

Mount Whitney is one of the most accessible high peaks in the United States. The path to the summit ascends very gradually. It's a wide, well-tended twenty-two-mile trail that meanders along a route especially chosen to be accessible to hikers of all fitness levels, with permanent handholds installed for any potentially tricky bits.

We aren't going that way.

We're headed up something called the Mountaineer's Route, and it isn't actually a marked trail, though it is a well-known path to the mountain's summit. We will start out on the main Mount Whitney Trail, then veer off the trail at the north fork of a mountain stream called Lone Pine Creek. We'll follow this creek straight uphill about eight miles, rather than pussyfooting around the perimeter of the range. This route is shorter and harder and has a lot more exposure (i.e., chances to fall a very long way). It's the route that John Muir took to what was then the roof of the country, and it's a classic of American mountaineering.

Zac, Uriah, and I carpool from my place up to Whitney Portal. It's a remarkable drive. North of Los Angeles, the suburbs and lush green lawns fall away as the road drops out of the San Gabriel Mountains and into the Mojave Desert. Water is scarce, and Joshua trees claw the impossibly blue sky like dessicated hands. As we drive north, the High Sierras rise out of nowhere, ten miles or so to our left. Among them, the highest point in the contiguous United States. To our right, just over the horizon, Death Valley, and the lowest point. It's a climate of extremes.

Zac points the car into the mountains, and we ascend. Up and up, into a bowl situated high in the range, surrounded on all sides by stark granite cliffs and hundred-foot pines. This is Whitney Portal. The air is thick with the scent of pine trees and a feeling that somehow the world is bigger here than it is in cities at sea level.

We start unloading our gear. After my first enthusiastic trip from car to campsite, the altitude hits me. Just a touch dizzy. Just a touch out of breath. The High Sierras are no joke. My second trip is a little slower. More purposeful. Soon, the five of us are sitting on a crude wooden bench with an entire REI scattered around us.

I start to cook as night falls. Because of my recent bovine acquisition, I'm in charge of dinner at base camp. Steaks, as one might surmise. New York strips, to minimize variables—I can't afford to mess this up. I'm cooking over a campfire, at elevation, with a dull knife and a handful of wishes. I need something I know.

It probably isn't the best steak I've ever cooked, but it might be one of the best I've ever eaten. Moderately seared and red-rare on the inside, but eaten in a tall pine forest as a mountain stream gurgles nearby. Eaten in the dark. With a spork.

We talk about prep and the trek to come. There's anticipation in the air. Something about the moment compels us to speak in low tones. There are jokes sprinkled among the logistics. And optimism. And just beneath the surface, a little trepidation.

Before dinner, we learned that the Whitney summit was snowed in.

We aren't geared for snow.

The next morning, we set off. The trail winds along the side of the mountain, steadily uphill. I'm a little winded from the altitude, but nothing too bad. We all joke and chatter, excited to be under way. Soon enough, a stream of water gurgles and splashes out from the thick brush to our right. Lone Pine Creek. "Up," Rich commands, pointing.

This is where the trail ends for us. But the route continues. We leave the nicely maintained trail, affectionately called the Mule Trail, and head directly up Lone Pine Creek. Thirty seconds later, a large sign warns us, in all caps: THIS IS NOT THE MOUNT WHITNEY TRAIL. Then, lower down: THE MOUNTAINEERS ROUTE IS NOT EASY. It goes on to clarify: "Visitors without proper skills, knowledge, equipment and experience have died here."

"There are a lot fewer people on the Mountaineer's Route," I note.

"Just ten a day," Rich says. "And we're five of them."

We continue upward at a much steeper grade than the trail we just left—probably over triple the incline. The Mountaineer's Route climbs the same elevation as the main trail, but in about a third of the distance.

Forty-six pounds—the weight of my pack—was light at the bottom. It's not so light now. Did I really need to bring that extra pair of shoes? There's no signal on my phone. Why did I bring it? How many cameras are too many?

Continuing up, we cross back and forth across Lone Pine Creek a half-dozen or so times, stepping across slick, wet granite and dodging spray from waterfalls. It's fun, but tiring. We break every minute or so, just for a few seconds, to give our lungs a chance to wring out every last molecule of oxygen from this so-called air.

At about 9,600 feet elevation, we bump up against a tall granite wall. Our path is not immediately obvious. We sit to rest, drinking water like camels and scarfing down enormous handfuls of sugary homemade granola. I have more than a little sugar in my pack, intended to help me power through any exhaustion I might encounter. The glucose is a welcome and immediate lift to my mood.

I look around. "Where do we go from here?" There is only the path that we came up, ending at a sheer granite wall.

Rich, leaning against the wall, points a single finger skyward. "These are the ledges, man."

I look up. Zac had mentioned something about the Ebersbacher Ledges in passing. According to some, they're the most difficult section of the route. Though not the most technically challenging, they offer some of the most daunting exposure of the journey. In other words, it's an easy climb, so you probably won't fall. But if you do fall, you'll probably fall several hundred feet.

"Can I bum some jerky?" Rich asks.

"Of course." I offer my stash. He takes a piece, and I shake the bag, weighing it roughly in my hand. I may have brought too much. In my zeal to prepare for every possible contingency, I may have burdened myself further. Still, I'm going to be hauling this entire bag to the top, either on me or in me. Better in me. I pop another stick in my mouth.

As I munch my jerky, I look up at the cliff. There isn't a trail to be seen. From my perspective, it's just a wall.

I offer jerky to Uriah, who's also looking upward. He nods once to himself, definitively. "This'll be fun."

Rich leads us uphill, parallel with the cliff, beneath a canopy of gigantic woody bushes. We aren't really on a path so much as a thin divide where the enormous plants looming over us can't grow any closer to the granite cliff. I feel like a child again, hiding under the bushes that grew along the wall of my elementary school.

Another forty feet or so, and we turn around. There are boulders leading up and onto the granite wall. And upward from there in a series of sloping ledges.

"Ready?" Rich asks. But Uriah's already up. That guy's like some kind of goat.

We take our first tentative steps across the ledges. To my left, the ledges step up in increments five feet tall, one behind another. They're like Little League bleachers for giant children.

The path in front of me is about three feet wide, narrowing to two as I continue. The ledge slopes gently, but noticeably, to the right. I trail my hand against the cliff wall to my left. Its solidity is comforting.

To my right is nothing but open space.

"Is this safe?" Natalie asks. I look back, and she has stopped, eyes fixed on the sheer drop to our right.

"Sure." Rich nods. "Just don't fall."

I take a deep breath and turn back to my task. Ahead, Uriah's strolling happily along, completely nonchalant. As if at any moment an entrepreneurial Sherpa might appear and sell him ice cream. He might even be whistling.

I begin to walk.

Just don't fall. Why would I fall? I haven't fallen yet. There's no reason I should fall now. I have solid new boots. I even hiked in them beforehand to break them in. Mostly. I'm sure I won't roll my ankle in them, like I did a couple weeks ago. On the sidewalk. The flat sidewalk. I shouldn't have fallen then, either. And I have terrible ankles. Ever since I broke them in high school and—

Shut up. Just walk.

I press on, acutely aware of every ounce of my pack and the newness of my boots. I'm slightly top-heavy and I wobble with every step, the wobble amplified by my awareness of the precipice to my right. Once, I catch my right boot on my left calf and stagger for half a second before my foot finds the ground.

"You alright, man?" Uriah asks, shooting me side-eye.

"Oh, sure," I answer, masking my clumsiness with humor. "You know, I'm thinking maybe I should get into parkour. Climb some walls. Jump some gaps. It'll be great."

"Yes!" Zac concurs. "Let me know when. I'll go, too. We can get matching compound fractures together."

I laugh.

"Up here, I think," I hear Uriah say. I look, and he's five feet or so above me, one level up, next to a small cairn. I grab the rock above me and pull myself up onto the ledge.

We continue upward. Another cairn. Another ledge. A gnarled tree root to grab. A sketchy crack to inch along. Uriah gives me a hand up. I do the same for Zac, who does the same for Rich, then

Natalie. Then, suddenly, it's over. A trail winds up and away now, leaving the ledges behind.

We pause. That wasn't so bad. I look down. The ledges extend maybe twenty feet in front of me before ending at a sheer drop. To our left, the valley descends hundreds more feet to the portal, then thousands to the valley below.

Uriah shoves his hands in his pockets. "Cool."

"That's amazing," Zac agrees. "How much farther to Lower Boy Scout?"

Rich looks up the hill. "Fifteen minutes or so."

An hour later, we crest the lip of a cliff and come to the edge of Lower Boy Scout Lake. A broad expanse of water spreads out before us, placid and clear, to a broad granite cliff a half mile distant.

We sit for lunch. A fat handful of granola and some sticks of jerky. "Dude, how much did you bring?" Rich asks.

"I'm not sure. A lot. I just made it and packed it. Better to have and not need than need and not have." That's a Boy Scout thing, right? I was never a Boy Scout.

"Until you have to carry it," he replies. "Then it just slows you down."

Rich has a point; I may have overpacked. I'm tired, there's no doubt about it. And the elevation is a variable that my sea-level body couldn't anticipate. Sitting on a rock for lunch, I realize that even though I've been eating jerky whenever I wanted, my bag still looks full. As I munch another stick, I can feel my strength returning. Sitting here, resting for a moment, eating this jerky—this is key. It's good for my psyche. If I'm pissy and hungry, I won't be good company, either physically or emotionally. However, there's a very fine line between being prepared and having too much baggage. It's a line I may have crossed.

I pull out a few more sticks before offering the bag back to Rich. "Take some more. Please." He shrugs and obliges.

Our trek paused, I pull out my phone and check my e-mail. No signal. I shove it back in my pocket and look around, momentarily without stimuli.

And then I remember that I'm on a mountain.

I take a deep breath. And I start to relax.

We scramble across a field of talus boulders, varying in size from washing machine to small house. I wield trekking poles to negotiate the uneven terrain and uncertain footing of the big rocks. The poles are lifesavers here—it's like the entire world has handrails. I cross the boulder field like some kind of gently brain-damaged giant arachnid.

Our ascent is punctuated by three large plateaus. Lower Boy Scout Lake is the first. The second, Upper Boy Scout Lake, is our target now. The third, at Iceberg Lake, is our camp for tonight. "How long before Upper, Rich?"

"Oh, forty-five minutes. Hour tops."

Two hours later, we crest a low ridge to the campground at Upper Boy Scout Lake. The sun is low above the crest of the mountains all around us. There are no trees—we left them behind five hundred feet below.

Rich leans against a rock. "Forty-five minutes may have been a little optimistic."

Zac surveys the sky. We're supposed to camp at Iceberg Lake tonight, another 1,300 feet up. "Rich, how much longer to Iceberg?"

"It's a pretty easy hike. Maybe an hour."

Uriah nods. "So two hours."

"And change," I add.

Rich looks over at us and breaks out into a wide grin. "Okay, maybe."

We laugh. "I'm not sure we have the daylight," Zac notes.

Rich nods. "We can camp here at Upper Boy Scout. No big deal. We'll have a longer hike tomorrow, but nothing we can't handle."

"I think that's probably a good idea. That cool with everybody?" Uriah asks.

"Yes." Natalie drops her backpack to the ground and slumps against a rock. Rich sees and offers her some water.

"You okay, Nat?" Zac asks.

"I'll be alright. The altitude is getting to me."

"Make sure you stay hydrated, honey," Rich suggests, still holding out the water. "Dehydration sucks up here."

She takes the water. Rich pats her back. Uriah looks out over the valley floor, thousands of feet below us. "It's getting cold."

It could be a trick of my eyes, but shadows are racing across the granite cliff walls high above us. "Does it get dark up here earlier than in the valley below?"

Rich nods. "Much earlier."

Twenty minutes later, I'm wearing every piece of clothing I have. The temperature has dropped at least twenty degrees, and we're racing to set up camp—half as shelter from the wind and half to stay warm.

"Zac, do you have an extra shirt?"

He swivels to me, suddenly concerned and in doctor mode. "No. I'm wearing everything. Are you okay?"

"Yeah, I'm fine. It's just that my nipples have sliced through the three shirts closest to my skin, and I thought you might have an extra."

He cracks a grin, and we work faster. Some Good Samaritan previous camper hand-built a rock wall windbreak, and now I see why. Freezing winds whip through our camp at twenty miles an hour.

Moments later, two tents are up. That done, I set out to find a suitable place for my bivy sack. I'm not in a tent on this trip—I'm in a much lighter, much smaller waterproof bag only slightly larger than my body. It's definitely not for the claustrophobic or those who have a persistent fear of mistakenly winding up in a body bag, but I like it. It doesn't stake down like the tents do, so to keep it from blowing away I need something by a windbreak, but not too far from the rest of the crew. Some ten yards off, I find a boulder the size of a large house propped up on some smaller boulders the size of small cars. This'll do.

I roll out my bivy sack and drop some rocks on it. Standing there, I look up at this gargantuan boulder looming above me. That's a big rock.

I pull out my phone and check for a signal, idly curious what the seismological history of the mountain range is. It'd be great if Google could tell me whether this rock was likely to crush me like a bug in my sleep. No signal. I slip the phone back into my pocket, unaccustomed to being out of touch.

I rejoin the crew. Zac, something of a camp chef, offered to do both of our backcountry dinners. Rich and I go to a nearby stream to pump some water for our Nalgene bottles. Up here, water is everything. There is no other beverage.

I dip the intake end of Zac's pump into the stream, and Rich slips the output end into his bottle. I begin to pump, actively resisting an urge to check my phone. Little by little, water begins to trickle out into the bottle, passing through a series of antimicrobial filters that should clear out any harmful bacteria that could make us sick. Afterward, a few drops of a water treatment solution directly into the bottle should knock out any bugs the filters miss.

As I'm pumping, a lone figure stalks toward us on the other side of the stream. He sports a bandanna and full beard that would be the pride of Sturgis. But he's also wearing a broad-brimmed hat to protect against the sun. It's the hat that gives away his occupation: park ranger.

"Gentlemen," he greets us. Without another word, he walks a few feet downstream of our pump site and dunks his Nalgene bottle into the water, filling it instantly. He stands and turns back toward his tent.

"Aren't you worried about disease?" Rich asks.

The ranger shoots Rich a look like Santa shoots to children in movies who ask why their parents don't believe. "Nah. I'm not worried. Not here." Then he continues toward his tent.

Rich and I exchange a look. "Good enough for me," I offer.

"Yep," Rich, the doctor who actually knows something about gut-exploding bacteria, says. We drop the pump and fill our bottles directly.

Bottles filled, we head back to camp. I take a swig of stream water from my bottle. It is the coldest, clearest water I've ever tasted. "Wow," is all I can say.

I stand silently for a moment, chilled from the stream water and the wind whipping by me. It's very quiet here. The only noise is that which we make ourselves. I'm tired but content, exhaustion momentarily dulling my urge for stimuli. Still standing, I close my eyes and revel in the silence and the wind.

Darkness falls at elevation long before it reaches the town of Lone Pine, visible far away in the valley below. Natalie retreats to her tent, but the rest of us shelter under the windbreak as night falls all around us. Above, there are more stars than I've ever seen.

Uriah stares upward, resting his head on a rock.

I point. "The stars are brighter because they're closer here."

He looks at me, unsure if I'm serious. I am not. He laughs.

The four of us eat and chat as night spreads from our plateau into the valley below us. Up here, eating is a sacred act. Not only are we hungry on a physical level, but I'm acutely aware that I'll need every calorie I can get. Those calories are the difference between summiting and failing. It's like carbo-loading before a big race. This food is fuel.

But here, perhaps more than at sea level, it's also an event. Really, it's the only event we have. This little ceremony, this small moment in the dark, huddled against a rock in the wind, where our only obligations are to eat and chat. No pack to carry. No hill to climb. Just conversation and reflection. And maybe a joke or two.

After dinner, Rich calls it a night. Natalie still isn't feeling well. She's spent the entire evening in her tent, so he retreats to his tent with our best wishes.

I'm beat. And I'm not alone. With limited entertainment options, night falls hard. Zac and Uriah are ready for bed as well. And it's all of eight o'clock.

"You want to crash over by us, man?" Zac asks me. "You can

tuck your bivy up into the vestibule of the tent and get some shelter from the wind."

"Nah, that's okay. I have my sweet rock shelter all prepped. I should be good."

I bid my friends well and fight the wind back to my bivy sack under the enormous house-sized boulder. I crawl in and leave the top open, better to watch the slow migration of the stars across the sky.

Except I can't. I'm under a huge, house-sized rock.

That's okay. I need sleep anyway. I can already tell I'm going to be sore tomorrow. I close my eyes and shove the fleece I've been wearing into a makeshift pillow.

But I can't relax. That rock's awfully big. It's not going anywhere, right?

My eyes blink open. I look. The rock is being supported by two boulders that would be absolutely enormous if they weren't being dwarfed by this rock the size of a midrange duplex.

I peer at these rocks through the darkness, looking for scrape marks or any sign that the rock might have slid recently. I can't see very well, so I scramble out of my bivy to look. Nah. I don't think so. This rock's probably sat like this for a hundred years. It certainly isn't going to slip off its perch now and crush me like an overripe grape.

I slip back into my bivy sack. This is stupid. I'm being crazy. Time to sleep.

I pointedly close my eyes. I take a deep, relaxing breath.

Eyes closed, I can still feel the cool of the rock above me. Its presence—leaching heat out of the air. Radiating cold.

That's stupid. That isn't how thermodynamics work.

Another relaxing breath.

Stillness.

I do wonder if this place is seismically active . . .

No.

No? These mountains have to come from somewhere . . .

I am sure the High Sierras will not experience a freak earth-quake tonight and slam a thousand-ton minimountain of granite death onto my unconscious body. That isn't going to happen. Sleep. Now.

Long, slow, deep breath.

Lotta big boulders down in the valley . . .

No.

You willing to bet your life on it?

I lie there for a long, pensive moment. I have a life ahead of me I'd rather not miss out on. And if Summer found out I died from falling asleep under a big rock, she'd kill me.

Dammit. My eyes blink open.

Forty seconds later, I am trudging back to Zac and Uriah's tent, my pack on one shoulder and my bivy draped across the other.

Zac hears me coming and unzips the tent flap. "Hey, Jared. You okay?"

"Make room in the vestibule."

The sun rises in an incredible wash of pink and rose reflected off the high granite cliffs all around us. I stretch. As predicted, I'm sore. But in a good way. I'm sore like I did something, rather than being sore like I didn't.

Zac's cooking like he's expecting in-laws. Bacon. Fresh pan-cakes. Peanut butter. Eggs. I wouldn't be surprised if there were a fruit platter and a tasteful muffin basket around here somewhere.

Uriah pours me a cup of coffee. Natalie and Rich are up and about. She's considerably less green than the night before. "How you feeling, Nat?"

"Better, thanks."

"Make sure you eat first," Zac says, dishing a fresh pancake into a bowl. "Today's gonna be a long day."

I survey my own bowl of breakfast joy. It'd be a feast at any elevation. I nosh happily, my only lament that I have to cut/scoop my bounty with a spork.

Then Uriah earns his genius badge for the day. He smears a pancake with peanut butter, drops eggs and bacon on top along with a little maple syrup, and then he rolls the whole assembly up like a taco. "I call it the McGriddle."

In a heartbeat, we imitate him. "Yes," Rich says emphatically. "This. Yes."

"Uriah, I want to have your genius babies."

"Well-fed genius babies," Zac notes.

"This is the single greatest food assemblage ever devised by the mind of man."

Zac roots around in the bear canisters that protect our food stores from hungry ursines. "We need more pancakes."

We cook through our breakfast stores, partly from hunger, partly so we don't have to carry them, and partly because we're enjoying ourselves. We will summit with daypacks, leaving the bulk of our gear here at camp. We laugh and joke well into the morning. By the time we turn our faces toward the summit, it's 11:00 a.m.

Buoyed by rest and ample breakfasting, we set out. The weather is some sort of platonic ideal of sunny. We move quickly, but through ever-increasing dustings of white.

Then finally, as we crest a cliff, a broad plateau stretches out in front of us leading to the very foot of Mount Whitney itself. In the distance, a pale gray-blue ring peeks out from beneath a field of white, denoting the edge of the aptly named Iceberg Lake.

And all around us—snow.

As we hike the mile or so to the frozen lake, my trepidation grows. We aren't geared for this. The snow will only get worse as we go higher. And the last five hundred vertical feet before the summit is a borderline-technical climb straight up, over icy rocks, with a twenty-five-hundred-foot drop immediately behind us.

Zac points at the mountain. "Climbers. Coming down."

I don't see anyone. But then, after scanning for a long moment, I notice several black specks barely visible against the white of the snow. They're tiny.

And they're coming down fast. "They're glissading," Uriah notes. As I watch, they slide down the mountain on their asses, using their ice axe to slow their speed.

"That is awesome," Natalie says.

Right about now I wish I had an ice axe. And waterproof pants.

As they hike toward us, the specks resolve into people. One of them is the ranger we chatted with the night before, at the stream. He waves and breaks into a broad grin.

I whip out my bag of jerky. We've eaten maybe 40 percent of it. I offer pieces to the crew.

Rich asks the ranger about the ascent, noting that though we did rent crampons at the last minute, we don't have ice axes. We also have only limited water-resistant gear. Can we make it up?

"Maybe," he replies. Earlier in the day it would have been eas- ier. But the midday sun softens the snow and melts the ice. Makes surfaces slicker than they would be first thing. The longer we wait, the more treacherous the climb. Our leisurely breakfast may have cost us the summit.

As he talks, I extend my bag to the ranger. "Beef jerky?" I offer.

The ranger smiles. "That's kind of you." He pulls a stick out of the bag and takes a bite. "Wow. You did a nice job with this. What'd you use?"

"Top round."

He nods. "Good choice for jerky. I used to be a meat cutter. I love top round."

"Please, have some more. We have plenty."

The ranger smiles again. I get the feeling he isn't used to hikers offering him food from their stores—he's the guy who checks for their permits and enforces the rules. Up here, you have only what you can carry. And you can't carry much. You can replenish water on the mountain but not food. Suddenly, I'm struck by how valuable this jerky is. But from the look on the ranger's face, it's something he already knows.

The ranger takes another stick of jerky. "Thank you," he says simply. He looks up at the mountain, then back to us. "You might be able to make summit, if you hurry. Ice axes would be more valuable than your crampons at this point. You have trekking poles, though, so that's something.

"But if you're gonna go, go now."

Five minutes later, four of us are hiking as fast as our wobbly post-McGriddle bodies can take us, heading for the tall couloir the ranger came down. Natalie elected to stay at Iceberg Lake and take photographs rather than taunt her recently eradicated altitude sickness with a summit attempt. There's a calm wisdom in her restraint and her ability to listen to her body. To come all this way and not feel the temptation of the summit is something I'm not sure I could do. She may be a Jedi. I'm impressed.

The couloir is a tall seam in the side of the mountain, gray ordinarily, but now solid white with snow. As we approach, the seam grows, looming impossibly large against the eye-searing cerulean of the sky. Distances are tricky to judge here. The mountain was farther away than we thought.

We move from rock to rock as we approach the mountain, like frogs on granite lily pads in a snow-white pond. As the angle of ascent increases, our lily pads fall away. In moments, we are hiking straight up the couloir at a forty-five-degree incline, each of us stepping into the footprints of the person in front of us lest we sink too deeply into the snow. Without waterproof gear, I'm getting soaked.

Rich leads, with Zac and me following ten feet or so back. Uriah takes up the rear, burdened with an extra twenty pounds of climbing rope. He's probably the strongest climber, but he's slowed by the extra weight.

On a whim, I extend my trekking pole to its full four-foot length and jam it into one of Zac's footprints. The pole disappears. "How deep you think the snow is?"

"Twenty feet, minimum," Zac calls over his shoulder. "At least that's what my research said."

We keep moving up. Once or twice, I accidentally punch through the compressed snow in Zac's footprint, sinking to my hip without touching any solid ground. Ahead, Rich is increasing his distance from us, while Uriah's falling behind.

I stop to look around. The view is breathtaking. Here, the world is three colors. Blinding white snow, pale gray granite—and above, an impossibly bright blue sky.

This is the steepest ascent we've yet faced, and between the angle and the snow our pace is slow. I check my watch. It's a little after two thirty, but the sun is already dipping low toward the ridgeline. Yesterday, it was dark at six. And our plan—the plan for which we are geared and provisioned—is to hike all the way back down the mountain to Whitney Portal before dark.

It dawns on me: We aren't going to make it.

Zac's the only one in earshot, and he hasn't spoken in a while. That's unusual. "What's on your brain, Z.?"

"I think we have a long way to go."

"Yeah. I don't think we're gonna summit."

"Doesn't look like it."

I pause. "We should stop climbing. We're just making our return longer. We have to get all the way back to the portal today, and I don't want to be trapped trying to negotiate the ledges in the dark."

"Agreed."

About this time, Uriah catches up to us. Either he heard us talking or, more likely, his thought process was already two steps ahead. "We need to turn around."

The three of us stand there for a moment, hip deep in the High Sierra snowfall, and just wait. The air is cold and still, and none of us speak. Below us, almost the entire continental United States spreads out in hazy greens and pale, rusty browns.

Almost the entire continental United States, but not all.

I look up at the peak still towering above us. We're only 150 horizontal feet from summit, but a little more than 500 vertical feet. To get there, we'd have to continue upward another 200 feet—an hour, by our estimates—to what's called "the Notch." There, we would all rope in and climb several hundred more feet up a rock wall that will be slippery with ice and snow, with a sheer 2,500-

foot drop behind us, meaning instant death if we fall. If we succeed there, we'd then have to do it all again, only backward. In the dark.

We've hiked a long way to get here, but unfortunately this is where our ascent ends and we all know it. Eventually, Rich notices that we're no longer following and returns to us. Reluctantly, he agrees.

We stand there for a long moment, the four of us, and try to fix the experience in our memories.

Uriah speaks first. "We'll come back."

"Hell, yes, we will," Rich says.

"I'm free next weekend," Zac offers.

I nod. "I think they have a loyalty program. Try two ascents, get your third free." They chuckle.

Uriah turns to us and smiles a little. "You guys wanna learn how to glissade?"

Thirty seconds later, I tuck my trekking pole under my arm, face down the forty-five-degree slope to Iceberg Lake, and hurl myself forward—sliding furiously, chaotically, ridiculously—down the mountain on my ass, using the pole as a rudder. Laughing. All the way down.

Killer Jerky

Time: 16 to 21 hours, largely unattended

Serves lots. Enough to feed several people as they climb a mountain.

Jerky made at home is simple, healthy, and ridiculously delicious. It compares very favorably with anything you can buy in a store.

I adapted this method from Alton Brown's justifiably famous recipe.

2 pounds round steak or flank steak

1 cup Worcestershire sauce

1 cup soy sauce

2 teaspoons freshly ground black pepper

1 teaspoon onion powder

1 teaspoon garlic powder

2 teaspoons liquid smoke

2 teaspoons red pepper flakes

1 tablespoon honey

TOOLS

Two (20- to 25-inch) bungee cords

Full-size (20-inch-square) box fan

Three (20-by-20-by-1-inch) furnace filters (economy grade or those labeled "better" are fine—just avoid any that contain fiberglass)

1. If your meat is frozen, thaw it until it's still firm but not frozen solid. If your meat isn't frozen, stash it in the freezer for 30 to 45 minutes or so, just until it firms up. This will make the meat easier to slice thinly, as it won't wobble around.

2. Slice the meat very thinly, following the grain lines in the muscle as closely as possible—cutting with the grain, not against it. Top round will have a thinner grain than flank steak, which means that top round will dry faster, but flank steak will hold together better in the finished product.

3. Combine the rest of the ingredients in a freezer bag, then add the meat. Close the bag, sealing out as much air as possible, then massage the bag to make sure all the meat has contact with the liquid.

4. Stash the bag in your fridge for about 6 hours.

5. Discard the marinade and move the meat to a sheet pan lined with paper towels. Using more paper towels, pat the meat as dry as possible. Liquid removed here is liquid that won't have to be removed in the actual air-drying process.

6. Lay out one of the furnace filters and place a layer of paper towels on top. Place strips of beef on top of the paper towels, parallel with the ridges in the furnace filter. Be careful not to crowd the strips; air needs to be able to pass freely around the meat.

7. When you've placed about half of the meat on the towel, place another layer of paper towels on top of the meat.

8. Repeat this process on a second furnace filter, with the remaining meat.

9. When all the meat has found a home on one of the two furnace filters, stack one filter on top of the other. Then place the third furnace filter on top of that. At this point, all of the meat should

be sandwiched between furnace filters. The end result: filter-towel-meat-towel, filter-towel-meat-towel, filter. The goal is to make something like a beefy, industrial club sandwich. The furnace filters are the bread, the paper towels are the cheese, the beef is, well, the meat.

10. Using the bungee cords, strap the entire filter stack securely onto the front of the box fan. The fan should be able to sit upright without spilling beef slices.

11. Turn the fan on high, and leave the contraption alone for 10 to 15 hours (or possibly more, if you live in a humid climate).

❧

If you leave this contraption indoors, your house will smell like a smokehouse. However, if you leave it outdoors, especially overnight, you may attract nocturnal scavengers. In my opinion, smokehouses smell like heaven. But pointing the fan out a window works, too.

12. Check the meat every hour, starting at about 10 hours. When it's appropriately dry and chewy (I prefer my jerky stiff but pliable), remove from the drying rig and store in an airtight container in a cool, dark place. Like a backpack.

13. Throw away the furnace filters. Those things get nasty.

5

New Frontiers

Zac pulls his car to the curb in front of my house and kills the engine. All of us—Zac, Uriah, me, our gear, and our collective stench—sit motionless for a second.

I'm sore.

As an experiment, I poke every major muscle group on my body, starting with my biceps, crossing laterally across my chest, and then down to my ankles. Every single muscle responds with a dull ache. I ran a marathon a few years earlier and the resulting pain crippled me for three days. This is comparable.

I open the door, and we stumble out into my yard. Summer is at my front door in an apron, looking for all the world like some pseudo-Irish take on June Cleaver. "Welcome back," she says with a smirk.

We head inside, dropping our gear in haphazard piles on the

floor. "So yeah. 'Mount Whitney—Come for the Summit, Stay for the McGriddles,'" I say.

"To be fair, they were delicious," Uriah opines. "What's a successful summit attempt compared with a quality breakfast sandwich?"

Summer laughs. "Sandwich, schmandwich. I have a surprise." She gestures to the kitchen, where she's laid out possibly the largest cut of beef I've yet seen. It's a mammoth thing, three or four pounds, easy. A squat, fat oblong of meat, several separate muscles all run together, with great seams of fat streaked throughout. It looks like a steak from a cartoon.

It's great to be home again.

Next to the slab of beef, there's a cookbook propped open on the counter. It's the book Chris sent me home with when I picked up the beef: *The Grassfed Gourmet Cookbook: Healthy Cooking and Good Living with Pasture-Raised Foods*. It's open to a recipe entitled "Super-Slow-Roasted Rosemary-Crusted Chuck Steak."

Now we're talking. I don't really know that much about chuck steak.

What I do know is that the chuck primal is the biggest muscle group on the animal—it's essentially the shoulder of the beast. It does a tremendous amount of work moving the animal around and thus has an enormous amount of connective tissue holding it all together. Put differently, it has a very pronounced "beef" flavor, but it's like chewing a shoe unless that connective tissue is dealt with.

It's usually a roast, not a steak. It's generally used in a braise, and it's exemplary in that role. But the recipe Summer has called up is different—it calls for the steak to be roasted for a long time at a very low temperature in a dry oven. No liquid whatsoever. I've never done this before. I'm excited.

I don't even have to do any prep on this dish. Summer has already thawed the steak and prepared a dry rub heavy on fresh rosemary, salt, and garlic. I generously slap it with the spice rub, loosely cover it with foil, and give the steak and the spices some alone time.

I rejoin my wife and friends in the living room and collapse onto the sofa. Declan clambers excitedly up onto my lap, the only member of my family brave enough to sit near me—I'm pretty sure I smell like the Unibomber looks.

Uriah reaches into his pack at his feet and produces another wonder: a small bottle of whiskey. "I was saving this for a toast at summit," he says. "I won't be able to take it on the plane back to Colorado. It'd be a shame to let it go to waste."

"Good point," Zac says.

"I'll get some glasses," I offer. I make a very convincing imitation of a man trying to stand up, though I don't actually move.

Summer sighs. "Stay put, Grizzly Adams. I'll get them."

When she returns, we explorers of the high, wild places toast to our most recent adventure. And then to our safe return. And then to the women we love. And I think there was something about Robert Frost, and two roads diverging in a yellow wood, and maybe a Walden quote or something. It was inspiring.

An hour later, Uriah's brother arrives to pick him up, and we send him off with promises of more adventures to come. Then, it's time for a beautiful piece of chuck steak to enter a dry, preheated oven.

I slip the steak in at 250 degrees, per the instructions. As with a braise, a key to cooking tougher pieces of meat is to keep the temperature very low. After a half hour, the directions call for me to lower the temperature to 170 and roast for about four hours, or until the internal temperature of the meat is between 120 and 125. Any higher, and the steak is ruined.

Thirty minutes later, I return to knock the temperature down to 170 degrees. But I have a problem: My oven doesn't go down to 170.

Okay, not really that big a problem. I'll just knock the temperature down as low as it goes, and I'm sure that will be close enough. This is not a complicated recipe. Surely the temperature control on modern ovens is sufficiently sophisticated that "low" will serve all my low-temperature roasting needs.

I return to my living room and to scintillating conversation.

Two and a half hours later, my house smells fantastic. Like herbs and roasting meat and all the pleasures of the hearth. Because my particular obsessive-compulsive permutation doesn't allow me to leave things alone, I slip into the kitchen to check on the steak. It's a big cut, so it will likely take most of the four hours mentioned in my recipe. However, I want to be sure to pull it before the temp inches above 125, lest the meal be ruined. I'm too tired and have waited too long to eat a steak that's been turned to shoe leather.

I open the oven and insert my meat thermometer into the steak.

Internal temperature: 157 degrees.

I wrecked it.

Not only did I wreck this meal, I wrecked it egregiously. I ruined this meal on a colossal scale. If they gave out awards for culinary imbecility, if there were some opposite of the James Beard Award—say, the Jimbo Mustache Award—I'd have that thing locked right down. I didn't just slightly overcook a steak, I missed the mark by thirty fucking degrees.

Far too late, I pull the steak.

When chuck is properly cooked, the connective tissue melts

away. When it's subjected to high heat by mouth-breathing idiots like me, all that connective tissue remains intact. If this cut is to be edible at all, that connective tissue must be *cut* away, a laborious and potentially tricky prospect. I'm trying to make the best use of this animal that I possibly can—and throwing away an entire chuck steak without even trying to salvage it does not meet that lofty goal. I let the steak rest for a moment and grab my chef's knife.

Would a boning knife have been a better choice? Sure. Do I have a boning knife? I do not. Cutting the connective tissue away with a chef's knife is like performing surgery with a hatchet.

I slice the steak into comically small pieces in an attempt to excise as much of the connective tissue as possible. I'm only moderately successful. The pieces are tiny, which I find funny because this steak started as such a Flintstone-like mass of beef. Now we're eating beef Grape-Nuts.

The resultant meat is still chewy—very, very chewy—but the beef flavor is still remarkably strong. I'm intrigued. Overcooked as it is, the intense flavor of grass-fed chuck still punches through. We eat the steak dust in little piles, alongside roasted broccoli and heads of just steamed corn. Though the dish is definitely ruined, the meal isn't. If anything, I've provided plenty of fodder for conversation. Zac and I recount more of our High Sierra exploits, and Summer fills us in on what Dec's been doing in the time I've been away. As we chat and chew at about a 1:3 ratio, reflecting on the adventure just passed, I consider the adventure still to come. And I make a mental note of something.

Oven thermometer. Use one.

I'm a pretty solid home cook, but I'm no pro. My debacle with the oven thermometer—or lack thereof—suggests that perhaps I have a few things to learn. Before I flamboyantly ruin any more of this beast, I decide to consult someone who cooks for a living.

My friend Eben is a professional chef, having run restaurants in New York and Pennsylvania. I hit him up for some words of wisdom. It isn't the first time I've turned to him for food advice—in college, flush with student loan money, I suggested that we invite a couple of ladies over to my place for dinner. A real dinner. A grown-up dinner. He'd cook; I'd bankroll it.

The girl I invited expected overcooked spaghetti. She got five-spice shoyu-marinated Chilean sea bass, shiitake beggars' purses tied with green onion threads, and a from-scratch five-spice chocolate mousse served with tuile cookie spoons.

She was impressed. So much so that she later married me.

Eben has some great advice. He rather astutely notes that the middle meats on a cow aren't really going to pose any problems for me. Tenderloin, short loin, rib, and the like—they're all easy. These are New York strip steaks. Rib eyes. Filet mignon. Not a lot of connective tissue, plenty of fat to keep the cuts moist during cooking.

The cuts I need to give more thought to are those from the ends of the animal. Cuts off the chuck, which is the shoulder of the cow. The round, which is pretty much the animal's hip. The brisket, which is the two enormous muscles off the animal's chest, between the front legs. These primals are huge, so they'll yield a lot of beef—and they're rife with connective tissue, widely varying shapes, distinctive grain structures, and other attributes that will need to be specifically addressed in the cooking process. They are not slap-a-steak-on-a-grill cuts.

There are also cuts that aren't off either the round or the chuck and aren't especially familiar to the average home cook. There's a flat iron steak. Crosscut shanks. A hanger steak, which presumably hangs from something. Petit tenders, which I can only assume are like regular tenders, only smaller. (Of course, this begs the question: What are regular tenders?)

Basically, the beef animal is divided into primal muscle groups, each of which contains several distinct muscles and cuts. In America, there are eight primals:

Chuck. The shoulder of the cow, back through the first five ribs. The chuck primal, situated as it is at the top of the leg of an animal that stands most of the time, is used almost constantly. As a result, it develops a lot of connective tissue as well as a pronounced "beefy" flavor. Relatively fatty, the chuck is also quite large. I have a lot of cuts from here. For example: big chuck roasts, chuck steaks (one of which I ruined), various pot roasts, and probably more than a little ground beef.

Rib. Just behind the chuck, the rib primal encompasses the upper part of the animal's body from the sixth rib through the twelfth. This is one of those middle primals I don't have to worry too much about—rib eyes, standing rib roasts, and prime rib are the heroes here. Tender cuts with a thick layer of fat and not a lot of connective tissue to deal with. Tender, rich, and luxurious.

Short Loin. Also known as the strip loin. Just behind the rib primal at the top of the animal, this is the next of those middle cuts that should be pretty easy to handle. Very tender cuts without a lot of connective tissue. Respond well to high heat and dry, fast cooking. Kansas City/New York strip, T-bones, porterhouses, tenderloins. Sexy and expensive.

Sirloin. Just behind the short loin. If the steer had a waist, this would be the back part, by the spine. It's sort of a transitional primal—cuts nearer the short loin are more tender, and smaller, than those nearer the round, which lies just behind this primal. Cuts from the top are top sirloin, and I have a hunch that a lot of my packages labeled simply "stir-fry meat" and "kebab meat" came from here. Cuts from lower down are considered bottom sirloin and include the tri-tip, ball tip, and flap.

Round. Behind the sirloin, this is the hip and back leg of the animal. Another muscle group in near constant use, so it has a fair amount of connective tissue, but not a lot of fat. It's huge, so I have a lot of cuts from here, mainly pot roasts, the odd round steak, eye round, and other cuts that generally benefit from moist, low, and slow cooking, like the descriptively labeled "stew meat."

Because they're large sections of a large animal's legs, the chuck and round primals are suitably enormous. The chuck is the largest primal on the animal. The round is the second largest. My future is filled with roasts.

Flank. On the belly of the beast, just in front of the round. This cut is relatively thin with a pronounced grain structure. There's really only one cut here—the flank steak. Not a lot of fat, but a fair bit of connective tissue.

Plate. This primal is just in front of the flank, farther up on the animal's stomach, just below the rib primal. This is where you'll find short ribs, as well as the skirt steak, which is essentially a thinner, longer flank steak with a more pronounced grain structure. The Spanish word for "skirt steak" is *fajita*, or belt—and this cut was the traditional cut used for the Mexican dish. Meat here has a lot of connective tissue and a fair amount of fat, depending on the cut.

Brisket. Finally returning to the front of the animal, the brisket consists of the chest muscles of the steer, between the two front legs. A brisket is only two muscles, the flat and the point, frequently cooked together. I have two briskets, each split into two pieces, making for four packages total. Good for Texas or Kansas City barbecue—as well as for Jewish cuisine, such as pastrami and corned beef (because kosher meat in the United States comes only from the front half of the animal). Absolutely riddled with connective tissue, so low and slow is a must.

With that general beef road map in my mind, Eben goes into detail on some of the less common cuts. The crosscut shank is the shank, or leg, cut across the bone. Essentially, it's beef osso buco. The flat iron steak is a piece of chuck from inside the shoulder blade, with a really thick band of connective tissue running through it. It turns out that once you remove that, this is the most tender cut of beef on the animal besides the tenderloin. Hanger steak is muscle that hangs between the kidneys of the animal. There's only one per cow, and it needs to be used wisely. Petit tenders come from the chuck and are a poor man's tenderloin.

But the cut Eben has the strongest opinion on is the eye round.

Specifically: The eye round just sucks. Or, more eloquently: "The most useless and misleading cut on the entire animal."

Naturally, I want to cook this immediately.

The eye round is off the round primal, so it does a lot of work. It looks like a tenderloin, so people think they can treat it like one. They can't. Because it does a lot of work, it has a lot of connective tissue interwoven in the muscle fibers. If it's treated like tenderloin—that is, grilled hot and fast—that tissue will remain intact, resulting in a tough, nasty piece of meat. However, this cut is also very low in fat. Which means that if you cook it low and slow, it'll dry out.

The trick, then, lies in figuring out how to cook it fully without drying it out, while simultaneously dealing with the connective tissue in such a way that it doesn't turn into a fleshy pink football.

The answer Eben suggests: pho. (Pronounced "fuh." Not "foe." Not "foo." Not "fah"-la-la-la-la. Nobody's decking any halls here.)

As fans of Vietnamese soup know, making pho involves painstakingly crafting an exquisite broth, keeping it lava hot, and dropping delicate slices of beef into it. The beef poaches in seconds, yielding a beautiful, savory soup. If done properly.

If done improperly, one may look forward to a tepid bowl of raw beef, accompanied by a side of *Listeria* and the everlasting enmity of one's friends and family.

Undaunted by my recent, beginner-level failures, Summer and I give pho our best attempt one Saturday afternoon. The weather is sunny and SoCal gorgeous, and I'm walking on air. This is exactly the sort of dish I would never try were it not for the whole cow in my backyard. This is a little bit nuts and a whole lot exciting.

We start with the broth. And, frankly, we'll end with the broth. Because the broth is where this soup succeeds or fails. I have exemplary beef and high-quality produce—I made a special trip to the store just for the occasion. The ingredients, which will go into said broth, are simple. The broth itself—that's where I can mess things up.

"Alright, Stone," I declare with some degree of brio. "The boy occupied?"

"Legos," she responds. That's a big, fat *yes*.

"Ready to make some soup?"

"Pho sure," she responds. Pronouncing the name of the soup correctly in that phrase—"fuh" *sherr!*—she has never sounded more like a Valley girl transplant than at this moment. I do not say this out loud, however, as I enjoy breathing and walking under my own power. "Let's do the thing."

I begin by quartering some white onions while Summer starts filling a big pot with water. I toss the onions with some whole gingerroot in a little canola oil and lay them out on a sheet pan under my broiler to char. This is key. One theory of the etymology of pho is from *feu*, the French word for "fire." Per this theory, when Vietnam was a French colony, they adopted the French tradition of charring their vegetables prior to inclusion in a stock to caramelize the sugars and get all the roasty-toasty goodness that the Maillard reaction could provide. In fact, this charred onion is one of the defining characteristics separating pho from other similar meat soups. Vietnamese cooks translated the French word for "fire" phonetically, and the national dish was born.

Because I'm making a broth, I'm working with bones. In this case, five and a half pounds of grass-fed beef marrow bones. I slip them into the water and crank up the heat. My sad little gas range, so eager to blast my chuck steak into oblivion, now struggles to boil these eight quarts of water. I hover nearby expectantly, literally waiting for a pot to boil. It's very clear, however, that this will take a while. The two of us stand in the kitchen, momentarily taskless.

"So we have a few minutes?" Summer asks.

"Until the water boils, however long that takes."

"On this range? That's a while," she says. "I have an idea." She pops into the other room and returns with a slim wooden box. A chess set.

"You want to play me in chess?"

"I want to *destroy* you in chess."

"Oh, honey. You're so cute when you're ruthless."

She grins and sets up the board. We begin to play. She's good at this.

Thirty minutes or so later, I'm about to lose my queen. Meanwhile, in my stockpot, I have bubbles. I let the concoction boil vigorously for fifteen minutes or so, actually lose my queen, then pour out the water we boiled the bones in. This initial blanch is just to coagulate the proteins of the blood and fat and similar undesirables that I would otherwise have to skim off the broth as it cooks.

I return my attention to the chessboard. "Dec's been awfully quiet."

"Legos. I'm telling you," Summer muses, eyes on the board. "He's absolutely nuts about them." With deft fingers, she slides a bishop to the center. "I'll go check on him." She stands up and kisses me on the cheek. "That's mate, by the way."

As she leaves the room, I look down at the board. She's right. "I'm so glad we had this time together," I call out, half sarcastically. Her only response is laughter.

Back to the soup. Blanching done, I pour another six quarts of water over the bones and put the pot back on the heat. I have to return this new water to a boil—again. I can't rush this. I couldn't if I wanted to. But I do have to pay attention to it; I can't play video games or leave the area entirely to go do something else. I have to be here.

I toss my phone on top of a bookcase in my dining room, wondering how to pass the time. There, on my to-read shelf, I have more than a couple of books I've been meaning to put eyes on—I just haven't had the chance. I pick up Lev Grossman's *The Magicians* and sit down on the couch. This book has been on my shelf for a few months now, though I haven't yet had a chance to open it. I sit and turn to the first page, indulging in what has somehow become a rarer delight than I'd prefer.

I have another twenty minutes before the liquid boils again. Once I have a rolling boil, I add the charred onions and ginger, a cinnamon stick, some whole coriander seeds, some fennel seeds, a cardamom pod, some cloves, and half a dozen star anise pods.

Star anise is my first I-love-that-flavor-but-I-don't-know-where-it-comes-from revelation of the day. It tastes slightly of licorice, but in the best way possible. Not at all in a Grandma's-leftover-Halloween-candy way. There's a slight earthiness to it. A tang in the same olfactory universe, for me, as cloves. If I'd omitted it, I wouldn't be able to say what was missing. But I'd miss it.

Spices in, I follow up with some salt, sugar, and fish sauce.

Fish sauce is my second that's-what-that-is! moment. First, it's an astounding creation. It's made by piling several tons of fish into a vat—usually some variety of sardines, but it varies—adding salt, and letting the mass ferment. The resultant liquid runoff is salty and somehow brothy—with just a touch of fishy sourness that sounds utterly revolting but tastes like every good thought your mother ever had about you. It's just loaded with *umami*, otherwise known as "the fifth taste," after sweet, sour, salty, and bitter. Umami perhaps is best described as a sort of savoriness, a particular meaty fullness that you can feel on the palate and the back of the throat. In this case, however, umami is what makes fish sauce glorious. It's another thing I've tasted a thousand times but would never have recognized as missing had I not been present at the creation of this soup. It's a revelation.

Summer drifts through the kitchen with a groggy little boy on her hip. "Hey, little man," I greet him. His only answer is to rub a sleepy fist into his eye.

"He's pretty pooped," Summer says. She smells the air. "Something smells good in here."

I hold up the jar of fish sauce as explanation for the scent.

"It's a sauce for fish?"

"It's a sauce *of* fish."

"How so?"

"It's the decocted syrupy runoff of a couple tons of rotten sardines."

"Oh," she says. "Got it. I'll leave you to it, then." Dec buries his face into her neck. "Could you whip up some noodles for the kiddo?"

"No problem." I switch gears briefly to make dinner for Declan. At this rate, he won't make it to dinnertime. That done, I return my attention to the soup.

Once all the spices have been added to the liquid on the stove, I reduce the heat to a simmer and sit back down with my book. This simmer will take several hours, with my only task being to skim now and again to remove anything that looks unappetizing. I can't really speed up this soup, so I have to slow down.

An hour or so later, I kiss my son on his blond moppet head and tuck him into bed. Then Summer and I chat while I prepare some condiments and accoutrements to accompany the soup.

I pour us each a glass of wine, and we talk about everything and nothing. All the little things we haven't gotten to speak about lately, what with our commutes and disparate schedules and sometimes conflicting daily imperatives. So now, as the soup simmers, we catch up on our days. On our everythings. On the million little details with which we fill our waking hours. It's nice. A moment just for us.

Soon enough, the broth is ready. I prep some rice noodles and pull the eye round from the freezer to thaw until it's still firm, but not frozen, which will make it easier to shear into slices of nano-metric thinness.

The grain on eye round runs lengthwise through the roast from end to end. I slice the roast laterally, across the grain, as thinly as I possibly can. This is key; I'm not doing anything chemically to break down the connective tissue that riddles this cut (i.e., melting it in a long braise), so I need to break down that connective tissue mechanically. I need thin slices.

I set the condiment platter on the table. The magical part of pho, at least from my wife's point of view, is that it's served with a pan-oply of condiments and accoutrements and largely prepared in the bowl. There is no anticipating what people may enjoy in their soup—they prepare it themselves. We're accompanying our soup with basil leaves, cilantro, mint, sliced jalapeño, bean sprouts, lime, fish sauce, hoisin, more fish sauce, and plenty of Sriracha. And fish sauce.

I strain the liquid to remove anything chunky, and I'm left with a delicate golden broth just erupting with umami. I was excited before—now I'm ecstatic. I play it cool, though, to allow Summer to be duly and appropriately surprised. "What, this little thing? Just something I threw together," I imagine myself saying. "Please, have a seat. I'll be by with a warm towel and apéritif momentarily. So glad you could join me for a little *quelque chose à manger*." Of course, I say none of this.

"Someone's in a good mood," Summer notes.

"Oh, yeah. You know," I stammer with characteristic grace. "This soup's gonna be stupid good." *Nice.*

We slip delicate slivers of glistening-pink beef into two bowls, then I ladle screamingly hot broth into each. The meat instantly poaches, darkening to a soft gray with just a touch of rose remaining in the center.

I pause, the recent failure of the Roast I Wrecked looming large in the back of my mind. Finally, I dip my spoon beneath the surface of the golden liquid and taste my handiwork.

Glorious.

"Wow," I hear my wife say from somewhere far off in the distant reaches of my soup-induced Pleasuretorium. "Nice work, Stone."

It's possibly not only the best soup I've ever made, but the best dish I've ever made of any variety. It's joy in a bowl. It's savory and delightful and rich—and a far better dish than I have any business creating.

We ply the broth with our accoutrements and pour another glass of wine. I'm heartened by this success after such a spectacular failure.

There's hope for this project yet.

My job may be a hot ball of stress dipped in anxiety and amphetamines, but my weekends are wonderlands of culinary experimentation. As I explore the beef that occupies my freezer, I realize that dealing with connective tissue is a major consideration. More than only thinking about it when I make a pot roast—connective tissue is a constant that I face with every cut in some capacity or another; it isn't something I can skip or evade or put off—it has to be dealt with. Since the two largest primals, chuck and round, contribute tremendously to moving the animal around—they are hunks of legs, after all—they have correspondingly large amounts of connective tissue, which is decidedly not delicious.

Connective tissue comes in two main types—elastin and colla-gen. Elastin is, oddly enough, elastic. It's the reason, for example, that skin snaps back into place after it's been pinched. It usually forms in thick bands and is fairly obvious to the eye.

Collagen, on the other hand, generally forms in threads between the muscle fibers themselves, though those threads can be quite thick in places. It's also an ingredient commonly added to lotions and beauty creams for the purpose of making them more expen-sive. (Also, it might decrease signs of aging. But mostly the first thing.)

When a piece of meat is cooked in a liquid at relatively low tem-peratures for a long period of time—that is, braised—the collagen in the meat transforms into another type of protein: gelatin. This aptly named protein is a powerful gelling agent and is the primary ingredient in Jell-O, as well as many similarly textured foods.

In a pot roast or other braise, this gelatin thickens whatever flavorful liquid the roast is cooked in, resulting in a sauce with a smooth, lovely mouthfeel. It's the reason why chefs boil bones when they're making soup and why enthusiastic amateurs boil bones when they're making pho. This transformation is a really remark-able bit of culinary alchemy—turning chewy, unappetizing colla-gen into rich, gorgeous sauces. Making lowly, tough cuts of meat into something divine.

From a chemical standpoint, the liquid that the roast is braised in isn't important so long as there is enough water content to fa-cilitate the conversion of collagen into gelatin. From a culinary standpoint, it's nice to choose a liquid that complements the dish. Beef stock is an obvious choice. It doubles down on the beefy good-ness already present in the cut. Wine is lovely—it adds a little acid and then turns a little sweet during the process as most of the alcohol and some of the water evaporates out, condensing the sugars. Some chili recipes braise in beer and water. Some classic pork recipes braise in milk. Or, in the South—Coca-Cola.

I try them all. Pot roasts become my go-to weekend dish. I have a free Sunday afternoon? Pot roast. No plans for dinner? Pot roast. Extra-long commercial break? You bet that's a pot roast. Solid experimental proof of the Higgs boson? Pot. Roast.

One fine Saturday evening, my wife is invited to a Drag Queen Tupperware Party. This is, I'm told, a Tupperware party hosted by a drag queen—and not, as I initially supposed, an opportunity to ensure that one's drag queen remains refrigerator fresh. With Summer in Eagle Rock catching dinner storage and a show, I'm staying home with Declan. Just the two of us. Guys' night.

It's the first night Declan and I have had alone together for quite a while. I'm usually running hither and yon, pulled in a thousand different directions, working on a million different things. Dec is usually getting ready for bed by the time I get home. But not tonight. Tonight we can do anything we want.

And guys gotta eat.

Declan is almost two years old. A few times while I was cooking, he's brought a chair over and tried to help. I gave him some carrots to "hold for me," as there was never really anything he could actually do to pitch in. But tonight, that changes. Tonight, Daddy and Dec have a mission. Tonight, we're making stew. Appropriate for the evening, as a stew is just a pot roast in a wig. More liquid than a braise, but the same process underneath. Moisture. Low heat. Long time.

I'm going to let Declan take the reins of the project. We'll use all his favorite foods and let him do as much of the prep work as he's able. Nothing with knives or heat, of course, but that doesn't mean he can't wrangle some veggies. Maybe lots of veggies.

I prep the accoutrements I think we'll need—an assortment of stew meat, some stock, and all the vegetation we could find in the fridge. And, because we're a couple of dudes making stew—bacon. Lots of bacon.

I pull a chair over for Declan so he can sit at the counter and work with me, and I hand him a clove of garlic to peel. Unencumbered by civilized notions of proper sanitation, he ignores the chair, taking a seat on the floor next to the compost bowl, and begins to peel the garlic. I watch him for a moment, debating whether I should make him move to the counter.

Nah. Don't put your rules on me, man. It's guys' night.

Alright, I can do this. I take a seat on the floor next to him and likewise begin peeling garlic. My enormous Rhodesian Ridgeback, always entranced by any sort of edible matter whatsoever, lopes over and sprawls out behind me. We make a happy threesome on the floor. I'm okay with the dubious hygiene of the situation. It shouldn't cause any food safety issues in this particular case—and this isn't a meal for guests. This is a meal just for us. I'm careful to keep our veggies off the tiles and away from the dog; still, if my wife were to walk in and see this, she'd have a stroke.

Silence falls as we focus on our tasks. Declan has never peeled garlic before, and his fine motor skills are still developing. But he's diligent. I think he's happy that he gets to participate. With fat, stubby fingers, he delicately removes flake after flake of garlic skin.

I'm the first to break the silence. "So, how you been, buddy?"

"I'm peeling!"

"You certainly are, my friend. You certainly are."

We finish the garlic and move on to peeling halves of an onion. This one is fun. Declan is painstakingly careful to peel only the very top layer of the onion and nothing more. Again, delicate. Deliberate. Focused.

"Wow, you're really doing a good job, buddy. Working hard over there."

He beams. I melt a little inside. Finally, he hands me back an onion as pristine as if I had peeled it myself.

"More, Daddy?"

I look around. The rest of the veggies require tools. Metal tools, like vegetable peelers, that might scrape clumsy, not-quite-two-year-old fingers.

"More?" He eyes the carrots, hopeful.

"Can you be very, very careful?"

"I careful," he insists.

"Okay," I relent, handing him a carrot and the vegetable peeler. "Careful."

"Careful. Carrot. Careful." Like a tiny surgeon, he delicately pantomimes peeling the carrot, removing perhaps a nanometer of skin with each stroke. Whispering to himself, "Careful. Careful."

I reposition the peeler in his hand, showing him more explicitly how it works. A moment of instruction later, he's legitimately peeling a carrot. Slowly, and in tiny strips, but he's doing it.

"Good work, buddy."

"Careful, careful," he responds. I pull out a paring knife and start peeling the potatoes.

Vegetables prepped, I survey our *mise en place*, such as it is. Of course, today half of it's on the floor, so I try to arrange my cooking area into some sort of order. I like to cook in an organized work space; I find it helps counteract my intermittent bouts of flamboyant stupidity. I have my onions, carrots, garlic, potatoes, and—off to one side—the stew beef. We can do better.

"Hey, D. What else do you want in your stew?"

He looks up. "I want peas."

"Peas?"

"I want peas, Daddy." I don't frequently cook with peas. The sight of them gives my wife "the vapors," as she is wont to declare while fanning herself when affecting the accent of her antebellum roots. I'm not nuts about them either, but Declan is absolutely mad for them. He eats his weight in peas about every two weeks.

Summer isn't here. And I'm letting Declan call the shots tonight. "Peas it is!" I say, headed to the fridge.

"Yay!" he replies.

"Yay!" I echo. "Guys' night!"

"Guy nye!"

I dice some bacon. Some. A reasonable amount. Organization is great, but tonight measuring is for chumps. Tonight is relaxing and free. I throw the bacon into my Dutch oven and cook it until it's crisp. Then I remove the lardons and sear the beef in the bacon fat.

"This is gonna be good stew, dude."

"Yeah. Stew dude!" Declan laughs. So do I.

I pull the beef, toss in the onions, and sweat them until they begin to soften. I toss a little flour into the bacon fat to make something like a roux. Then stock, bay leaf, fresh thyme. I bring it all to a boil, then return the meat to the pot, drop the heat to low, and put a lid on it.

Declan and I retire to the television parlor to watch a show in which things explode in an educational manner. Thirty minutes later, we return to the kitchen, and Declan helps me add the carrots and potatoes to our stew.

"Careful, careful," he intones.

Another fortyish minutes later, veggies are soft, and the meat is like butter. I add the bacon back in. And, finally, the peas.

"Peas!" Declan exclaims.

I give the peas five minutes in the liquid to heat through and then ladle two bowls for Declan and me. We sit down at the dining room table, and I offer a toast to my almost-two-year-old son.

"Thanks for hanging out with me, buddy."

"Cheers!" He raises his glass, leaning awkwardly across the table to make triple sure the glasses touch, otherwise—by toddler logic—it doesn't count. I grin. This is fun.

"Declan, we should definitely do this more often." This sort of moment with my son is all too rare. Precious. Special. Right now, I'm acutely aware he won't be this age forever. But running from place to place, checking items off to-do lists, and performing the necessary maintenance duties of our daily lives, I find that it's easy to forget.

"Peas!" he yells, plunging a fat, plastic spoon into his stew.

Peas. And thank you.

Pho

❦

Time: About 4 hours, largely unattended

Serves 4

Pho is a glorious thing. Savory and rich, equally suited for winter and summer, and fantastic for sharing with guests, as everyone can prepare their bowls exactly how they like.

It takes a little time to make, but it's worth it.

This recipe is adapted from one in Into the Vietnamese Kitchen, *by Andrea Nguyen.*

BROTH

2 white onions, halved and peeled

4 inches fresh ginger, cut in half lengthwise

Canola oil

5 to 6 pounds beef bones (marrow and knuckle)

1 cinnamon stick

1 tablespoon coriander seeds

1 tablespoon fennel seeds

5 whole star anise

1 whole cardamom pod

6 whole cloves

2 tablespoons sugar

1½ tablespoons kosher salt

¼ cup fish sauce

SOUP

1 eye round, about 3 pounds (refrigerate unused meat for
two to three days to re-create soup)

Rice noodles of your choice (if possible, get "banh pho" or
"rice stick" noodles from a local Asian market)

AT THE TABLE (TO BE ADDED PER EACH DINER'S TASTE)

1 large bunch fresh cilantro, finely chopped

1 large bunch fresh mint, stemmed

1 large bunch fresh basil, stemmed

3 hot peppers (jalapeño or serrano), thinly sliced

Mung bean sprouts

Lime wedges

Hoisin sauce

Fish sauce

Sriracha sauce

1. To make the broth, begin by lining a sheet pan with aluminum
   foil, move your oven rack to the highest position, and fire up
   your broiler. Rub the onion and ginger with oil and broil until
   nicely charred—about 8 minutes. Flip the veggies and char the
   other side.

2. You have two options for preparing the bones. Option A—Blanch
   the bones: Bring 8 quarts water to a boil in a stockpot capable
   of holding at least 12 quarts. Add the bones (gently!) to the boiling water and boil vigorously for 15 minutes. Discard the
   water along with all the accumulated crap that leached out of
   the bones. Rinse the bones, rinse the pot. Rinse everything.

   Option B—Roast the bones: Knock the oven temp down to

400°F and move the rack back to the middle. Put the bones on a sheet pan and roast for 30 minutes, or until gently browned.

Both methods remove impurities from the bones, resulting in a clearer soup. Blanching provides a cleaner, more neutral taste. Roasting adds a toastier, nuttier flavor from the browning.

3. Put the bones in the gigantic pot and cover with 6 quarts cold water. Lid up, and return to a boil over high heat.

4. Once the liquid is boiling, reduce the heat to a simmer. Add the charred ginger and onion, the cinnamon stick, coriander, fennel, star anise, cardamom, cloves, sugar, salt, and fish sauce.

5. Simmer, uncovered, for 3 hours. From time to time, skim the surface of the liquid to remove whatever scum rises to the surface. Otherwise, find a good book. Something you've been meaning to read. Use this time to escape into a world of pure imagination.

6. After 3 hours, strain the broth and return it to the pot, discarding the solids. Taste the broth and adjust levels of salt, fish sauce, and sugar as necessary. When in doubt, add slowly. You can always add more seasoning to the broth, but you can't remove any.

7. Stash your eye round in the freezer for 10 to 20 minutes so that it's still firm but not frozen solid. Utilize the meat's resultant stiffness to slice it no more than ¼ inch thick. Thinner is better. Set aside.

8. Cook the rice noodles in water according to the package instructions. When they're ready, drain and set aside.

9. Stash the requisite number of (oven-safe!) bowls in the oven at its lowest setting to warm. This step is solely to warm the bowls.

10. On a large plate, arrange the cilantro, mint, basil, peppers, mung bean sprouts, and lime wedges. Place on the dining table along with a jar of hoisin, a bottle of fish sauce, and enough Sriracha to wake the dead.

11. Goose the heat to bring the broth back to a rolling boil. Place a warmed bowl on a small dish (so you don't burn your hands). Place a few slices of raw beef in the bottom of the bowl, followed by some rice noodles. Ladle the screaming-hot broth onto them and take the bowl immediately to the table. Repeat with the remaining bowls.

12. At the table, add accoutrements according to your taste.

13. Eat. Eat now.

6

Ancestral Foodways

Kids are fast.

I realize this as I try to maneuver my six-foot-one-inch-tall body through a door frame that, at that particular instance, seems built for dwarves. Of course, it isn't—I'm just clumsy and slow. My son, however, is neither.

"Dec, we need to brush your teeth!" It's his bedtime and time for this evening ritual. Part of this ritual, evidently, has become a rousing episode of everybody's favorite game show: *Let's Evade Daddy!* And we're in the bonus round.

He rounds a corner on stocking feet, squealing with delight. I galumph after him, knocking a picture off the wall in my chase.

Headed down the hallway, I stretch out my stride. The tiny man has me on the corners, but he's toast on the straightaways. I catch him in two strides and swoop down upon him like a demented paternal raptor. "Gotcha," I proclaim, picking him up as he squeals with delight.

I carry him back to the bathroom. "If you don't brush your teeth, they'll fall out. Then you'll look silly in yearbook photos and you'll have to eat pudding for the rest of your life."

I corral him in the corner of the bathroom, pick up his toothbrush, and get to work. As I'm brushing his teeth, I muse aloud, "I need to talk to your mom. We need to take you to a dentist one of these days."

Dentists have been on my mind lately. When I picked up my cow, Chris sent me away with an armful of books and recommendations to make the most out of my beef. Foremost among them, a volume titled *Nourishing Traditions*, by Sally Fallon. It's the hybrid cookbook/manifesto of the Weston A. Price Foundation—the man after whom their foundation was named was a dentist.

As all good manifestos should be, the tome is earnest and enthusiastic. It opens with a solid eighty pages of small, dense print regarding what's wrong with the state of modern nutrition and agriculture and how to fix it. It's the Dr. Bronner's soap of cookbooks. And I've been reading it a lot.

Weston A. Price did medical work all over the world in the 1930s, especially with indigenous peoples still subsisting on traditional, locally sourced diets. In many of these populations, he found that they enjoyed superb health, with far lower incidence of chronic disease than first-world populations, despite lower access to medical care. And as a dentist, he especially noticed that most of these individuals had perfect bites without braces and very low incidence of dental cavities.

He also noted that when these populations transitioned to Western industrialized diets, these benefits vanished.

These isolated groups placed a high value on animal products, especially animal fats. They focused on vegetables, nuts, raw or fermented dairy, and unrefined whole grains. In short, their diets roughly resembled those of subsistence farmers. And they thrived.

The Weston A. Price Foundation has me considering a question I'd never really thought about before. Today in the United States, people are trying harder than ever to live healthier. Supermarkets are packed with low-fat, low-cholesterol, low-sodium foods. Yet heart disease remains the leading cause of death in the United States. Stroke comes in at number four. And diabetes at six. If Americans are trying harder than ever before to adopt healthy lifestyles, why then are so-called lifestyle diseases killing so many Americans?

Nourishing Traditions attributes the prevalence of these chronic conditions to the nutritional deficiencies of a modern diet. They posit that conventional theories of nutrition, such as the food pyramid, are flawed. Not completely wrong per se, but lacking in some fundamental ways.

According to the Weston A. Price Foundation, fat in particular is unnecessarily villainized. Fats found in whole foods from animal or vegetable sources should in fact be considered healthy, including saturated fat and cholesterol, because they serve not only as a ready source of metabolic energy, but also as building blocks for bodily structures such as cell membranes and critical structures in the nervous system. Further, fat is necessary to make use of fat-soluble vitamins and is also the raw material through which the body regulates hormone production. It's only when these fats are excised from whole foods, refined, condensed, and chemically altered that they become dangers to health.

A famous (and, since it began in 1948, famously long-running) study in Framingham, Massachusetts, on the causes and contributing factors of cardiovascular disease found that, whereas participants with elevated blood cholesterol levels were more at risk for heart disease, no correlation was found between cholesterol intake in diet and elevated cholesterol levels in the blood. Furthermore, participants in the Framingham study who ate the *most* cholesterol on average weighed less and were more physically active.

Instead of fat, *Nourishing Traditions* lays much of the blame for cardiovascular disease—as well as diabetes, kidney disease, liver disease, and a host of other maladies—on refined carbohydrates, and especially sugar. It strongly recommends replacing refined sugar with unrefined sugar and eating only whole grains, preferably either soaked, fermented, or sprouted before consumption to make their nutrients more biologically available.

Very old school. Positively Amish. Many foods I enjoy do have a significant fat content (I never really had a sweet tooth, but fat is flavor), though I never considered them especially healthy. Was I wrong?

Further, the book encourages the use of raw or fermented milk and milk products and strongly discourages use of pasteurized and homogenized milk. This is madness to me—pasteurization kills disease-causing pathogens, right? Per *Nourishing Traditions*, raw milk is naturally antibacterial due to helpful lactic-acid-producing bacteria already present, and pasteurization is largely unnecessary. (It lays the milk-borne disease epidemics of the past on dirty equipment and unclean work environments.) Further, the book holds that the pasteurization process kills a lot more than bacteria. It also destroys or reduces the availability of milk's vitamins and minerals, requiring them to be chemically added back into the milk in less-than-ideal, chemically synthesized forms. For example, synthetic vitamins A and D are added to most milk sold in supermarkets. Then, in 1 or 2 percent milk, powdered milk solids are added back to give the liquid a mouthfeel more like whole milk. This powdered milk features oxidized cholesterol, which is the kind of dietary cholesterol that actually *has* been linked to heart disease. (Oxidized cholesterol is damaged cholesterol, different from normal dietary cholesterol.)

I'm not sure what to make of all this. On the one hand, this would imply strongly that people should buy milk from a farmer they trust. Sound reasonable? Sure. I don't think that's controversial. But to advocate buying raw or fermented milk exclusively and avoiding homogenized and pasteurized milk? That I don't know about. That's a tougher sell. Disease born of contaminated milk has been a problem in the past, hence pasteurization. However, the latest outbreaks of milk-related disease have occurred in pasteurized milk. But how many deaths did pasteurization prevent? That's a negative that's hard to prove. At what point does the health value of pasteurization outweigh the potential health value of raw milk consumption? To me, it seems that as long as the consumer is making an informed decision, the choice of milk and the choice of milk providers are personal and depend heavily on that person's relationship with the farmer—at least until more definitive research is done. Of course, this biological calculus is somewhat complicated by the fact that many of those who drink milk and would be disproportionately harmed by any milk-borne pathogens are children, living with the choices of their parents.

In much of the United States, however, the choice between raw and pasteurized milk isn't one that consumers are allowed to make. Sale of raw milk for human consumption is outright illegal in seventeen states. On August 3, 2011, federal agents conducted an armed raid on Rawesome, a private, raw-milk-buying club in Venice, California. Sale of raw milk is legal in California, but only from certified dairies. In California at the time, only one dairy qualified, and Rawesome had been distributing raw milk from other dairies. This was unambiguously illegal. As a result, armed federal agents raided Rawesome's warehouse, arrested the leaders of the collective, and destroyed more than $70,000 of perishable foodstuffs to be sold to the members of their private club, all of whom had signed a disclosure form signifying that they understood the risks of consuming raw dairy. Further, the club's members had no history of illness caused by their raw dairy habits.

Meanwhile, industrial food giant Cargill was at that time trying to plan how to best manage an outbreak of drug-resistant salmonella in ground turkey at one of their processing plants—one of the largest meat recalls in history. Cargill sells its products under a number of names, none of which feature the word *Cargill*, to clients that include the national school lunch program. As a result of this outbreak, 136 people became infected with drug-resistant salmonella. One died.

Three people were arrested as a result of some crunchy, granola-esque folk at a club in Venice selling uncertified raw milk, privately, to fully informed members, with no incidence of product-related disease. Elsewhere, 136 people contracted drug-resistant salmonella from ground turkey sold under another label by an enormous corporation that the USDA allows to self-police, and no criminal charges were filed.

I'm not by any stretch saying that raw milk has all the answers or that it's the panacea that some say it is. But in learning about food production, I can feel myself starting to slip down the rabbit hole a little bit—the Rawesome/Cargill debacles do strike me, at the very least, as a gross misallocation of resources. Which is the greater threat to public health, some hippies with a raw milk habit or a self-policing multinational corporation repeatedly botching food-safety protocols and selling meat tainted by drug-resistant salmonella? If nothing else, it's a pretty stark illustration of the extremes to which an overreliance on the industrial food system can take us.

No, Americans aren't starving. We have an abundance—perhaps an overabundance—of food choices in every supermarket, gas station, and retail store in the country. But if we don't exercise some preference as to where our food comes from—who makes it, what's in it, and how it's made—we could lose the opportunity to choose.

I find all these assertions of the Weston A. Price crew fascinating, but for me, at least, something of a solution in search of a problem. I'm a big, healthy guy. At six feet one, 184 pounds, I'm in pretty good shape. I hike a lot—or as much as my schedule allows, anyway. I bike on the weekends. I have the regular aches and pains of a guy in his early thirties who works in an office. I appreciate beautiful meals, but I'm not really embarking on this cow odyssey for my health, necessarily. Though I'll certainly admit, much of the stuff in the middle aisles of the grocery store—home of all the processed foods the Weston A. Price crowd inveighs against—does not seem, by any stretch of the imagination, healthy.

I think back to the taco pie we made when I first brought home the cow. Something about it struck me as off. Not right. Borderline obscene, maybe. I can't quite put my finger on it, besides a vague notion that there was something odd about the juxtaposition of the sacrosanct nature of the grass-fed beef with the cheap, almost tawdry quality of the Fritos. Like Funyuns in a Fabergé egg. Perhaps on some not-quite-conscious level, the dish seemed like something that should not be.

It's true that we modern Americans didn't always eat the way we do now—that much is undeniable. My own great-grandparents owned an acre or so adjacent to some train tracks in Lawrence, Kansas. They had a cow for milk. They grew all their own vegetables, kept chickens, and bought very little at the market. In fact, my grandfather hated the taste of chicken until the day he died—because as a boy, if his family didn't have enough money to buy something at the market, they could always go out into the yard and kill a chicken for supper. For my grandfather, the taste of chicken meant poverty and hard times. It was a meal of necessity; chickens bred quickly and ate bugs and whatever table scraps were available. Chickens converted nonresources into protein. His family didn't eat chicken because they were foodies or had some fetish for free-range poultry. They ate chicken because they were poor. And if they didn't eat chicken, some nights they didn't eat.

Summer, Dec, and I stand in our local supermarket. We're at the dairy case, way at the back of the store.

"Honey, do we need anything besides milk?" I ask.

"Nah, that's it. I never knew one kid could go through so much milk."

Summer grabs a gallon of 2 percent and moves to put it in the cart. "Actually," I interject, "why don't we get whole?"

"It has a ton of fat. This only has 2 percent fat."

"Truth be told, whole milk has only 3.25 percent milk fat. Plus, it hasn't been futzed with as much. Let's live a little."

She shrugs. "Sure. Why not?" She replaces the 2 percent and grabs a gallon of whole milk. "Watch out, world. We're drinking whole milk. The sky's the limit."

We turn and begin the long trek back to the front of the store. Our journey takes us down aisle four: snacks. I peruse yards upon yards of eye-catching packaging. "I think in my next life, I want to be the guy who dreams up the name for snack foods."

"I think you'd have a knack for it."

"Thanks. It's all in the vowels. Add enough vowels to something, and it automatically sounds ethereal and wholesome."

"If you could make a name that was all vowels, you'd be a billionaire."

"Please enjoy my new snack cracker, 'Aieiaoia,'" I say. Summer chuckles.

Declan imitates me. "Aaaeah!" he howls as we shush him, laughing.

I grab a package off the shelf—containing some form of extruded, bite-sized crisp. I flip it over to read the ingredients. "You ever notice how much of the stuff from the interior of the supermarket is made of vegetable oil and corn?"

"What, as opposed to the stuff on the roof?"

"As opposed to the items around the perimeter." I gesture to the exterior walls of the building. "The outside ring is filled with the food that can go bad. All the meats, veggies, dairy, eggs. The stuff in the middle rows is generally shelf stable for a long time. And they contain a lot of corn. Corn is a starch, but it can become a simple sugar if it's turned into high-fructose corn syrup. And it's cheap."

"I like sweet corn in the summer."

"Me too. But supercheap corn is a big reason why supercheap food makes people fat. We're suffering from diseases of abundance now, rather than scarcity."

"But it isn't just about price. All these foods in the middle aisles are convenient, too. You can't forget that." She pauses, pulling a bag from a shelf. "Besides, if you took away Declan's Goldfish crackers, you'd have a riot on your hands."

She has a point. Kids of a certain age have very limited palates, and that's completely normal. It's a biological defense mechanism: Not all bitter-tasting things are poisonous, but many poisonous things taste bitter. As a result, human children have evolved so that when they first start eating solid foods, they dislike bitter things. They like bland or neutral things. Further, they *love* sweet things. Sweet means sugar. Sugar means energy. Energy that they need to either burn off or store.

Even if the foods in the middle aisles of the supermarket are cheap, sweet, and convenient—that doesn't necessarily mean that they're healthy.

As with the rise of feedlot beef, we can trace the origins of much of the modern diet to the period immediately after World War II. As the war drew to a close, the industry that had sprung up to feed the troops—producing a variety of field rations for all terrains and situations—needed a new audience for its products. The food industry turned to the civilian marketplace and began offering consumers the same sort of frozen, canned, and processed foods that had once filled military field rations. This is the birth of Spam, TV dinners, and airline food.

At first, many industrial food producers didn't have much luck with their new offerings. Housewives considered many canned, frozen, or dehydrated convenience foods "cheating." Cooking was considered one of the most important responsibilities that a wife could have, and data from the time indicate that they took pride in their work. A poll conducted by the magazine *Woman's Home Companion* in 1949, and another by Gallup in 1951, found that cooking was the household chore that women had the most positive feelings about, in contrast with the relative drudgery of other housework.

Cake mixes can be seen as somewhat illustrative of the process by which Americans became more familiar with and more accepting of highly processed foods. In her excellent *Something from the Oven: Reinventing Dinner in 1950s America*, Laura Shapiro recounts the transformation. Before the advent of just-add-water or just-add-water-and-eggs cake mixes in the 1930s, cakes were made from scratch by necessity. However, cake mixes rose in popularity after the war, though not without some reservation that the cakes produced were inferior to cakes made from scratch. The assertion wasn't without merit, and producers of cake mixes had a difficult time convincing home cooks that they weren't shirking the duties expected of them as housewives. Famed psychologist and marketing pioneer Ernest Dichter conducted research on behalf of General Mills and hypothesized that home cooks should be encouraged to think that the use of cake mixes—you know, actually making the cake—should merely be considered the *first step* of the cake-making process. The real showcase of a housewife's culinary skill, the real ability for a home cook to make the cake *hers*, was in her ability to decorate it. To frost it, add sprinkles, and pile it high with chocolate chips and Jell-O. Don't have time to make frosting? They can sell you premade frosting too.

The motif of the ticking clock was central to the midcentury advertising of premade and packaged food. Ads served to manufacture a sense of panic—the solution to which was premade and highly processed foods. Without that sense of urgency, there wasn't necessarily any impetus to use cake mixes—or canned meats, or Cheez Whiz, or condensed soups—because they simply didn't taste as good as the made-from-scratch items they replaced. The desire had to be manufactured for its solution to take root.

In the case of cake mixes, the companies that produced them took out glossy magazine ads promoting their new wares, and helpful how-to articles in women's magazines provided inspiration. Further, copious amounts of sugary frosting would mask any deficiencies in the taste or texture of the cake (such as chemical undertones), blunting the comparison between homemade and premixed products. In the 1950s, assisted by classroom teaching aids supplied by the food industry, home economics classes began to teach baking using store-bought mixes instead of building the cake from scratch. As this became the default method for producing a cake, tastes changed to anticipate it. The taste of the cake from a cake mix became the new normal and—as pupils of those home economics classes grew up—acquired the aura of childhood nostalgia. Simultaneously, the number of people with the skill to bake a cake from scratch declined.

Elsewhere in the food landscape, similar patterns emerged. Canned, frozen, or dehydrated versions of familiar foods emerged, usually for some real or imagined labor-saving purpose. New cuisines and new dishes were developed to utilize them in a manner separate from their initial intent. Then, as consumers became comfortable with the artifice of the product, new needs were manufactured and new products developed to meet them. Canned soup from concentrate replaced homemade soup. Then it found its way into casseroles. Fresh fruit for pies gave way to canned pie mix. And look! You can also use it as a festive centerpiece for a Bundt cake! (Also from a mix, of course.)

These processed foods offered convenience and speed in mealtime prep, as well as a much longer shelf life, but all this came at a price. Processed foods tend to be high in sodium to inhibit spoilage from bacteria. Added sugar can mitigate the otherwise bland or even slightly chemical taste of highly processed foods, while contributing mightily to weight gain and the myriad detrimental health effects that come with it. And partially hydrogenated oils—or trans fats—used to keep foods shelf stable at room temperature have been linked to heart disease, Alzheimer's, and cancer.

All this is to say that how we cook and prepare food changed pretty radically in the last seventy years or so. Our relationship with food has changed pretty drastically as well—if getting something to eat is cheap and easy, we'll value it less as a result. In my own experience, people I've known who've lived through the Great Depression rarely leave a scrap of food on their plate. But people nearer my own age will think nothing of throwing half a bagel in the trash. At the same time, over one-third of adults in the United States are classified as obese.

I don't know the solution to our bizarre relationship to food. I do know that a solid first step is to respect what we put on our plates and into our bodies. When I bought this steer, consensus among my friends was that I was doing something spectacularly dangerous and unhealthy in the extreme. That it was stunt food. I thought their fears were largely overblown, but I didn't vociferously contest them. I never really considered the fact that rather than being outlandish and hyperbolic, my meat choice was surprisingly normal for a time other than ours. Perhaps even banal.

Once upon a time, buying an entire cow wasn't a vote for locavorism or even a show of foodie street cred. It was a function of the fact that I owned a cow—and now that cow is dead. I'd better eat that cow, because otherwise it's going to go to waste. You buy most or all of a cow because that's how they come. Upright. On the hoof. Mooing.

For a long time in many parts of the world, there wasn't a debate about getting an entire cow. If you had a cow, you'd eat it. If you had a duck, you'd eat that. Chickens, goats, peacocks, pigeons, pigs, and pheasants—same deal. Protein came from animals. And if it came from a bigger animal, it meant that you could wait longer until you had to resupply, especially if you had a freezer or a method of preservation. That's why, though Western minds consider whale slaughter immoral, it's actually accepted in some varieties of Buddhism as the lesser of several evils—if a single large animal dies, many small animals may live.

Admittedly, I also thought that buying a whole cow was a little bit nuts. But as I get into living with and cooking this beast, I'm starting to change my mind. It isn't nuts that I drove to a ranch, bought a steer, and drove nine hours with it in the back of my car. In a way, given how dependent we as a culture are on animal protein—it's nuts that more people haven't made the same trip. It's nuts that we depend so mightily on a food production infrastructure that's largely invisible to us. It's nuts that we can accidentally eat so much without realizing it because calories are so cheap. And it's nuts that we know—that I know—so little about the material that eventually makes up my body. The very stuff that becomes "me."

But I'm learning.

The best thing about *Nourishing Traditions* is the absolute glut of recipes. Sauces, fermented dairy dishes, appetizers, soups, and more ways to treat vegetables than a vegan potluck. I enjoy vegetables, though admittedly more in the abstract than on an everyday basis.

One lazy Sunday, I'm flipping through recipe books, trying to let the accumulated knowledge of generations of French chefs somehow osmose into my mind. I could get lost in a *Larousse Gastronomique* hole for days. As it is, I've been reading about vegetables for a solid hour, and now I'm craving a salad of some sort.

I head to the kitchen to see what my vegetable options are. Maybe I'll be inspired by my botanical bounty and some salad idea will spring fully formed from my brainpan like Athena from the brow of Zeus.

I have an onion and a single head of romaine lettuce.

Okay, that won't really do. But I can throw together a little side salad, I suppose. There's a whole section of *Nourishing Traditions* on salad dressings, not to mention the *Larousse*, Bittman, and the entire Internet. I can make this work.

With my salad plans duly modified, I head into the backyard to see what my options for a main dish are. Dec and Summer are out shopping; maybe I can put together lunch for the whole clan.

I sift through the packages of beef. I'm finding that in trying to make the best use of every part of the animal, I'm becoming somewhat protective of each little package in my freezer. I really don't want to wreck any more dishes. With several of these cuts, I have only one. If I mess it up, that's it. No do-overs. For example, hanger steak? There's only one on the animal. Gotta save that. Chuck roast? It's huge. Way too big for three people. Gotta save that. Flank steak? There's only one, cut into two pieces. Gotta save that.

I find a package of tenderized round steak and pause. This is interesting. The round is enormous, so I should have plenty of these—doubtless enough to spare one for a quick Sunday meal. The package, at just over a pound of meat, should be just the perfect size for two adults and a child. I pull the package and head back inside the house.

In college, I waited tables during the graveyard shift at a pancake house popular with college students, drunks, and insomniacs. In a college town in the conservative Midwest, all the crazy comes out at night. At my job, it was in my best interest to notice crazy coming in the door, give it a high five, and pour it a cup of strong coffee. It was at this pancake house that I developed an appreciation for our most popular dish—chicken-fried steak.

Chicken-fried steak is, essentially, a steak treated like fried chicken. It's usually one of the more humble cuts of meat—such as top round—tenderized, floured, and pan- or deep-fried. I haven't fried any beef at all yet, and I have a brand spanking new Jaccard begging to be used. A Jaccard, also known as a needler, is something like a self-inking date stamp someone might use in an office—only instead of the date, it stamps two dozen razor-sharp needles into the surface of your choice.

I slip my package of beef into a bowl and turn on a thin stream of cold water. A half hour later, my steaks are thawed, my Jaccard is ready, and I'm eager to perforate some steak.

I lay the steaks on the board. They're already tenderized by my butcher, but I can do better. I stamp them with the Jaccard like a nefarious bureaucrat from Terry Gilliam's *Brazil*.

Once they're thoroughly perforated, I dredge the steaks in some seasoned flour, then an egg wash, then more seasoned flour, and then drop them into some hot canola oil in my Dutch oven. A couple of minutes per side, then I stash the steaks on a plate and stow them in a warm oven.

The main course is ready, now it's time to turn my attention to the side salad. What the hell can I do with white onions and lettuce? I start considering dressings. I have herbs, I have vinegar . . . and I also have all this oil. Just sitting there. Barely used for frying my steaks. Still warm, in fact. Sitting right there.

I glance back to my onion. Back to the oil.

Since I'm on a kitchen gadget kick, I pull out my mandoline, which, like my Jaccard, I rarely use. The mandoline is essentially a small, elevated table with a blade set into it for slicing. If you recall those ancient credit card machines that used to take an imprint of the entire card rather than just swiping the magnetic strip, you have some idea of what a mandoline looks like. Only instead of pressing carbon paper onto a credit card, it slides the veggie of your choice through a razor-sharp blade.

The theme of today's meal is Deadly Office Supplies, apparently.

Five minutes later, my white onion is sliced into delicate concentric rings of identical thickness. I dump the flour from the dredging station but create a new, identical one on another clean plate. I put the canola back over the flame and bring it up to about 350 degrees. I drop the onion rings into the oil, one at a time, working in small batches to keep them from sticking to one another. Ten minutes later, I have a stash of beautiful, golden-brown onion rings. I stow them in the warm oven as well.

Finally, I drain off most of the oil from my fry station and whisk in a little flour to make a quick roux. I add a little chicken broth until I get the right consistency, then a little milk to make a cream gravy. Pleased, I survey my work.

I have created nothing remotely resembling a salad.

The head of romaine sits unused on the counter opposite the detritus of my fry frenzy. Somewhat embarrassed, I chop the romaine and pull together the saddest vinaigrette mankind has ever known.

Also, I've cooked an entire meal in canola oil. It's a highly processed oil that oxidizes easily, leading to all sorts of maladies *Nourishing Traditions* lays at the feet of the Western industrialized diet. I feel a bit guilty.

Still, when Summer and Declan return home, I'm ready with the chicken-fried steak, onion rings, and my punchline of a salad.

"Nice job, Suzy Homemaker," my wife comments, surveying the meal. She pauses and cocks her head. "Is there anything in that salad besides lettuce?"

"Um . . . no. There is not."

She laughs. I set the table.

As chicken-fried steaks go, this is glorious. Better than anything I've ever had in a restaurant. Summer forgoes the steak in favor of the ludicrous little salad I made, but Declan dives into the steak with gusto. He rarely eats meat, so this is a welcome surprise. Similarly, the onion rings blow the doors off most restaurant fare.

We eat and laugh as Summer tells me of their afternoon adventures. I love these little moments when I can put food on the table literally, instead of just figuratively.

I'm encouraged by how well this meal turned out, but it isn't really what I set out to do initially. I wanted a salad. I'm dismayed by the dearth of vegetables in my house. I glance over at my copy of *Nourishing Traditions* lying on the kitchen counter. Mocking me.

Something needs to be done.

"What is it?"

"I'm not sure," I reply. Summer and I are standing over an open cardboard box. It is overflowing with all manner of vegetables. Some of these vegetables are familiar. Others—such as the enormous white carrotesque roots in the center of the box—are not. "I think they're turnips."

"I've seen turnips. Those are not turnips."

"Maybe rutabagas?"

"I don't think so," she says.

"Have you ever had a rutabaga?" I ask.

"No. But they're like big round globular things. Not giant carrots." She thinks. "Go check the list."

I jump on the computer and pull up my e-mail. We've signed up for a vegetable delivery service, and our first delivery has just arrived. We don't get to pick what we receive, though. Each shipment is simply an assortment of whatever's fresh and in season at the time. They e-mailed an inventory of the first shipment.

"Parsnips."

"Oh, cool," she says. Then, a second later: "I have no idea what that is."

"Me neither," I reply, examining the gigantic roots before

moving on to the rest of the box. There are huge green leaves everywhere. "We have kale for days, though."

"So much kale. What are we going to do with all of it?"

"We'll figure it out." I smile. "It's an adventure."

"It certainly is."

"What doesn't *kale* us—"

"Stop," she interrupts. "Let's get this stuff in the fridge."

Thursday night. All is not well.

I walk in the door to the sound of a screaming toddler. Dec is cranky, sobbing his lungs out in his room. Meanwhile, Summer is riffling through our kitchen stores.

Summer hears me come in. "Check on him," she says, gesturing to the far side of the house. I drop my bag and head for Declan's room.

The little man is in a bad mood. There's nothing really wrong with him, but he's hungry. Toys aren't calming him. I try to read him a book, but he won't hold still. He's hungry. I hoist him up onto my hip and head back in Summer's direction.

"Do we have any chicken nuggets?" she asks.

"Trade me." I pass Declan off to Summer and take her place in the kitchen.

Go time.

We need food for the munchkin, and we need it yesterday. I raid our vegetation-crammed fridge.

Snow peas! Dec likes peas.

Broccoli! Superfood. Everybody likes broccoli.

Asparagus? Why not.

Edamame—definitely. Another toddler favorite.

Declan likes all this stuff. Surely he'll be in the mood for one of these.

Now, what to do with it all? I could do tapas—in our house tapas is another word for lazy buffet. But raw broccoli and raw asparagus are nasty. Luckily, I have brown rice in the fridge. Brown rice plus a boatload of vegetables equals stir-fry. Beef for a protein. Done.

I raid the freezer and pull out a pound of round. At least, I think it's round. The package is conveniently labeled "stir-fry beef." Good enough for me. I throw it in the sink under a thin stream of water to thaw.

That done, the knife comes out. I slice everything into approximately equal-sized pieces. In a stir-fry, prep is everything. Once the cooking process begins, there's no stopping it. You have to have all the ingredients ready to cook, standing by in the proper order, and know how long everything needs to stay in so that the entire dish is ready at once. Good prep makes that easier.

I begin the rice in a pot on a back burner. Meanwhile, I pull together a quick sauce out of soy sauce, some rice vinegar, a little mirin—Japanese cooking wine—I had on hand, and the juice of an orange. I also dice a couple cloves of garlic. Garlic is always good.

Summer pokes her head in, still holding a grumpy child. "How long 'til dinner?"

"Soon. Ten minutes. Ish."

She nods and darts back out. I slam my wok down on my biggest burner, splash in some oil—organic, virgin coconut oil rather than canola—and crank the heat to high.

When the oil shimmers, I toss in the thawed beef. There's a frenzy and commotion in the wok as the meat hits the oil. When the beef is browned, I pour it into a bowl to wait.

More oil into the wok. Then, all the veggies. I cook them until they're only slightly soft—overcooked veggies are gross. Just undercooked veggies are crisp. Besides, they'll continue to cook as they cool.

I pour in the sauce, which responds with a hiss and a cloud of steam. I let it just warm, then add the beef back in to heat through.

The rice is done. I drop a scoop in three bowls and fat ladles of stir-fry over the top. I add extra veggies for Declan, in hopes that there's something in the bowl he likes. I'm playing the screaming-toddler lottery here. Dinner is served.

It's a good dish—a little rushed and a little sloppy for it. But we enjoyed it; the sauce was bright and lovely. Declan wolfed down the edamame, largely ignoring the rest of the dish. But that's okay. He ate. Perhaps through sniffles, but he ate.

Summer likewise approved. "I love broccoli so much."

"Me too. And it's so good for you it's silly."

She nods. "Nice work, Stone. And on a weekday, to boot."

"It's a weekday." I grin a little. For a weekday, this is quite a meal.

It's also the type of meal I've found myself eating more and more in this project. And it seems to be having an effect on me—I've dropped nearly ten pounds since last I weighed myself, which admittedly, I do not do often.

Though counterintuitive, this weight loss does make a kind of sense. I'm cooking far more than I did in the era BC (Before Cow) and eating a far higher-quality beef than I ate before I started the project. Chicken-fried steak notwithstanding, having a freezer full of beef has led me to eating far more vegetables as well. I'm eating a diet much closer to that of my great-grandparents than that of people of my generation. Whole grains. Raw sugar. Grass-fed beef.

I may not know what I'm doing all the time. But I feel like I'm doing something right.

Chicken-Fried Steak and Onion Rings

Time: About 1 hour

Serves 4

This is not, in any sense, a salad. However, if you grew up in a few particular areas of the Midwest or South, this dish will taste like home.

1 pound round steak or tenderized round steak

3 large eggs, plus 1 additional, beaten

3 cups plus 3 tablespoons all-purpose flour

2 tablespoons kosher salt

2 teaspoons freshly ground black pepper

1 teaspoon garlic powder (optional)

1 white onion

1 cup canola oil (approximately)

1½ cups chicken broth (plus 2 tablespoons, if needed)

½ cup milk

½ teaspoon fresh thyme leaves

1. Preheat the oven to 200°F or the "keep warm" setting.
2. Using a Jaccard tenderizer, stamp your steaks from tip to tip. Rotate the Jaccard 90 degrees and stamp them again. Flip the steaks to the other side and repeat. (Alternatively, you can pound each side all over with a tenderizing mallet, but be gentle.)

3. Put the 3 beaten eggs in a wide bowl and beat them lightly with a fork to combine. In another bowl, combine 1½ cups of the flour with salt and pepper (and garlic powder, if desired), to taste. Transfer half of the seasoned flour to another bowl.

4. Dredge each steak in the first bowl of seasoned flour, then dip in the beaten egg, then dredge again in the second bowl of seasoned flour. Gently shake off any excess.

5. Stow the steaks in the fridge for 30 minutes to allow the egg/flour mixture to harden into a crust.

6. Meanwhile, peel the onion, keeping it whole, and slice into rings ⅜ inch thick. A mandoline is your friend here.

7. Create a new dredging station in clean bowls, again seasoning 1½ cups of flour and dividing it in half between two bowls. Use the remaining egg as the egg station for the onion rings. Repeat the same flour-egg-flour dredging process used for the steaks.

8. Put the oil in a wide stockpot until it reaches a depth of 1 to 2 inches. Heat the oil to about 350°F on a deep-frying thermometer, or until it's shimmery. Lower the heat to maintain the temperature.

9. Working in batches, fry the onion rings until golden brown, then transfer them to a baking sheet lined with paper towels. Sprinkle the onion rings generously with salt, then put them in the warm oven until ready to serve.

10. Pour off most of the oil into a heatproof bowl, leaving only ½ inch in the stockpot. Heat the oil in the stockpot to about 350°F, or until shimmery, then lower the heat to maintain the temperature.

11. Working in batches so as not to overload the pot, fry the steaks for about 4 minutes per side, or until each side is golden brown.

12. Remove the steaks to a plate and season with a sprinkle of salt.

13. Quickly pour the remaining oil into the heatproof bowl, then add 1 tablespoon back to the stockpot. Boost the heat to medium and whisk in the remaining 3 tablespoons flour to make a roux.

14. Add 1½ cups of the broth and whisk to deglaze the pan (add a splash more if the fond is stubborn about dissolving).

15. When the broth begins to bubble, add the milk and thyme and cook until the liquid is reduced and coats the back of a spoon, about 5 minutes. Season with salt and pepper to taste (pepper is your friend here) and kill the heat. You've got gravy.

16. Serve the steaks alongside the onion rings, applying gravy to whatever suits your fancy. Or serve the gravy on the side.

17. Next meal, eat a salad. Seriously.

7

Go Big

Here's a little-known fact: God made summer to give the rest of the world a taste of what it's like living in the City of Angels.

I mean, sure. Beautiful days exist in other places. But not like here. We get the platonic ideal of beautiful days. We get Elysium and the Land of Milk and Honey. Other places have the odd song written about them now and then—"Take Me Home, Country Roads"; "New York, New York"; "April in Paris"—whatever. We've got the entire Beach Boys canon.

And in certain specific instances of this Southern California idyll—on certain days when the sky is impossibly blue and the sun shines down with all its beatific glory and people slip their shades on and crack a grin that splits their faces ear to ear—on days like that, it's a crime against nature not to go to the beach.

On this particular Saturday, the beach of choice for us is Leo Carillo. It's dog-friendly and toddler-welcoming. Close enough to our house that we don't have to pack a lunch and a canteen to get there, but far enough away from Los Angeles proper that we won't have to throw elbows to find a place to drop our towels.

At the beach, Summer relaxes while Declan, Basil, and I chase the waves back into the sea. It's an altogether lovely way to spend a Saturday. And it's becoming more and more common.

Since I've been focusing on cooking and eating whole foods, I've noticed that trends in my life reinforce one another. When I'm active—when I run, climb, surf (or try and awkwardly fail to surf)—I also cook more often. I'm inspired, in some weird way, to seek sustenance in proportion to my ambition. And the reverse is also true—when I slouch around the house, I cook less. I can't really explain it. But it could be that when I do things that I personally ascribe meaning to, I want to keep the chain going. I ride a wave—I want a steak, a beer, and a sunset. I blow some time killing virtual zombies, I want a pizza.

And today, I was active. I'm tired but not ready to quit. On the way home, I turn my thoughts to dinner. "Surf 'n' turf," I suggest, grinning to my wife in a way I hope splits the difference between cocky and genius. Have Jeeves bring around the Bentley and fetch me my driving Rolex. No, no, the good one.

This meal is stunt food. It exists because it's a way for restaurants to package the two most expensive items on the menu—tenderloin and lobster—into one ostentatious price tag. Otherwise, these two items don't even go together. It's the most conspicuous of conspicuous consumption, and maybe even a little cliché.

But it also sounds delicious, and I already have the tenderloin.

Summer grins a little. "I like the way your brain works, Stone."

When my wife is down for an adventure, that adventure moves from "great idea" to "absolutely epic" with a quickness. "That means we'll have to buy a lobster."

"Yeah. I was reading the other day that lobster prices have fallen through the floor in the last few months. Global recession, financial catastrophe, yada yada—nobody's buying lobsters."

She grins wider. "I'm down." Then she turns to watch telephone poles whip by in front of a shimmering ocean. "Do you know where to get a lobster?"

"Sure," I say. "I know a guy."

I don't know a guy.

After trying two Vons supermarkets, a Henry's, and a Ralph's, I finally find a supermarket that has a tank of lobsters—and a seafood attendant who's never sold one. He has to call over his manager to figure out how to package the crustacean. He settles on a plain white box that I believe once held cans of tomato sauce.

Minutes later, the box is resting on my wife's lap. Something scrapes the lid from within. It's like a sound effect from a zombie movie. Creepy.

At home, I open the box, gross out the wife, frighten the child, and freak out the dog, in that order. Then, as is my wont, I do a little research.

Lobsters are colloquially referred to as "bugs," and that's actually relatively accurate, as they are both arthropods, or beasts with no backbones and their skeletons in their skin. Their brain is about the size of a grasshopper's—and I use "brain" very loosely here. It's more like a clump of ganglia that don't really have other plans.

Lobsters used to be considered the vermin of the sea. In the 1800s, so many would wash ashore after New England storms that they were fed to indentured servants, or even ground up and used as fertilizer. In Massachusetts, servants actually filed suit against their masters to prohibit them from feeding their servants lobster more than twice a week. The servants won. Poor bastards.

I'm researching lobsters because I'm going to be killing this thing, and I want it to be as painless and humane as possible. I look into methods. Alton Brown, kitchen guru, suggests fifteen or twenty minutes in the freezer to render the lobster insensate. My trusty copy of the *Larousse* says that two hours in a freezer will cause the lobster to lose consciousness and painlessly die. Mark Bittman, in *How to Cook Everything*, essentially says to just chuck the damn thing into boiling water and stop being a pansy.

I opt for three hours in the freezer, a considerably longer period of time than even the most conservative suggestion. This is—quite literally—overkill. When those three hours have passed, I pull the bug from the freezer and start bringing my pot of water to a boil.

Through the kitchen window, I see Summer and Declan playing in the late afternoon sun. It's a charming, storybook scene. Basil dozes near my feet. I smile at the sheer, gosh-darn swellness of it all. Today is a good day.

From the corner of my eye, I notice the lobster twitch. Eerie, but I'm ready for this. It's a postmortem nerve reflex, like frog legs kicking in the sauté pan. Perfectly normal. The water is nearly boiling, so I prep a side dish. I toss some fingerling potatoes with oil, sprinkle them with salt, and chuck them into my preheated oven.

The lobster twitches again. Very creepy.

I take a deep breath and walk over to the cutting board. To set my mind at ease, I tap the lobster's shell.

The lobster stands up.

I make an embarrassingly high-pitched noise and shove the bug back in the freezer. Slam the door. Lean against it like they do in every horror movie ever made.

I take a moment, chest heaving. Out the window, I can see my wife and son playing in the yard. So innocent. So blissfully unaware of the eldritch horror lurking in our freezer.

Another full hour later, I crack open the freezer door. Lobster corpse. For sure, this time. Water already boiling, I pull the cutting board the lobster is resting on out of the freezer and slide it gently onto the counter—just in case the bug is only sleeping. I don't want to risk waking the dead again.

My sources suggest rinsing the lobster briefly before placing it into the pot. I turn on the faucet, pick up the bug, and slip it into the stream of water.

The lobster detaches its claw from its body and throws it at me.

This is not hyperbole—the claw bounces off my arm and falls clattering into the sink. I make another high-pitched noise and stash the lobster back into the freezer. Then I run back and pick up the claw and stash that in the deep freeze as well.

Two strides later, I'm at the computer. Google informs me that lobsters often detach their limbs as a defensive measure.

This bug is still alive.

Furthermore, after four full hours in subzero temperatures, this bug is seriously pissed off. So angry, in fact, that it winged its arm at me rather than go gently into that good night. Despite my best efforts, I'm not making this easier on the bug, I'm making it harder. This bug is some sort of zombie Rocky Balboa, and I'm his culinary Apollo Creed. I'm pissing off the most badass undead crustacean motherfucker the planet has ever known.

Enough. Without further ado, I pull the bug from the freezer and slide it quickly into the boiling water. I follow up with its disembodied claw. Then I shoot it with a silver bullet, drive an oak stake through its heart, and hang garlic above the doorway. Deep breath.

After my culinary Romero movie, I turn to my dog-proof microwave and pull out the beef tenderloin, already at room temperature. I dust it with salt and pepper, then lay it delicately into a skillet with some melted butter. It's easy. It's relaxing. It's autopilot. It occurs to me that handling this beef has become second nature to me. That dealing with this particular steer—once the difficult and unfamiliar part of the cooking process—is now the easy part. It's a nice feeling. And the meal, despite the horror-movie drama, is outstanding.

"Gross," Declan says as he watches me pull apart a lobster claw as we sit down to eat. It's his new word. Right now everything is gross.

"That's cool. You just keep thinking that," I retort, dipping a chunk of lobster in some melted butter. "That conclusion is perfectly okay by me."

Summer attacks the tail of the bug. "Oh, my God, this is great."

"Thanks. Easy meal, too. Boil water. Sear steak. Done."

"I've never been so happy about a global economic recession," she says.

"Silver linings, I suppose."

I cut my steak; the center is warm and red and lovely. I've turned a corner with my steer. It isn't intimidating anymore. I know what I have, and I know what I can likely do with it. Not everything may work, but by and large my executions are getting stronger and stronger. Braises are automatic. Broiling, pan-frying, or grilling hot and fast is second nature. The change in my skill level is like the difference between speaking French in a classroom with other Americans and being turned loose on the streets of Paris. I'm achieving some degree of proficiency, and I'm ready to try more advanced techniques.

I need to push myself further.

Shortly after our return from our trip up Mount Whitney, Zac deployed to Germany. Such is the life of a career military doctor.

So that fall, Summer and I visited Zac and his wife, Katie. We flew to Munich, romped through the city's capacious parks, and rented bikes so we could cover more ground. Bicycles turn Munich from lovely to *spectacularly* lovely. The city is built for two wheels. And good friends, excellent sausages, and outstanding beer certainly help endear a place to me.

Though we visited Munich in the fall, we didn't experience Oktoberfest, which began a week after we left. Munich during Oktoberfest is when tourists invade and ladies in lederhosen serve a preposterous amount of beer to a preposterous number of people. I wasn't especially sad about missing it because in all likelihood I wouldn't have enjoyed it—I'd rather see a city as locals do than see it in costume for tourists. However, upon my return to California, some small part of me wondered what I'd missed.

Summer and I decide to prepare our own Oktoberfest Octoberfeast, only with fewer tourists and more awesome because we're cooking it ourselves. I'm creating what is essentially the national dish of Bavaria: sauerbraten, kartoffelkloesse, and red cabbage with apples (which probably has some delightful single word in German to describe it that I don't know).

Sauerbraten is a roast from the bottom round of the steer, marinated in a vinegar solution for several days and then braised and served with a sauce made from the braising liquid. Kartoffelkloesse are potato dumplings—and about as traditionally Bavarian as one can get without yodeling. The red cabbage is sautéed with tart apples, then tossed with vinegar and sugar. Also very traditional.

However, if Summer and I do Oktoberfest alone, oompah bands across Germany will shed fat, salty tears for their wayward American cousins. So we invite our friends Andy and Jen over for the festivities. Andy is another film school friend from the deep, dark wayback of my time in the Kansas heartland. He's a former actor, which is to say that he's gregarious and charming and tells the best stories at cocktail parties. His wife, Jen, matches his charisma and manages to play grown-up kickball without making it seem ridiculous. We haven't seen them in a while, and it'll be good to catch up.

The Thursday prior to our Sunday dinner engagement, I pull a rump roast from the freezer. The rump roast is a cut from the bottom round of the steer, which is part of the round primal, or the hindquarter of the animal. When butchers lay the piece out on the butcher table, they do it with the portion from the outside of the animal's body on the bottom, touching the table. As a result, roasts cut from this part are called "bottom round." Cuts from the inside of the muscle primal, from closer to the spine, are called "top round" because they're on top from the butcher's point of view.

After the rump roast thaws, I sear it on all sides and stash it into a pot to marinate in a mix of vinegars, along with an onion, a carrot, bay leaves, cloves, juniper berries, and mustard. If I botch cooking it, I can always make a weird pickle out of it, I suppose.

Early afternoon on the day of our feast, I remove the pot containing the roast and stash it in a fairly cool oven. Time to begin the sides.

I boil some russet potatoes to within an inch of their lives, cool them, peel them, and rice them with the back of a fork (i.e., I smush them until they look like tiny grains of rice). Next, I dice some bread into cubes, brown them in a mixture of butter and olive oil, then set them aside.

Once my riced potatoes have cooled, I season them with salt and some freshly grated nutmeg, then add a touch of flour and some cornstarch to make a dough. Finally, I break an egg into the mix to act as a binder.

Each dumpling consists of a ball of dough with a bread cube at its center. My batch yields ten, and they're ready to cook. Here's where the German-ness of the recipe and the American-ness of my cooking impulses clash—I want to throw these things into pea-nut oil and fry them until they're a glorious golden brown and crispy. But kartoffelkloesse should be boiled, not fried. Who boils anything when they have a choice? Germans, evidently.

Still, tradition is tradition. I heat some water and drop in the dumplings. When the dumplings are finished, they float. Conve-nient.

Andy and Jen arrive. I am a whirlwind of activity. Maybe I'm a bit manic from the vinegar fumes. "Hey! Great to see you guys," I bellow, following up with hugs and handshakes.

"Heya, Jared . . ." Andy says, surveying my kitchen. "This is quite an operation you have going on in there."

"Yeah. It's bananas. I'm adrift in a world of vinegar and cabbage. Have a seat!"

Great to see them, but I'm a kitchen cyclone right now. They sit outside the kitchen to chat with Summer, while I run some red cab-bage and Gala apples through my mandoline and toss them into a lidded skillet with salt, butter, sugar, and cider vinegar. Vinegar is proving to be a theme for this meal. I add a little flour to help the sauce thicken up a bit.

When the roast is finished, I stow it under foil to rest. My recipe calls for thickening the braising liquid into a sauce with a handful of crushed gingersnap cookies. Cookies! This is madness, but I comply.

Then, all of a sudden, everything is done. Somehow, there have been no mishaps. No happy accidents. No terrifying debacles. Everything worked out as I hoped it would. I cooked a relatively complex meal in front of other people, and I didn't completely embarrass myself in the process—in fact, quite the opposite. I take a moment to revel in the triumph. Then I plate the dishes and pour a little more Märzen beer for everyone.

After putting Declan to bed, we sit down to a meal exactly as I had planned it. Dear friends, good food, and a plan of action, well executed. I'm not sure how to react—I'm not used to endeavors this complicated going off without a hitch. But I like it.

"So, uh . . ." Andy says, munching on the sour beef. "You thickened this sauce with cookies."

"Uh . . . yes. Yes, I did."

"That should not work," he says, chewing. "But somehow it does."

"Yeah. Frankly, I don't get it either. And these boiled dumplings—I never boil food. Who boils food anymore? But I gotta say they don't suck."

Jen picks one apart. "The little bread cube in the middle is a nice touch."

"Not one I would have ever thought of," I say, munching my own dumpling. "This whole meal is a surprise. Just when I think I've wrapped my head around what's possible, I find out that you can marinate and braise a roast in vinegar and serve it in a sauce thickened with crushed cookies."

Summer raises her mug of fine Bavarian beer. "To surprises," she says.

The rest of us raise our glasses.

"I just don't think we can do it." Summer is slouched on her piano bench, sipping a glass of water. She's a pianist by training, and she's just finished practicing. Bach, I think. She's great at Bach.

"Yeah, I know. But it just doesn't seem like Christmas if I don't have to shovel out a car." I crack my sore neck. Desk jobs, man.

"There are worse places to spend the holidays than California. Besides, we don't want Dec's earliest holiday memories to be of airports." She stands up to take her glass to the kitchen. As she does, she points to a corner of the room, near a tall window. "I thought that'd be a nice spot for the tree. We'll be able to see it from the outside. Cozy."

I nod. I've never been away from home for Christmas. Tradition is big in our family—we all have specific spots we sit in around the tree and traditions of breakfast and coffee all done on the big day, just so. All my family is in Kansas.

Well, not all. Not anymore. Summer comes back in and sits on the couch beside me. "We'll make new traditions," she says.

"I know." I have no reason for melancholy, really. I live in a beautiful area with my lovely wife, boisterous little boy, and enormous canine accomplice. Still, it'll be a little odd celebrating the holidays without seeing my Kansas family—we're a tight-knit group.

She rubs my neck, right where I carry all my stress. "We can make a big meal here. Do it up right."

An idea slips into my head. A big, ridiculous idea. "Yeah?"

"Sure," she says. "Do you know what you'd want to cook?"

Why, yes. Yes, I do.

The standing rib roast is probably the most ostentatious cut on the entire animal. Essentially, it's up to seven bone-in rib eyes left together as a roast instead of being partitioned into steaks. Colloquially, people often refer to it as "prime rib," which isn't technically accurate, as the "Prime" designation is a USDA qualification based largely on the degree of intramuscular fat—a test my steer wasn't subjected to.

We may be doing the holidays in Hollywood, but we won't be doing them alone. There are quite a few Kansas expats in the City of Angels. This year, we're having some of our oldest and dearest from film school over for a dinner to celebrate hanging this year's tinsel in Tinseltown. Ben will be joining us again, as well as our dear friends Allan and Chris, Ben's roommates. Allan is compact and muscular and, like many people in Los Angeles, has an interesting job—he's a sculptor specializing in creature effects. Mostly, he makes monster heads for a living. Chris, tall and lanky, performs similar visual feats to Allan's, only with computers—he's a digital effects artist. Together with Ben, the three of them live in a house everyone refers to as the Embassy because it's usually the first stop that recent University of Kansas film school grads make when they move from the heartland to Hollywood.

Big cuts like a standing rib roast take a long time to cook, so it's imperative that I get started early. I should take this opportunity to note that I am not by any stretch of the imagination a morning person. But somehow, on a Saturday in December, I drag myself out of bed at the crack of seven and trundle out the door for a grocery excursion the magnitude of which has never before been attempted by the hand of man. I'm planning dinner for 7:00 p.m., so I have exactly twelve hours to prepare.

I'll need those twelve hours. Rib roast, like royalty, does not proceed unaccompanied. I have a host of sides and accoutrements that will join our roast at the table. Back at the house, the Great Work begins. I whip together a quick simple syrup, infused with a little star anise. I combine this syrup with grapefruit juice and stow it in the freezer. I'll get to that later.

Next, I cube a French loaf I've left out overnight to dry. After a little olive oil, salt, and fifteen minutes in the oven, I have croutons.

The roast has been thawing in the fridge for twenty-four hours. I pull it from the fridge and stow it in the microwave, not for any culinary reason—I'm just intensely focused on cooking a thousand and one dishes simultaneously and my dog, Basil, will steal and devour any bit of animal protein she can get her enormous brown snout around. She can reach the counter with her mouth. She can unlock the latch on the baby gate we use to keep her out. She can open closed doors. She's like a velociraptor from *Jurassic Park*. If I don't watch her, that roast is gone. But one thing she can't do is open a microwave. Yet.

Before it goes into the oven, the roast needs to come to room temperature to make sure that it cooks evenly. Cold spots in the roast would result in uneven cooking and make the entire cooking process unwieldy. The roast weighs more than six pounds—that's unwieldy enough.

The meal I'm making is as British as bad teeth. I'm even preparing Yorkshire pudding, which is a traditional accompaniment to a standing rib roast. During feudal times, the lord and lady of the castle would eat first, followed by the landed gentry present at the meal and then the rest of the household in order of privilege. In a situation like this, every molecule of protein was salvaged. To maximize the nutritive impact of the meal, cooks would pour a rough batter into the roasting pan, scraping up whatever little burned-on bits of meat remained. This batter would go back into the oven or hearth to rise and result in a somewhat meat-flavored breadish item: Yorkshire pudding. I'm doing them as individual, popover-style puddings, but the concept is the same.

I've never made Yorkshire pudding before. In fact, I've never made any of the dishes I'm preparing today. A problem? Maybe. But I feel up to the challenge.

I will be making the pudding during the twenty minutes or so the roast will be resting after I pull it from the heat. Time will be valuable, so I make the batter in advance. It's simple: flour, salt, eggs, and milk. I cover it and stash the bowl in my ever-more-full refrigerator.

Serving roast beef without horseradish is sort of like buying prescription pills out of the back of a van. Sure, you may still get what you're looking for, but the process is off-putting. It isn't how things should be done. I pull together a quick horseradish cream sauce with sour cream, lemon, and ground horseradish root.

Four hours until dinner. I plan to prepare tableside Caesar salads, old school, so I prep all the ingredients now: minced garlic, eggs, Worcestershire, salt, anchovies, olive oil, lemon juice from our lemon trees in the backyard, and grated Parmesan. Houston: We are go for salad.

Three hours to go. I can't believe it, but I'm actually on schedule. Everything is in its place and ready to go. Dare I say: I have some spare time. Weirdly, thrillingly, impossibly—I could do more.

I consider my audience. Ben is Jewish, but he loves bacon more than any human being I've ever met. He doesn't eat it just with eggs. He's worked bacon into pies, cheesecake, sushi, vodka—and, I believe, ice cream. Allan and Chris share his obsession—for a Super Bowl party one year, the three of them built a replica of the Lombardi trophy out of bacon. You may have seen it on the Internet.

In honor of these porcine prodigies, I figure I'll try to work bacon into the meal somehow. But this entire meal is so over the top, I don't want to do something easy and expected. I want to do something stupid. Something absurd. I decide on bacon–chocolate chip cookies.

I fry up some bacon in my beloved cast-iron skillet, dice the bacon into the smallest pieces that my knife skills allow, and incorporate them into the cookie dough. I cut way back on the amount of butter used in the dough; the dough's fat content will come from bacon fat instead. A half hour later, I have two dozen cookies and a dog who doesn't understand where all the bacon went.

I try a cookie. They turned out pretty well, I suppose, but I'm not sure they're qualitatively better than standard chocolate chip cookies, despite the extra labor required to make them. They're smoky from the cured meat addition, while simultaneously chocolaty and sweet.

These cookies are also a meat-scented chocolate-delivery device. And chocolate is extraordinarily bad for dogs—even lethal in some cases. The cookies go into a sealed container on a high shelf. There's no more room in the microwave. This entire meal is a daylong torment for Basil.

Two hours to go. I place my room-temp roast into the roasting pan. Ordinarily I'd have to tie this roast to keep it from falling apart due to the breakdown of connective tissue during the cooking process. My butcher already tied mine, so I'm set. I slide the roast into the oven, bone side down. The fat on the top of the roast will drip down and marinate the meat, though I'll likely have to do a little basting myself now and then.

I start the roast at high temperature to sear the outside and give it a sexy, golden-brown crust. Then I lower the oven temp and bring the roast slowly to an internal temperature of 120 degrees. That temperature is well below medium rare, but the roast will continue to cook as it rests under foil after I pull it out of the oven. For this beef cut, overcooking is disastrous. Not only would it dry out the roast and make it taste like a bad cafeteria meal, but this is the only standing rib roast I have. If I screw this up, I don't get a second chance.

One hour from mealtime, the doorbell rings. Guests have arrived. The dinner train pulls away from the station.

Course One: Bacon–Chocolate Chip Cookies and crackers with cheese. Cookies don't really belong here, but I already have a dessert planned, so now cookies are appetizers. Accompanied by eggnog and good conversation because I am wildly in favor of both.

I watch my guests sample the cookies with all the subtlety of a toddler with a jack-in-the-box. I don't say anything, but I know what's coming. Now? No. How about now? Huh? Anything kooky about those cookies? Anything? How about now?

Allan speaks first. "What's up with these cookies?"

Bingo! My moment has come. "Bacon! There's bacon in the

chocolate chip cookies," I spout enthusiastically. Sometimes I embarrass even myself.

There's a moment of silence as everyone reassesses their cookie-eating experience. "Chewy," Allan notes. A long beat.

"Yeah, there's a texture thing going on here," Chris notes. "And a salty thing I wasn't really expecting."

Summer nods. "If you've ever wished your cookie tasted more like a pig . . ." She gestures to her cookie. "This has you covered."

I nosh on my own cookie. They're not wrong. Too much salt and too much sweet. There's a certain sense that these two things—bacon and cookies—don't really belong together.

"I like it," Ben insists.

I shake my head. "Nah, it's okay. It was an experiment. Lesson learned."

Ben shrugs and helps himself to another cookie. "I enjoy my pork products."

I chuckle. "Who wants more nog?" Nog fixes everything.

Course Two: Caesar Salad with Homemade Everything. I already prepped the dressing ingredients, so it takes only about thirty seconds to whip together a quick emulsion and toss it with the leaves of romaine lettuce. I separate this onto small plates, drop some croutons on top, and serve with chilled forks.

Chris turns his fork over in his hand. "The chilled forks are a nice touch."

"Wow, man," Allan says. "These are fancy."

"We are not barbarians!" I proclaim with a flourish.

Ben examines his plate. "Did you chill the plates, too?"

"Maybe."

Summer laughs, hiding her face in her hands. "Nice one, Stone."

I only smile, enduring their jests. We shall not skimp on details. Not today.

I cut short my own salad experience to pull the roast to rest and transfer meat drippings to muffin tins and then add the batter for the Yorkshire puddings. Into the oven.

Course Three: Palate Cleanser of Grapefruit–Star Anise Granita. The simple syrup and grapefruit juice mixture I made earlier is now frozen solid. I scrape it with a fork, making instant peach-colored shaved ice. I plan to serve this in some champagne flutes we haven't used since our wedding. However, some of them are inexplicably absent. They may or may not have shattered in an ill-advised juggling attempt. Instead, I think I can serve this concoction in brandy snifters. Except several of those are currently being used as eggnog receptacles. I have Burgundy glasses. Fine. Those will work. I serve the granita with chilled spoons because one cannot have enough chilled utensils at a meal. *Obviously.*

Course Four: Standing Rib Roast with Yorkshire Pudding. The main event. The roast is rested, and the internal temperature has risen to 132, solidly in the optimal medium-rare territory. I disassemble it into half-inch slabs and pair it with the popover Yorkshire pudding and a nice glass of Zin.

The meat looks fantastic—a deep rose in color, juicy, and lush, with a hard brown sear at the edge. It tastes like pure joy, kissed by angels and carried aloft by ecstatic butterflies. It's dead simple, but the trick with beef this good and a cut this luxurious isn't figuring out how to make it fantastic, it's figuring out how not to mess it up. One just has to get out of the way. The Yorkshire pudding also is lovely, though it doesn't taste the way I expected it to. It's soft and pillowy and only slightly beef-flavored. Like a luxurious dinner roll.

Course Five: Cherries Jubilee, which is vanilla ice cream topped with thickened cherry preserves and flambéed with brandy. I'm excited about this one. In one of the first film projects Ben, Allan, and I worked on together in college, we blew up a car for a climactic shot. My dinner companions today have a healthy love of and respect for well-executed pyrotechnics.

Brandy needs to be hot to burn. In room-temperature brandy, the alcohol is held in solution, mixed with other liquids—mostly water. This water keeps the alcohol from igniting. Since alcohol boils at a lower temperature than water, heating the brandy causes the alcohol to vaporize, leaving the water behind in the pan. This now gaseous alcohol mixes with oxygen in the air and becomes flammable.

I heat the brandy, kill my burner, and touch it with a long match. Nothing.

I slip the skillet back onto the heat and try again. Still nothing. A third time. Zilch. The ice cream is melting. In a tactical maneuver to minimize meal disruption, I mix the unflamed brandy with the preserves and top the ice cream. Declan gets only ice cream—the "jubilee" portion of the meal just got literal. This dessert is eighty proof.

I serve my guests, then join them at the table.

"Jesus, man," Ben says. "That was delicious."

"Glad you liked it," I reply. I'm beat, but thrilled that everything worked out. Well, mostly everything. The cookies were unnecessarily porcine, and I can smell the liquor in my dessert from several feet away. But it was close enough for jazz.

"Yeah, really nice, man." Chris nods. "Thanks for having us over."

Allan squints. "Dude, these forks aren't even chilled. What are you, some kind of animal?"

"I know." I laugh. "I'm not sure how you put up with me."

Allan grins and takes a bite of his dessert. The rest of my guests follow suit.

A moment of silence.

"So . . ." Chris begins. "There's liquor in this, huh?"

Laughter around the table. I take a bite of my own boozy cherries jubilee. It's quite alcoholic. It'd probably be more accurate to describe it as a semisolid cocktail. Like Ben and Jerry and Rémy Martin had a baby.

Summer rubs my back and smiles. I smile back. I've been on my feet for twelve hours, cooking what I hope will be a meal to remember. Our first foray, perhaps, into making California our home, way out here in the West, instead of being permanently "away from home" for the holidays and every other day of the year. We live here, in California. We have a family here, in the only home Declan has ever known. Traditions are lovely, but it's high time to make new ones. I'm happy to start that process today, surrounded by dear friends and fine food, lovingly prepared.

Tired as I am, this meal was definitely worth it.

Christmafestikwanzikkuh Feast

Time: Clear your schedule. This could take all day.

Serves 4 to 6

Suitable for holidays, special occasions, and impressing the in-laws. This feast is adapted largely from a menu by Linda Stradley, of whatscookingamerica.net. (Note: I didn't include the bacon–chocolate chip cookies I made earlier in the chapter because, as a first course, they're just weird.)

GRANITA

½ cup sugar

2 whole star anise

½ cup pink grapefruit juice

ROAST

Standing rib roast in the 5- to 6-pound range (you may have
to visit a butcher for this cut, since supermarkets
frequently don't carry it)

Butcher's twine (if your roast isn't already tied)

CROUTONS

1 loaf good, but slightly stale, French bread

About ¼ cup olive oil

Kosher salt

YORKSHIRE PUDDING

¾ cup all-purpose flour

½ teaspoon kosher salt

3 large eggs

¾ cup milk

½ cup pan drippings from standing rib roast

HORSERADISH SAUCE

½ (6-ounce) bottle of prepared horseradish

2 cups sour cream

Juice of ½ lemon (use the other half for the Caesar salad)

1 teaspoon kosher salt

CAESAR SALAD

1 large egg

2 teaspoons minced garlic

2 anchovy fillets

Kosher salt

Juice of ½ lemon

⅛ teaspoon Worcestershire sauce

6 tablespoons extra-virgin olive oil

4 tablespoons freshly grated Parmesan cheese

Freshly ground black pepper

3 heads romaine lettuce

CHERRIES JUBILEE

1 pound frozen pitted cherries

½ cup sugar

½ cup brandy

Vanilla ice cream

1. Make the granita first, since you need time to freeze it: Combine the sugar, star anise, and ⅓ cup water in a small saucepan over medium heat and bring to a boil.

2. Remove from the heat, discard the star anise, and let the syrup cool. Add the grapefruit juice and whisk to combine.

3. Pour into a 9-inch square casserole dish (or similar wide container; surface area is the important factor) and stash in the freezer until frozen solid, about 4 hours.

4. About 2 hours before cooking, take the roast out of the refrigerator and allow the meat to come to room temperature.

5. Make the croutons: Preheat the oven to 375°F.

6. Cut the bread into 1-inch cubes and toss them with just enough oil to lightly coat. Lay the cubes out on a baking sheet, sprinkle with salt, and bake for 15 minutes. Now you have croutons. Set aside.

7. Start the Yorkshire pudding by sifting the flour and salt together into a large mixing bowl.

8. In another bowl, whisk together the eggs and milk. Stir in the flour mixture until just combined. (Lumps are okay; make sure you don't overstir.) This is your Yorkshire pudding batter; cover with plastic wrap and stash it in the fridge until you're ready to use it.

9. Preheat the oven to 450°F.

10. To make the horseradish sauce, combine the horseradish, sour cream, lemon juice, and a little salt in a small bowl. This is your horseradish sauce, the perfect complement to your roast. Stash it in the fridge.

11. When the oven is ready, place the tied roast in a roasting pan, bone side down.

❧

Many standing rib roasts are already tied by the butcher before purchase. If yours hasn't been, simply tie a string around the roast between the bones, pull snug, and tie a simple knot. This will help keep the roast from losing its shape as it cooks.

Insert the probe of a digital thermometer into the center of the meat, and set the transmitter somewhere nearby outside the oven where it won't be in your way. Set the target temp on your thermometer for 120°F. This is one meal you definitely do not want to ruin. Make sure you have and use your thermometer. An appropriate thermometer features a digital readout outside the oven and can be had for about thirty bucks nearly anyplace that sells gear for cooks.

12. Put the roast on the middle rack of the hot oven and roast for 15 minutes to sear the surface. Knock the oven temperature down to 325°F and roast until the meat reaches 120°F, checking on it every half hour and basting with any resultant drippings. The total cook time will likely be a little over 2 hours, depending on how large your roast is.

13. To make your Caesar salad dressing, first coddle the egg, by placing it, still in the shell, in a coffee mug and pouring boiling water over it to fill the mug. Let stand for 1 minute, then flush the hot water with cold water from the tap until you can pick up the egg. Coddling thickens the egg ever so slightly, resulting in a creamier dressing. You could skip this step and use the egg raw, but why would you? (If you're worried about raw or undercooked eggs, many supermarkets carry eggs that have been pasteurized in their shells.)

❧

If you like, the next five steps can be prepared tableside. Bring a medium-sized bowl, along with all the salad ingredients, and get ready to impress. Don't forget the chilled bowls and forks.

14. In a medium bowl, whisk together the garlic, anchovies, and a pinch of salt, then add the lemon juice and Worcestershire sauce and whisk to incorporate them.

15. Crack the egg and add it to the protodressing, whisking all the while, until the dressing is thickened.

16. While still whisking furiously, pour in the oil in a thin stream and keep whisking until it looks like Caesar dressing.

17. Whisk in 2 tablespoons of the cheese and salt and pepper to taste. Add the lettuce and croutons and toss gently to combine and thoroughly coat.

18. Portion the salad out into chilled bowls, and serve with chilled forks, adding a little more cheese at the table.

19. Enjoy your salad, but don't forget to check on/baste the roast.

20. To serve the granita, pull the frozen grapefruit syrup from the freezer. Scrape it with a fork to create fluffy, peach-colored shaved ice. Serve it in pretty glasses (brandy snifters and champagne flutes work well) with chilled spoons.

21. When the internal temperature of the roast reaches 120°F, remove it from the oven, transfer to a cutting board, and tent loosely with foil. Let it rest for 20 minutes. Do not cut your roast right away—it will continue to cook as it rests. This is a good thing.

22. To prepare the Yorkshire pudding, remove the batter from the fridge and give it a quick stir.

23. Increase the oven temperature to 425°F. Equally distribute the hot drippings from the roast among the cups of the muffin pan. Top each off with the batter.

24. Put the muffin pan in the oven and bake until puffed and golden brown, 12 to 15 minutes.

25. After the roast has rested, cut the strings and shear off the entire rack of bones in one slice. Rotate the roast and slice perpendicular to the cut you just made, partitioning the roast into ½-inch-thick slices. Plate each slice with a Yorkshire pudding and serve.

🐝

Now eat your dinner. Tell some funny jokes. Be a good host.

26. Now for the grand finale, cherries jubilee. To begin, heat the cherries and sugar in a small saucepan over medium heat, stirring until the sugar dissolves, about 4 minutes.

27. Remove from the heat, then quickly but carefully add the brandy to the cherries and ignite with a long match. Once the flames die out, stir very gently. Brandy won't become flammable unless it's warm. This step didn't work for me because my pan wasn't hot enough. Once you take it off the heat, don't dally.

28. Place one scoop of ice cream in each of 4 to 6 attractive serving dishes. Spoon the warm cherries over the ice cream.

29. Serve, but with practiced nonchalance. Pretend you always set dessert on fire.

30. Rest. You've earned it.

8

One Step Back,
One Step Forward

s my beef experiment rolls on, I begin to give thought to how it is affecting my health. I haven't been to the doctor in years. I've never really thought it was necessary—so long as nothing hurts, nothing is poking out of me, and everything moves pretty much in the way it should, I figure I'm healthy. But my beef experiment has piqued my curiosity. How can I know what kind of shape I'm in if I don't go to a doctor and find out?

I go in for the first medical checkup since the Clinton administration. Everything's good for the most part. My cholesterol levels are normal. But my doctor notices something that concerns him in some of my blood work and wants to bring me back in. Some fasting, more blood work, and another couple of visits, and he has news: My fasting blood sugar is high. I'm not diabetic, but I'm inclined toward it.

My grandfather was diabetic, and my father and brother are diabetic as well, so I have an enormous neon diabetic arrow pointing in my direction. I'd always thought I'd gotten lucky and had avoided the particular set of genetic markers that made me more susceptible to diabetes, but with this news perhaps I hadn't. Perhaps diabetes was coming for me as well, only slower.

This is not good.

"Well, shit."

I glance down at my son, sitting across from me, and quickly correct. "Shoot."

Summer, Declan, and I are sitting in our local haunt for burgers and hot dogs. Out of guilt and health-induced anxiety, I ordered a garden burger. It's dry.

"Is there anything you need to do?" she asks.

"I don't know. I don't know if there's anything I can do," I reply.

She's silent a moment. "Well, it's not like it's a definite diagnosis. It's just something to be aware of."

"Something horrible to be aware of."

"You're being dramatic."

"Not really. My brother was diagnosed diabetic as a kid. My grandfather after he retired. But my dad . . ." I still remember my dad, borrowing one of my little brother's blood glucose test strips, pricking his own finger, and that was that. "My dad was diagnosed at maybe eight years older than I am now. But who knows how long he was prediabetic before that?" I toy with a fry on my plate. "This is not good."

"Cookie, Daddy?" Declan interjects. He's nuts about the chocolate chip cookies they have here.

"Not tonight, buddy." And what about Dec? I'd never considered his risk for diabetes before.

I turn back to Summer. "When my dad was diagnosed, he dropped all sugar immediately. Started running several miles, twice a day. Did everything he was supposed to. And then some."

"And?"

"Went from type two to type one. From producing little insulin on his own to producing no insulin."

"Wow."

"Yup. We Stone men have terrible pancreases." I take another bite of my garden burger.

Summer thinks for a moment. "Well, listen—so what? You just have to take each day as it comes, and make the best of what you have." I'm silent for a change, so she continues. "You aren't diabetic yet. You're a fairly smart guy. Maybe you can beat this thing."

"How am I supposed to do that?"

"I don't know," she says, stealing a fry off my plate. "Figure it out."

My health weighs heavily on my mind as I blaze through my workday. Ten hours of television are a blur—I'm preoccupied. I write words. Cut some pretty pictures. My section of the Machine whirrs along without a hitch. I wander home in a daze. I don't know what to do. I feel broken.

After putting my son to bed, I leash up Basil and go for a walk.

She's a fantastic companion for a stroll, especially when I don't feel like talking. And right now, I really don't.

Foremost on my mind: Should I give up this beef experiment?

If I give up, that's a lot of beef I'm going to have to do something with. I can probably donate it to a homeless shelter or a food bank. I don't know offhand if many places have standing capacity for this much perishable food, though I'm sure they could somehow find it.

But bigger question: Would donating all the beef to a food bank even solve my problem? This is great beef. Far higher quality than what one can buy in a supermarket. I don't know what the fat content is; it doubtless varies by cut. Even the ground beef—which in a supermarket would be labeled with its fat content—is a mystery to me here. Whatever fat was in the cow is in the beef.

But with diabetes—or prediabetes—fat content isn't the problem. Dietary sugar is the problem, at least to some extent. That's the reason diabetics aren't really supposed to eat sweets. In people with normal pancreatic function, the pancreas secretes insulin, a hormone that allows the body to absorb glucose from the bloodstream. The bigger the dietary sugar load, the more insulin needed to process that glucose.

In people with type 2 diabetes—formerly known as adult-onset diabetes—the pancreas can't keep up with the demands that their blood sugar is making on it. People with type 2 diabetes might take medication to stimulate their pancreas further, combined with modifying their diet to ease the demand on their pancreas. In type 1 diabetes, however, the pancreas doesn't produce insulin at all. People with type 1 diabetes have to compensate entirely with supplemental insulin injections.

Unregulated or improperly regulated blood sugar is a tremendously bad thing. Without treatment, diabetics become hyperglycemic—they have too much sugar in their blood. High blood sugar for a long period of time can lead to heart attacks, kidney failure, and diabetic coma.

On the other end of the spectrum, *hypo*glycemia is low blood sugar. In diabetics, this can occur from a number of causes, including injecting too much insulin, stress, or depleting blood glucose stores with exercise. Left untreated, this can also lead to heart disease and coma.

The risks associated with frequent or long-term hyperglycemia or hypoglycemia are the reasons that diabetics frequently eliminate or avoid sugar in their diets. A sharp blood glucose increase—say, a candy bar—immediately and dramatically spikes insulin demand, for which diabetics have to manually compensate. If they overadminister insulin, they risk hypoglycemia. If they underadminister—hyperglycemia.

Put differently—too much insulin: risk heart attacks and coma. Too little insulin: risk heart attacks and coma. It's usually just easier to keep blood sugar in a safe, predictable range. No candy bars.

As Basil and I walk beneath a streetlight, she looks up at me. From this angle above her, I can see the hourglass of her waist as her hip carriage shifts with her gait. This indentation, just above the hips, is one of the markers for ideal weight on a Rhodesian Ridgeback. They're big, deep-chested dogs and should not under any circumstances be allowed to pack on too many pounds. (Since dogs don't sweat, they pant to thermoregulate. Excess weight insulates their body with fat and makes it harder for them to cool off.) It's better to underfeed than to overfeed them.

I'm always wary of Basil's diet. When she was younger—before we had Declan—we used to feed her raw, according to what is called the BARF (Biologically Appropriate Raw Food) diet. The logic behind this approach is that it more closely mimics the diet that the dog evolved to eat. It consisted of whole foods, real meat, and vegetables. In our particular case, that translated into oatmeal with vitamins and veggies in the morning and a quarter of a raw chicken at night. Basil had tolerated the oatmeal—Ridgebacks are astonishingly food-motivated—but she'd annihilate the chicken. I remember her lifting the chicken quarter out of the bowl, carrying it out into our backyard, and lying down with it between her paws. She'd tear it apart with her jaws, crunch the bones with her molars, and swallow it in enormous chunks, bones and all.

When we fed her raw, Basil was in glorious, preposterously good health. Bright, shiny coat. Zero body fat. Boundless energy. But when our son was born, our free time evaporated. We couldn't get my wife started on her hour-long commute before work, get Dec dressed and ready for day care, get me dressed and ready for work and on the road for my own hour-long commute, and still find time to make oatmeal for the dog. Reluctantly, we switched her back to store-bought kibble. She's still healthy and fit, but the difference is noticeable.

When Basil ate whole-grain oatmeal and high-quality protein, she was in ludicrously good shape. She's a dog, so the parallels are somewhat limited. But better diet can't help making better health, right? Similarly, my high-quality protein likewise probably isn't a problem. Maybe, weirdly, I need to eat more like Basil had.

More like *Nourishing Traditions* keeps telling me I should eat. I should read more.

First things first, however: I should run more.

If I'm worried about my health, getting into some sort of exercise routine seems like the right thing to do. Running is one of the few purely physical activities that humans are supposed to be good at—yet most people would rather perform their own appendectomy than run a hundred yards. Me, I run only sporadically. A few years back, my wife and I ran the Marine Corps Marathon in Washington, D.C. The next day, my entire lower body cramped up, leaving me couch-ridden for several days. Because I couldn't stand, let alone run, I took a hiatus from what was at the time a pretty aggressive running regimen. I'm still on that hiatus.

Almost anyone can complete a marathon, if completion is their only goal. It isn't the sort of exertion that most people assume it would be. It's like sitting in a reasonably comfortable chair while a large man beats your heels with a very large hammer. Slowly. If a runner isn't trying to finish in any particular time, there isn't much aerobic exertion involved in running a marathon. It isn't a matter of being in shape. It's just a matter of enduring a moderate amount of pain for a very long time.

Getting hurt while running is relatively common; Summer developed stress fractures from her marathon training. I've never understood why something as natural and instinctive as running has such a high rate of injury—by some estimates, almost 80 percent of runners hurt themselves running each year. I can't count the number of times I've heard people say that they used to run, but they stopped because it's "bad for their knees."

I, on the other hand, am trying to get back into it. I've slimmed down a bit eating whole foods, and I'm generally happy about it. And because of my recent news, I'd like to keep the health train rolling. Plus, swimsuit season is just around the corner.

That in mind, I slip on my ancient running shoes and head out the door. I'm not as fast as I was when I ran regularly, but I have to start somewhere. It's a beautiful day, and I breathe deeply as I settle into my once familiar rhythm. Besides the birds, the only sound is that of my feet on pavement. Ka-thump, ka-thump, ka-thump. (I run loud—always have.) As I run, I mentally subdivide the sound of my strides into whatever song I have stuck in my head at the moment. Today, it's Paul Simon's "Cecilia." *I'm begging you please to come home . . .* ka-thump, ka-thump, ka-thump. *Whoa oh oh!*

I round the corner of my block and head back toward home. As it's the end of my run, I sprint, giving it everything I have. The rhythmic ka-thump vanishes. There is no music now. Just exertion.

Finally, I slow to a walk, panting. My feet hurt. I think I need new shoes.

It's a Sunday afternoon. I'm in the grocery store buying supplies for one of my weekend culinary adventures. Today, I'm not at just any grocery store—I'm at Whole Foods. They charge a premium for their wares, but they have everything that a budding food dork could desire: screamingly fresh produce, gorgeous seafood, and a fairly robust selection of cheeses for a supermarket chain. Drifting through the dairy section, I freeze—I've spotted a unicorn in the refrigerator case. Culinary Bigfoot. The Dairy Loch Ness monster.

For some completely unknown reason, this store sells raw milk.

I thought that was illegal.

Raw milk is one of the staples and primary points of contention between the Weston A. Price crowd and the population at large, as notably represented by the FDA.

I pull a bottle out of the refrigerator case to double-check—yes.

Raw. Unpasteurized. Comes in a glass bottle like men in white suits used to leave on doorsteps. I hesitate, then move to put it back. Then stop. And put it in my cart.

Back in my kitchen, I open the bottle and smell it. It doesn't smell like much—milk, I guess. What was I expecting? But is it my eyes, or does it look slightly different? A little yellower, perhaps? More straw-colored? I examine the label: "Shake Well Before Use." I look through the clear glass bottle at the fluid inside, which must be why they put it in a glass bottle instead of a carton in the first place. The milk is two-toned. It's definitely lighter on top because it hasn't gone through a process called homogenization—when bottlers force raw milk through tiny holes at high pressure, breaking up the fat globules and enabling them to remain in suspension instead of floating to the top of the bottle, as they have here. Homogenized milk has a uniform density. This milk does not. It's the real deal.

I shake the bottle vigorously. How long am I supposed do this, a few seconds? A minute? Five? I check the milk's consistency. Nope, still clumpy. I shake more. A few minutes later, and, well, I won't say it's unclumpy. But it's something like a more uniform consistency. I pour a glass. Take a sip.

It's creamy and very, very rich. I drink a little faster. Cold, it's almost chewy. It's grassy and thick, with a little more sweetness than I'm used to. I'm drinking it fast, like an eight-year-old child at a school picnic, and I can feel the milk coat my upper lip. For science, I check my milk mustache in the mirror. Regular milk gives one a certain pencil-thin, John Waters–esque 'stache—elegant and easily removed, if noticeable at all. Raw milk drops the full Wilford Brimley. It's luxurious, thick, and ever so slightly gloopy.

Also, this milk is delicious. If, of course, you have the sort of psyche and constitution that can shrug off the threat of a little *Listeria*. That is, if you aren't very young, very old, pregnant, or suffering from some malady that compromises the immune system. Listeriosis can kill—it's one of the reasons that some governments began widespread pasteurization of milk in the first place. It's a decision between absolutely bacteriologically safe milk with a possibly decreased flavor and health profile versus more flavorful milk with potentially greater health benefits that is *likely* bacteriologically safe—but if it isn't, it could be very, very bad. That's a personal choice, and I'm not sure there's a clear-cut right answer. Listeriosis is potentially deadly, and those most susceptible to it, especially children, have the least agency in their own food choices. Conversely, risk can be minimized by buying locally from producers one knows and trusts. And proponents say the health benefits can be enormous.

I don't have an answer. But I do have milk. I top off my glass and put the bottle back into the refrigerator. I leave my kitchen and stride across my living room, before sitting by the window with a good book.

I take another sip of my raw milk. I'm down the rabbit hole now.

Some nights just don't go quite like you planned.

"Cool," my wife says. We're in our living room. She is gazing down at a small ceramic bowl on her lap with a look midway between nonplussed and actively disinterested. "So what is it, like a bowl?"

"It's a French butter crock!" I exclaim, as if that should explain it all. "You're making a lot of bread now, and I thought you could use this to keep your butter fresh."

"Of course," she replies, trying out a smile because I'm being a little weird. "Well, thank you. I really like it." She says it like the conversation should be over now.

"Allow me to elucidate," I continue, unwilling to give up on an item that I think is actively fantastic. I talk fast. "Before refrigeration, people had to keep butter from going bad somehow, right? Most of the time, they'd wrap it tightly and keep it submerged in water. It takes a lot of energy to change the temperature of water, so the butter would stay pretty cool. Also, because it's away from oxygen, it wouldn't go rancid. Make sense?"

"Sure." I can only imagine what mad gleam I must have in my eye.

"In the late 1800s, French butter lovers—great band name, by the way—developed this little guy."

"To hold butter."

"Exactly! Dig." I gesture to the device in question. "Two pieces. The outer is this mug-looking thing. You fill it about a third up with water."

"Okay."

"The inside is this inverted bell-type thing. You fill this with butter. Flip it over, insert it, and the lip of the bell slips beneath the surface of the water. You get butter, sealed free of air, so it keeps at room temp. What's more, it stays super spreadable. So you won't have to nuke it and risk it separating. All without refrigeration."

"So this just sits on the counter?"

"Yeah."

"And the butter won't go bad?"

"Not for thirty days, give or take. But when does butter ever last us thirty days?"

A pause. Her eyes dart from the butter crock to me. "Cool . . ." she says.

"You're not excited?" I ask incredulously.

She smiles. "I'm excited you're excited." Her smile widens a little. "I haven't seen you this excited about something for quite a while."

"It's butter! And it's a better, cheaper, more delicious way of doing something. It's an old tech that's better than the new one, and a mere forty-eight hours ago I had no idea it even existed. What's not to get excited about?"

"You are absolutely right. It's very cool, Jared. Thank you." She stands up and kisses me on the top of my head.

"You will understand the magnificence of the butter crock!" I bellow, fist shaking sarcastically like a B-movie villain. "You must recognize its genius!"

"Come to bed, Goldfinger," she calls over her shoulder. "We have to get up early."

I glance at the clock. She's right. She's always right.

Several days later, anticipating a breakfast featuring astonishingly spreadable butter, I get ready for my run. I've been looking into which shoes I should pick up for my new running habit, and I've been exploring how people used to run. From my days as an anthropology undergrad, I recalled that humans are supposed to be really good at running pretty fast for a really long time. It's one of only a very few purely physical traits we could exploit for hunting success. We aren't especially strong. Or especially swift. We don't have sharp teeth or claws. We usually have one baby at a time, and our babies stay helpless for years. But we can run. Pretty fast. Almost forever.

Specifically, we can run fast enough and long enough to wear out prey—a technique called persistence hunting. We can't beat many animals in a sprint, but we can keep on running, whereas a prey animal—say a gazelle or an elk—has to stop and catch its breath. Lacking the ability to sweat, these ungulates have to stop and pant to cool off. While persistence hunting, a running human catches up, forcing the prey to run before it has managed to re-cover from the first sprint. Eventually, the prey becomes too hot and tired to continue, which allows the hunter to spear them. Or shoot them with an arrow. Or atlatl them. Persistence hunting is an ancient technique—thought to be originally developed by *Homo erectus* but still practiced by some indigenous groups today, such as the famed !Kung people of the Kalahari Desert. However, per-sistence hunting clearly doesn't depend on modern running shoes. Nike was only founded in 1964. How did people run prior to that?

When I looked into how people used to run, I discovered the work of Harvard evolutionary biologist Daniel Lieberman. He's done research comparing the biomechanics of shoe-wearing run-ners and shoeless runners. His research shows that shod runners and unshod runners run very differently.

Most runners who learned how to run in shoes, myself included, stretch their foot out in front of them and land on their heel. Then they roll forward across the base of their foot before pushing off again with their toes. Or, in my case, I land on my heel, using my longest possible stride because I'm rather tall, and then quickly slap the rest of my foot down on the pavement because I'm also relatively fast. Ka-thump.

I'm only allowed the luxury of landing on my heel and slapping the rest of my foot down shortly thereafter, according to Lieberman, because I'm wearing running shoes. These shoes cushion the impact of my heel on the ground, called a heel strike, allowing me to take advantage of my six-foot-one frame by reaching my lead foot way out in front of my body, taking the largest strides possible.

Runners who learned to run without the benefit of shoes run very differently. Without the enormous cushion provided by a pair of modern running shoes, heel striking doesn't work. There simply isn't enough fatty tissue on the heel of the foot to absorb the impact forces of an entire human body crashing down onto it. Instead, people who learned to run without shoes land on the ball/middle of their foot, called a forefoot strike. Then, using the calf muscles as a spring, they place their heels on the ground only briefly before again launching off their toes and into the next stride.

In heel strikers, the entire body comes to a complete dead stop for an instant before forward momentum and the action of the leg muscles launch the body forward into the next stride. This presents a tremendous impact directly up the leg to the knees and hips, without the benefit of a calf muscle and ankle joint to mitigate the stress.

In forefoot strikers, the impact is dramatically lessened because the impact force is transferred instead into angular momentum, modulated by the ankle joint and the calf muscles, before pushing off again into the next stride. The result of the forefoot strike is decreased stride length—a runner doesn't have the luxury of sticking his foot way out in front of him anymore—but increased stride efficiency. This may make running injuries less common in forefoot strikers because they're no longer coming to a momentary dead stop with each step, jolting their body weight up their legs. Research is still ongoing.

Another way to look at it: People who learn to run barefoot run as though they actually have calf muscles and ankles to do some of the work. People who learn to run in shoes could be running on pirate peg legs, as far as their stride impact is concerned.

According to Lieberman and his colleagues, humans have been running for approximately two million years. However, they've been doing it in running shoes for only a tiny fraction of that time. To me, it boggles the mind to think that evolved persistence hunters would devise a system of hunting that causes debilitating injuries to up to 80 percent of its participants each year. If running in shoes is frequently injurious to those who partake, and running itself is supposed to be instinctive and natural to humans, could running in shoes be to blame?

A large part of Lieberman's research involves testing to see if runners' injuries are caused by repetitive stress on the joints and also whether running in shoes exacerbates that stress. Lieberman is a world-class evolutionary biologist with a professorship at Harvard—he has the burden and promise of peer review and professional commendations on the line as he tests his theory. As a result, he doesn't try to tell people how to run. He's a researcher, not a running coach.

I, however, am a schmuck who likes to self-experiment. And sometimes I like to run places. In other words, I have no reason not to ditch the shoes for a day and see how I feel. If I like it, if it feels natural and fun—great. If not, I'll stop. If it feels like my feet are going to shatter and leave me in a gasping, bloody heap splayed across the sidewalk, I'll stop quickly.

So this morning, I tell Summer I'm going out for a run.

"You gonna put shoes on?" she asks.

"Going without, today," I reply.

"Got it. Have fun," she says.

"That's it?" I ask. "No questions? Admonishments? Concerns over the wisdom of my course of action?"

She laughs. "Nope. This isn't the first nutty thing you've done," she replies, gesturing. "Please allow me to direct your attention to the cow in our backyard."

I chuckle and head for the front door.

I step outside and close the door behind me, feeling like the patchouli-est of hippie weirdos. Who runs barefoot? Hell, who walks barefoot? If I say hello to other people on the path, they're gonna think I'm recruiting for a cult. I'm one shaven head away from a police report.

I stroll down my front walk to the sidewalk. Man, if I so much as smell broken glass, I'm gonna bleed like a stuck pig. This is in no way safe.

Alright. Put up or shut up. I break into a jog.

Ow. Ow. Ow. Ow. Ow. This hurts.

I power through for a few paces, trying to figure out why. It doesn't take long: I'm heel striking. Really, really hard. With each step, my lead foot extends far out in front of me as I crash down hard directly onto the bone of my heel, only thinly shrouded in flesh.

Without the cushion of a half inch of space-age polymers, my heel can't withstand the impact.

So that doesn't work. I slow to a walk. I know I'm supposed to forefoot strike, but that isn't how I learned to run. I need to think this through.

I ease into a very slow jog as I focus on my stride. I'm a big guy—I take big steps. I tighten up my gait and focus on landing on the ball of my foot. It isn't especially natural. I feel like the world's least graceful ballerino. *Jeté. Frappé.*

However, not a ka-thump to be found. Running like this is eerily silent. The only sound I hear is my own rhythmic breathing.

Little steps. I force myself to stay slow. Pay attention. Land on the forefoot. After a few minutes, I'm not sending shock waves of pain up my legs anymore. But I notice something else. My calves are burning. This isn't a movement they're accustomed to making this hard, for this long. Or at all, really. With each step, it's harder to land correctly.

I'm nearing the end of my regular run, the point where I would ordinarily launch into a sprint. Determined, I hit my usual mark and I take off.

And I fly.

This! This is natural. This feels right.

At a sprint pace, my heels never touched the ground anyway. Without shoes, this familiar motion feels almost effortless. Barefoot, it's far easier to sprint than it is to jog. I feel several inches taller. The law of gravity is just a suggestion. I'm Hermes on amphetamines.

I slow up as I reach my house, winded but ecstatic. My virginal pink feet are torn up and bloody from trying to find traction on the rough concrete, but I'm hooked. Running barefoot is freeing and fun. It makes the act of running seem like a game rather than an obligation. Like play. Maybe it's the runner's high talking. Or maybe it's just joy.

Either way—I want to do this again.

It's getting downright Laura Ingalls Wilder at my Little House in the Valley. In addition to running barefoot and heeding the wisdom of nineteenth-century French butter lovers, I've started something of a backyard garden. Seven-foot-tall tomato plants block the view of my orange trees. Cucumber vines have burst from the soil, clambering up the cage I built for them and spreading a meter in every direction. Nearby, ferocious jalapeños thrust out more peppers than I could ever hope to use, turning fully red before I can even manage to get them off the vine. I'm accompanying my beef dishes with more vegetables than a boatload of Buddhists, and all the detritus goes straight into my backyard; my compost pile, halfheartedly begun when we bought the house, is now a towering edifice of bugs and branches and vigorous aerobic decay.

I cook a lot on weekends now, and I eat a lot more whole foods. My wife's fresh-baked wheat bread. Brown rice. Whole roast chickens. These culinary escapades are lovely, but they require a fairly regular influx of vegetables. With this garden, I'm trying to raise as many of those veggies here at home as I can. I should get some overalls. I could rock some overalls.

It's against this backdrop that I find myself standing, shoeless, in my kitchen, staring at a bowl of heavy cream that I'd left on the counter overnight to rot. On purpose.

Summer slips in behind me, joining my contemplation. "Is it ready?"

"I don't know," I answer.

"How do you tell?"

"It gets thick. I don't think it's thick enough."

"It looks thick."

"Yeah, but is it thick *enough*?"

We stare at the cream in silence for a moment. I used a down-and-dirty method of fermenting heavy cream into crème fraîche. It should be about done. Maybe.

On a shelf outside the kitchen, my phone chirps. I glance vaguely in its direction but otherwise ignore it. I'm focused on the project at hand.

Finally, I make a decision. "I think it's thick enough."

"I'm sure it'll be fine," Summer agrees, patting me on the back.

"Sweet. Butter time."

"Is that trademarked?" she asks. "Like, that could be your superhero catchphrase—'It's butter time!'"

"Hush, you." I laugh as I dump what I hope is crème fraîche into my food processor. I flip a switch, and the device's blades whip the liquid into froth. "I guess I'd *butter* try again." Lord, why do I do it? My brain can see the horrible pun coming, but my mouth says it anyway. It's a problem.

Summer shakes her head. "Do you get paid by the pun or something?" She points to the bowl. "I think we're getting somewhere . . ." she says.

She's right. Inside the food processor, the liquid is thickening further. This is good. A few more minutes and actual clumps form. It looks a little like cottage cheese.

"That's butter?" Summer asks.

"Yeah. Butter in the making. Protobutter, I suppose. We have to rinse it."

After a few minutes, I empty the bowl of the food processor into the second-largest glass bowl I have (the largest is filled with ice water for a later step), being sure to scrape out all the clumps.

Using a measuring cup as a ladle, I pour some cold water into my butter bowl, producing a mixture that looks like extremely runny cottage cheese. I mash it with a fork, making sure to get water onto the smallest clumps of protobutter that I can. The butter, being mostly fat, will refuse to mix with the water. Meanwhile, the buttermilk, being mostly water, will dilute, turning the water cloudy. This rinsing is how the pure butter separates out from the crème fraîche.

I empty the liquid through a strainer, careful to retain the solid in the bowl, and repeat the process several more times. Water in, empty the liquid when it's cloudy. Literally: Rinse and repeat.

When the mixture rinses clear, the solid section really looks like butter. I turn it out onto a cutting board, dash on some kosher salt, folding repeatedly to work it in.

"So that's it?" Summer asks. "That's butter?"

"That's butter." I tighten it up into something like a log.

"We made it ourselves."

"We did, at that."

"Awesome. Can we try it yet?"

"Sure! It's butter. It'll probably be better cold, though."

"Cold schmold. I want butter."

"Can I bring you something to put it on?"

"You can bring me a spoon."

I laugh and head back to the kitchen.

"And bring the butter crock!" she calls after me. "That thing is amazing."

I grin.

I don't know definitively if eating more whole foods is better for me, but it certainly couldn't be any worse. Without a doubt, meals are more delicious now, if more time-consuming to produce. People definitely ate better before World War II. Cattle were raised differently then, too, back before they became a petroleum product.

My experience with this freezer full of beef is also paying off in my family's health and general happiness. And I notice some commonalities in the changes we've been making. Frequently, Summer and I find ourselves reverting to previous iterations of a technology or technique that, for one reason or another, fell out of favor. I start jokingly referring to this state as One Step Back. Then, not so jokingly.

One Step Back, cows ate grass.

One Step Back, more people knew how to cook.

One Step Back, obesity was rarer.

I'm already one batch of hominy away from our place becoming a cover story in *Pioneer Kitchens Monthly*. So as a thought experiment, for every action in my day I start asking how people used to do it. Every task I perform, every methodology I employ—again and again: How was it done previously? And was it done better One Step Back?

Some of my retreats into historical precedent are completely fruitless. Before people worked on laptops, they worked on typewriters. In no way, sense, or fashion do I have any desire to return to the time of Olivettis and Underwoods. That's just crazy talk. I prefer my productivity machines with delete keys.

Other advances, however, aren't so clear-cut. Shaving, for example. Why does my razor need three, four, or five blades? Why isn't one blade sufficient for the task at hand, namely, denuding my face of hair? And why are there so many ever-more-gimmicky models flooding the marketplace? I shave with a curvaceous triple-bladed gewgaw that looks like the offspring of an unholy union between a ballpoint pen and a Dyson vacuum. To facilitate its use, I slather on neon-hued foam smuggled out of Chernobyl in a babushka's carry-on. It's just how I started shaving in high school (oh, who am I kidding—just after college). It's just how things are done. I don't know why.

Once, men shaved with straight razors. A single, gleaming shard of forged steel that folded out of a wood handle like the pocket-knife from hell. They have a fearsome reputation for a reason—they could slice your face off as easily as shave it.

After one too many men filleted his cheek, the safety razor was invented. It is, essentially, a section of straight razor, mounted perpendicular to the handle—a shape familiar to most primates capable of speech. While it was still entirely possible to inflict grievous damage to one's face—it uses a full-blown razor blade, for Pete's sake—one had to work a little harder at it. Safer, yes. But safety is relative.

In the first half of the twentieth century, a man named King Gillette made the next great strides forward in razor technology. He perfected a way to manufacture and sell sharp, thin razor blades stamped from a single sheet of steel rather than the much more costly forged blades used in razors at the time. Because Gillette's razor blades could be manufactured cheaply, they could be discarded when they dulled instead of being painstakingly re-sharpened. This created an entirely new income stream for the company; men constantly needed to replace their dull blades.

When Gillette's patents on his stamped blades expired, other companies leapt into the fray to try to claim market share. Amid fierce competition, the blades themselves became proprietary and noninterchangeable, enforcing brand loyalty. Buying a razor became a lot like joining a cult.

Put differently, razors have eleventy hundred blades because it's a way to hook a consumer into buying expensive proprietary blades forever and ever. And if marketers can convince someone to "upgrade" to the next, latest, and greatest depilatory device, all the better. Interested in more blades on the head? Perhaps something that vibrates? What about a razor that whispers positive affirmations while you shave and then plays "Eye of the Tiger" when it gets wet? Razor companies are well prepared to accept your perpetual commitment to whichever shaving system you should desire.

Which is to say, the endless iterations of shaving techniques have far more to do with marketing and cash flow than they do with performing the task for which the implement was designed. My triple-bladed shaving device is expressly designed to excise as much cash from my person as possible. And then, secondarily, to cut off my face hairs.

But those old razors are still out there, from before the format wars. There's still a semiobscure brotherhood of men—perhaps with a little gray in their beards—who still cling to the old tech, refurbishing ancient kits or remaking new ones in the old style.

And one cloudy Saturday afternoon, I find them. Standing in an old-school cutlery shop in downtown LA, the air heavy with the scent of old wood and oiled steel. I'm having my chef's knife sharpened; it's grown dull from near constant use, and this place, Ross Cutlery, has a reputation as the best at it. The store has been around since 1930 and I wouldn't be surprised if it looked exactly the same as it did the day it opened. Tile floors. Glass cases. An enormous scale that will weigh you for a dime.

But atop one of the cases is a small rotating turntable. Inside: razors. Safety razors—old ones, though they look brand new. Light glinting off polished chrome. I ask the gentleman behind the counter if he'd mind opening the case.

An hour later, I have both an impossibly sharp chef's knife and a safety razor with circa 1930s technology. The razor wasn't exactly cheap, but the replacement blades are a nickel. After spending ten dollars on blades, I have enough to pass on to whichever grandson inherits the device in the middle of the next century.

I also decide to retire the neon-hued shaving cream that smells like a low-rent frat house. Aerosol shaving cream first appeared in 1949, just after the war. Aerosol-propelled creams, called "brushless creams" because one didn't need a shaving brush to use them, competed on speed (no need to spend that ten seconds lathering!) rather than the quality of shave they gave. Like much of the instant and ready-made food of the time, they harnessed the power of an invented ticking clock to move product.

While I'm out, I pick up a brush and a tub of Geo. F. Trumper shaving cream. Trumper was a barber in London who developed the cream in the late 1800s, and his shop is still operational today. The cream is a little hard to find, but worth it—it features a faint aroma of violet, but without being reminiscent of either chemicals or the fairer sex. It smells the way I imagine Ferdinand the Bull did when he left the bullfight to sit in a field among flowers.

I head home, shower, and lather up. Being a rather scruffy gentleman, I set my razor setting to more than a little aggressive; my beard is a robust and dangerous beast. I'm excited and curious, but also preoccupied. I have a lot to do today. Still thoughtful, I lay the razor on my cheek.

I almost slice my face off.

Startled, I shove some tissue onto the gash on my cheek. I hadn't even started shaving yet—just inadvertently slid the razor laterally across my cheek, out of absentminded idiocy more than anything else. The tissue blooms crimson as I run through my gamut of swear words.

The pain brings me back to the present. This is no joke. This isn't something I can do absentmindedly. This is a skill. And if done improperly, it hurts like hell.

Bleeding stifled, I refocus, exhale, and replace the blade on my cheek. Ever so gently, I slip it down my face toward my jawline. It slides through my scruffy beard like a katana through silk.

This is badass.

It is the best, closest, least-irritating shave I've ever had. Yes, done poorly or absentmindedly it can shear your face from your skull. But done carefully and consciously, it is a beautiful thing.

My wife pokes her head in. "Jared?" she asks. "How much did it cost to get your knife sharpened? I was checking our balance and that purchase looks too high."

Evasive action. "I was thinking—how about I take the munchkin out for an hour tomorrow? Give you time to practice?"

Her eyes narrow. "Jared . . ."

"Two hours?"

She considers. Then sniffs. "Wow, you smell nice."

One Step Back, they were definitely doing something right.

It's a Tuesday. I'm back in the office, and I'm absolutely slammed. The phone is ringing off the hook. I'm keeping two projects locked down in edit while simultaneously writing a third. It's a pretty standard thousand-miles-a-minute morning for me. But shortly after noon, my day veers sharply from what I've come to call normal. I snatch my bag, heavier than usual, off the couch in my office and head for the door.

I set out on foot for a nearby park. I packed a lunch today—leftover pot roast—so I don't have to track one down. Instead, I can take that time for myself. And I'm going to take it outdoors. The world looks a lot better when viewed out from under fluorescent lights.

I commandeer a picnic table, then pull out the other reason I'm out here and the real reason my bag is so heavy: a massive cookbook. I feel bad reading a book in the office; it broadcasts that I'm not doing something to benefit the company. Out here, however, my time is once more my own. I crack the book, eating yesterday's dinner, and look into the best way to create tomorrow's. I find it calming to sift through my beef options—the different cuts, preparations, and presentations—and quietly consider how I should proceed with putting some small slice of my life in order. It's my little island of calm amid the tempest, sitting outside in the omnipresent California sunshine.

When looking into grass-fed beef in particular, I've found that information frequently comes from a number of very specific vectors. First, there are ranchers and farmers, many of them organic or organic-adjacent—perhaps ranchers like Chaffin, who hew to organic principles but lack the certification—and passionate about the products they produce. Their enthusiasm is blatant and infectious—and their agricultural expertise readily apparent, though their culinary skills vary tremendously. But I admire the passion behind the recipes these ranchers offer. Lord knows there are easier ways to make a living.

Slow Food aficionados also have plenty to say about grass-fed beef. The Slow Food movement was technically formed in Rome in 1986, as a protest against the proposed opening of a McDonald's at the Spanish Steps. Instead of picketing the restaurant site, journalist Carlo Petrini and like-minded supporters appeared at the Steps with bowls of pasta and other homemade regional dishes and picnicked to celebrate the virtues of *slow food* in pointed contrast with the proposed fast food franchise. Though the restaurant still opened, the Slow Food movement was one whose time had come. Today, through chapters around the world, Slow Food International seeks to preserve and promote the social, gastronomic, and ecological virtues of traditional and ethnic cuisine. Understandably, grass-fed beef occupies a prominent place in the Slow Food universe.

Finally, I glean an enormous amount of information on grass-fed beef from the Weston A. Price community. They're passionate about grass-fed beef primarily from a health standpoint, as opposed to a purely culinary or ecological stance. But I must admit—they know their stuff. The recipes I've tried have been solid, and I feel better than I have in months. Of course, nobody ever became *less* healthy by eschewing Wonder Bread and Cheetos in favor of less processed alternatives, but I feel undeniably good. The proof is in the free-range, organic pudding.

However, on Web sites of people loosely affiliated with the Weston A. Price outlook, I keep finding recipe variations for people eating *Paleo*, as in "Paleolithic." I'm intrigued, in part because of my current One Step Back obsession and also because of my anthropology degree. I learn that these variations are for people striving to eat diets approximating that of our Paleolithic hominid ancestors. Immediately, skepticism drops in like a piano onto a cartoon sidewalk. There's no such thing as a single Paleolithic diet—it varied by terrain and population.

Ah, well. Whatever. I flip the page of my cookbook. I'm in no hurry to return to the office. One of the Slow Food movement's goals is to help people integrate good food into their day-to-day routines. There's wisdom in that idea; I return to the office more refreshed and invigorated than if I'd sat at my desk through my meal. Making my lunch better makes the rest of my day better.

There's nothing not to like about that.

During the evening, I resume my research into how to increase the strength and endurance of all the leg muscles that aren't in use when one runs in shoes. There are Web sites dedicated to doing barefoot right, run by happy, bearded evangelists with "Barefoot" in their names. I find several approaches that all emphasize the same attributes—running bolt upright; not overextending my steps; and taking quick, light, whisper-soft strides.

I also notice something else—people knowledgeable about barefoot running also are frequently, though not always, evangelical about avoiding processed sugars and most grains, whole or not. My ears perk up. Then, on a message board, someone refers to this as *Paleo*. The Paleo diet, once again. It's following me. Stalking me.

Or, perhaps given the circumstances, hunting and gathering me.

I am not the smartest person to ever draw breath on this pale blue marble we call home. But I do know that when several distinct, seemingly unrelated intellectual vectors converge on a particular commonality, I should perhaps pay attention. So, disbelief momentarily suspended but skepticism still firmly in place,

I turn my attention to the dietary approach commonly known as Paleo.

The first thing I learn is that there are about a half a dozen sets of lifestyle guidelines and diets all calling themselves some variety of Paleo. In fact, it would be more accurate to characterize the collection of approaches as a Paleo movement, rather than a specific diet per se. Essentially, the Paleo movement takes the Weston A. Price argument one step further. Rather than noting that traditional foods are generally healthier than modern, industrial fare, adherents of the Paleo approach posit that many foods developed after the advent of agriculture—especially those foods created from cereal grains—at best contain suboptimal nutrition and at worst are actively toxic. In short, most modern humans subsist on diets from which they are not evolved to derive maximal nutrition.

Just like grain-fed cattle that don't derive maximal nutrition from corn.

Just like my dog, Basil, who didn't look bad when on a diet of (grain-heavy) dry dog food. But she thrived almost beyond belief when we returned to feeding her in a manner closer to the food she evolved to eat.

In a way, this approach posits that most people eat in a manner opposite that of the way we feed zoo animals across the world. For example, just because a chimp can eat a certain food—Cheetos, for example—without dropping dead doesn't mean that a benevolent zookeeper would consider them a suitable food for that animal. A benevolent zookeeper would feed that chimp a diet optimized for its species. Every day, however, humans feed themselves an enormous variety of nutritionally suboptimal foods. It's an interesting argument. And so I wonder, viewed objectively, how many of the foods that people frequently eat would be considered a suitable food for humans? If an alien landed in LA, abducted a Kardashian, and examined them in a lab, what would the aliens feed that "animal" after it was placed in an extraterrestrial zoo? What foods would keep a person in optimal health?

Like the Weston A. Price folks, the various branches of the Paleo family tree have strong views on what people should ideally eat. Whereas these branches don't overlap completely, they do share commonalities. First, whole foods. Eat stuff that either used to walk around or once grew from the ground and was edible with minimal processing. Broadly, this would be stuff that could be hunted or gathered, but not exclusively. This largely describes my diet now.

Second, however, Paleo adherents eschew cereal grains entirely. Corn, wheat, rye, barley—all of them. Period. Gone. Grains are avoided partly because they're nutrient-poor and irritant-rich. Gluten, a protein found to varying degrees in grains, is completely intolerable to sufferers of celiac disease, an autoimmune disorder. In celiac sufferers, the gluten proteins set off a chain reaction in the small intestine, causing ferocious gastrointestinal distress in the short term and a reduced ability to absorb fat-soluble vitamins (A, D, K, and E) in the long term, potentially causing further complications due to malnutrition.

Gluten intolerance can also be found in non-celiac individuals to varying degrees, with symptoms ranging from abdominal discomfort to joint pain to generalized inflammation. Cereal grains also contain compounds that inhibit the absorption of other minerals by the body. Among Paleo folk, the real or potential grain-derived health perils are generally not considered worth the relatively minor nutritional value those grains provide.

Further, Paleo adherents avoid nearly all processed sugar as a matter of course. Ditto sugar substitutes such as aspartame, saccharin, stevia, and the like. Especially sodas and sugared beverages; the human body is really bad at recognizing calories in a liquid form. The extremely high levels of sugar found in a modern American diet spike blood glucose levels through the roof and tax the pancreas—possibly to the point of partial failure, which manifests as type 2 diabetes. Prior to that, however, cells can grow accustomed to elevated levels of insulin in the body—required by a high-starch, high-sugar diet—and then become resistant to insulin's effect. As a result, the pancreas must produce even more insulin to compensate, taxing it even more and furthering the diabetic spiral.

So what's left? After cutting out processed foods, grains, and any sugar that didn't come from a bee or a bush—what's left to eat? Veggies. Lots and lots of veggies. Whole foods that come out of the ground in a naturally edible form and ready for consumption. Also, meat. Preferably meat humanely raised—without the use of unnecessary antibiotics or growth hormones—on the food that the animal itself evolved to eat, such as grass in the case of cows. Hence the Paleo community's love of grass-fed beef.

In a way, the various Paleo philosophies overlap pretty significantly with the edicts of the Weston A. Price community that have served me so well thus far. If anything, the Paleo suggestions go a step further. Avoid all sugar, refined or not. Avoid grains entirely, fermented or not. Eat lots of nutrient-dense vegetables. Eat high-quality protein that, when alive, lived in a way that was natural to the animal.

One thing the Paleo community does not shy away from is fat. Unlike starches and sugars, fat actually forms structural elements of the body—cell membranes and hormones, for example. In addition, fats are a ready source of quick energy and a medium for fat-soluble vitamins. Further, fat triggers certain receptors in our gastrointestinal tract, causing us to feel "full." People tend to find dietary fat extremely satisfying.

What Paleo adherents do pay attention to, however, is the type of fat: stuff you could find in or around nature. Coconuts. Avocados. Nuts. Animal fats from pastured animals. Stuff that could go bad, rather than products designed to last until the next ice age. To be avoided are industrial, highly processed, or refined fats: vegetable oil, canola oil, corn oil, shortening. I'm avoiding most of that stuff already. Studies have shown industrial fats can have a variety of undesirable effects on the body, and whatever nutrients were present in the original food, if any, are destroyed by the high-heat refining process.

Although all the Paleo approaches seem to vary somewhat around the edges, the core principles are very similar. They aren't diets per se, in the faddish sense (though some approaches could be described as fads), and the archetypal "Paleolithic ancestor" is just an illustrative tool, rather than an attempt to emulate a specific preagricultural population. The approaches are more descriptions of how the body works and how a person can run it at optimal efficiency. Like cows eating corn or runners wearing crazy shoes—the body didn't evolve to get plantar fasciitis at the first hint of a 5K—we've put the body in a position for which it isn't really adapted.

Running shoes have been around for only about fifty years. Agriculture has been around for about twelve thousand years, but *Homo sapiens* have been around for two hundred thousand years. *Homo erectus* first stood up somewhere in the neighborhood of 1.7 million years ago. Like shoes to runners, agriculture confers some definite dramatic and tangible advantages to those who utilize it. However, a civilization's adoption of agriculture historically was frequently accompanied in the archaeological record by signs of malnutrition in their skeletal remains, as well as increases in dental cavities. Though one should be careful not to generalize a process as widespread and varied as the adoption of agriculture, there is some evidence to assert that the adoption of agriculture frequently led to overreliance on one or a small number of foods and had some systemic detrimental effect on health—in addition to the positive effects of ready food sources as a hedge against starvation.

We evolved to avoid diseases of food scarcity. Today, however, many of our diseases are diseases of abundance. "In the wild," sweet things are rare. Berries. Honey. The saps of some trees. Our bodies evolved to like sweet things, because in nature sweetness indicated that a food would provide an intense simple-sugar burst of energy—a rarity. For millions of years, there was no worry about us overdosing on sweet things. Now, there is.

Preagriculture, corn actually looked like the grass that it is: pinhead-sized kernels on slender amber stalks. It would be hard to live on a diet composed of 69 percent preagricultural corn. But now, Americans consume about 69 percent of their calories from this mutant grass in one form or another.

Rather than consisting of a dour list of prohibitions, however, the various Paleo philosophies celebrate the foods that they consider healthy and wholesome in much the same way that the Slow Food and Weston A. Price movements do. Grass-fed and pastured animal protein. Offal. Copious amounts of vegetables. Good fats.

In addition, there is an emphasis on physical exuberance. On moving with joy as well as with ferocity. On sucking the marrow out of life—both literally and figuratively. I like that.

I'm intrigued. As with barefoot running, I can't really see any downside to self-experimentation. My One Step Back approach has served me well so far. I wonder what will happen if I take it one step further.

I was down the rabbit hole before. Now, I wonder how deep it goes.

It's Wednesday night. Declan is playing with blocks in the living room. I'm standing barefoot in my kitchen next to Summer, trying to figure out something for dinner. We aren't having any luck.

"I could make spaghetti," Summer offers.

"Nah," I say. Spaghetti is made from grains. As an experiment, I've decided to eschew grains for a while and see how it makes me feel. So far, it makes me feel like crap. Sluggish, fuzzy-headed— just a bit out of sorts. Still, I will persist. I'm nothing if not persistent. This experiment does not, however, make it easier to put together dinner for the family. "What about a salad?" I offer.

"Had it for lunch."

"Soup? I know of one we could—"

She cuts me off. "Why don't we just order a pizza?"

I shake my head. Then, an idea hits me: something I've been reading about. "Hey, do you remember how to make your dad's pizza sauce?"

"Sure."

"Perfect. I'll make meatza."

She blinks. "Wait, what?"

❧

Forty-five minutes later, a small pot of homemade pizza sauce simmers on the back of the stove as I pull out my cast-iron skillet. I love this thing. It's my favorite surface to cook on now, bar none. The cast iron heats up slowly and evenly, it's damn near indestructible, and it's largely nonstick. High heat? Low heat? Searing? Frying? Oven roasting? Cast iron don't care. Cast iron can do that and will do that better than anything else in the kitchen. I cook with it all the time now, and it's gotten shinier and blacker as a result. Cast iron, treated properly, gets better with age as carbon from cooking fats seals to the metal, making the surface slicker and more durable. The more it's used, the better it gets.

I drop the skillet on the stove with a thud. "Easy," my wife admonishes. But I love slamming this thing around. This isn't some pantywaist casserole dish. This is a hunk of slag iron. This is for making shit *hot*.

In a bowl, I whisk an egg, then add a pound of ground beef and some herbs. Once the mixture is thoroughly combined, I transfer it to the cast-iron skillet, pressing it down to line the bottom of the skillet—as thinly and uniformly as I can. If this were pizza, I'd be making a pizza crust. But I'm not making pizza.

I slip the skillet into the oven to brown. After about twelve minutes, the meat disk has shrunk considerably. I remove it, drain off all the fat that I can, and turn my attention to toppings.

Also, I mentally note that this dish seems ridiculous. I take a brief moment to cackle maniacally.

Right. Toppings. Because the "crust" is meat, vegetation is the order of the day. Specifically, red onions, black olives, and a little mozzarella cheese. After a thin layer of tomato sauce, I add the toppings and a little julienned basil for garnish. After a five-minute broil—the meat is already cooked, and this is just to melt and partially caramelize the cheese—dinner is served.

At the table, Summer's eyes dart from the meatza to me and back. The disk has been sliced into one-inch squares for easy noshing.

"So, it's pizza," she says.

"More or less."

"But with a meat crust instead of a bread crust."

I hesitate. Then, "Yeah."

She sighs, not sure what to think. "Okay, let's do this thing."

I serve the three of us tiny cubes of faux pizza. It's tasty—the cheese and meat picked up nutty flavors from the Maillard reaction, and the veggies are a welcome counterpoint—but it isn't pizza. Declan picks off the cheese but largely leaves the meat.

Without warning, Summer laughs. "You made a damn pizza with a meat crust."

"Yeah," I say. "I guess I did."

She starts laughing harder. "This isn't a pizza."

Now I start laughing. "Not really, no."

She brings a hand to her face as guffaws roll out of her in great waves.

"It's good, though! It's not a failure!" I protest.

She tries to control herself. "No. It's like a meatball with cheese and tomato sauce on it. And veggies." The laughter rumbles back. "But it is not, in any sense or fashion, a *frigging pizza*."

Declan starts laughing, too, catching the giggles from his mother. Finally, unable to resist, I join in as well. The three of us dissolve into hilarity, tears streaming down our cheeks, unable to speak or do much of anything for several minutes.

No. It is not in any way, shape, or form a pizza.

But I'm okay with that.

For the next couple of weeks, I eat no grains at all. No bread. No wheat whatsoever. No oatmeal. No corn, no corn chips, no tortillas. No sugar or anything containing sugar. I drink heavy cream in my coffee. I eat beef. A lot of eggs. A lot of salads. And a lot of salads with beef and/or eggs. More veggies than a vegan fever dream. For much of this time, I feel terrible. I'm hungry. A little groggy. I feel like something isn't right. Not ill per se, but out of sorts. I'm not accustomed to eating like this. I'm keeping up with my personal and professional obligations, but barely.

Then, one Thursday, I drop Declan off at day care and trundle off to the office. I don't eat much for breakfast today because I'm just not hungry. But I don't feel ill. I don't feel anything, really. I feel . . . fine.

I also forgot to make a lunch. So around midday, I swing by a local joint with a decent salad bar. I sidle up and fill my to-go box with an assortment of brightly colored veggies. Then, on a whim, I add a few cherry tomatoes. I don't usually eat tomatoes, but what the hell. Today I'm feeling frisky. Man cannot live on red peppers alone.

Back at my office, I sit down to lunch. I'm eating at my desk because the time that I would have spent in an idyllic workday picnic had to be used for acquiring a salad instead. This will be a working lunch, as I try to put my day back into some semblance of order. Eyes on my computer screen, I spear a tomato with my fork and take a bite.

Dear God.

This tomato is the most spectacular, heart-stoppingly deli-cious piece of plant matter I've ever placed in my mouth. It is the platonic ideal of yum. I had no idea that tomatoes—nay, *plants at all*—could taste so good. This tomato could stop wars or start them. It is Turkish delight, Soma, and the spice of Arrakis all rolled into one. I freeze and look down at my salad. What alchemy, what esoteric dark arts did the nice people at the Ralph's employ to make this tomato so transcendent? So divine?

I think. I haven't eaten any processed sugar, or anything sweet at all, really, for a couple of weeks now. What seems to have happened—what must have happened—is that I'm very sensitive to sweetness now. It's something rare and special. Something to be savored. Further, there are subtleties in the flavor of this tomato that aren't readily apparent to taste buds numbed by a deluge of sugar and sugar substitutes. It's richer and fuller than any tomato I've ever had. Or, more accurately, I'm more aware of its richness and fullness. It's like I've never quite tasted a tomato until this moment.

I poke through my salad. I only have six tomatoes. Why on God's green earth did I not get more tomatoes? Why didn't I fill my chintzy plastic tub to the brim with tomatoes? What was I thinking? From now on, it's all tomatoes, all the time.

Or, you know. Maybe tomorrow I'll get a few more tomatoes in my salad.

Wow.

The next morning, I open my eyes on a new world.

I'm alert, focused, and not sluggish at all. What's more, rather than experiencing merely the absence of the malaise I've encountered for a week or two—I feel actively fantastic. I get Dec ready for day care in record time, and I'm out the door in a flash. I drop off Declan and head into the office feeling like a million bucks.

Once I've settled into my routine, it dawns on me: I completely forgot breakfast. Ordinarily, this would be a problem. Ordinarily, this would make me a little shaky and cause my mood to plummet as my hypoglycemic tendencies took hold. Ordinarily, I'd grumpily search for a bagel.

Evidently, that is no longer ordinary.

I attack my day from a cloud. Extra couple of scripts? No problem. Deliverables changed? No biggie. I feel light and quick. I have energy and enthusiasm to spare. I find myself tackling random self-imposed physical challenges for no real reason at all. Can I jump over that? Let's find out. How many steps can I take running on the wall before I crash back to earth? Three, barely. How many pull-ups can I do? Not enough.

Lunch is another enormous salad—a salad of the gods. Extra tomatoes.

After lunch, I go on a walk. I have my phone, so I'm reachable, but the office won't collapse if I'm gone for twenty minutes.

I walk a little farther than I anticipated.

Then, I run.

I am exuberant.

Meatza

❦

Time: 1 hour 30 minutes

Serves 6

Just because you give up grains doesn't mean you have to give up pizza.

Well, okay. It kind of does.

James Beard made a version of this, which he called "hamburger pizza." This isn't quite a pizza, but it is a respectable meal in its own right—and filling: A little meatza goes a very long way.

1 large egg

1 pound grass-fed ground beef

1 clove garlic, minced

1 teaspoon kosher salt

1 teaspoon dried oregano

1 teaspoon dried thyme

¼ teaspoon freshly ground black pepper

About ¼ cup Tomato Sauce, or to taste
    (recipe follows)

4 ounces mozzarella, shredded

½ red onion, sliced

4 ounces pitted black olives, sliced

5 fresh basil leaves, thinly sliced

1. Move one rack of the oven to the topmost position and the other to the middle. Preheat the oven to 450°F.

2. In a large bowl, whisk the egg until smooth. Add the beef, garlic, salt, oregano, thyme, and pepper, and knead thoroughly to combine.

3. Press the beef mixture into the bottom of a cold 10-inch cast-iron skillet, pressing it all the way to the edges in a uniform thickness. In general, thinner is better. It helps to gently work the meat mixture up the side of the cast-iron pan, to give the eventual "crust" a concave shape. The disk will shrink during cooking.

4. Bake for 10 to 12 minutes, until the meat has browned and shrunk in from the edges of the skillet.

5. Preheat the broiler to high.

6. Pour off any excess fat that has accumulated in the pan, and blot the top of the meat with a paper towel until mostly dry.

7. Spread a thin layer of Tomato Sauce over the surface of the meat, then add the mozzarella, onion, and olives, in the amount desired, and top with the basil.

8. Broil for 5 to 10 minutes, until the mozzarella is lightly browned and bubbly.

9. Remove to a cutting board and slice into pieces a little smaller than you think is appropriate. Remember: This stuff is filling.

🐝

Substitutions in toppings can be made as one would with any ordinary pizza. Roasted red peppers especially shine here. Stick to a topping or two, at most, for best results. And you'll probably want to stick to veggie toppings. Trust me on this one.

TOMATO SAUCE

Makes about 2 cups

4 cloves garlic, diced

2 tablespoons olive oil

1 (15-ounce) can tomato sauce, plus ½ can water

1 (6-ounce) can tomato paste

1 teaspoon freshly ground black pepper

1 tablespoon dried oregano

1 tablespoon dried basil

1 bay leaf

1. In a medium stockpot over medium heat, sauté the garlic in the oil until just fragrant, about 3 minutes.
2. Add the tomato sauce and water, tomato paste, pepper, basil, and oregano, and stir gently to combine. Add the bay leaf.
3. Simmer, covered, for 1 hour. Remove the bay leaf before using. Leftovers can be frozen for future use.

9

Heart

The thing about having an entire cow disassembled and packed tightly into a freezer in the backyard is that one discovers a tremendous variety of beef cuts one wouldn't ordinarily encounter. There's an awful lot of crazy stuff in that box. Among the familiar steaks and roasts, there are culinary emissaries from the great unknown. Tongue. Heart. Miscellaneous wiggly bits. Offal.

Foremost among the cuts I'd otherwise likely never encounter are cuts that most people don't think of as edible at all—bones. I have bags and bags of them. It turns out that a full-grown adult steer has a lot of skeleton rattling around inside it.

Today I'm using some of these bones in a braise. Specifically, shank. I'm braising a cross section of the leg of the animal, like a beef osso buco. However, osso buco is generally braised veal shank, not beef, so I'm calling this a fauxxo buco.

As the shank bubbles and gurgles on the back burner of my stove, I find myself in what's become a glorious by-product of the cooking process—spare time. Moments like this have become more common as I've been cooking more, but I'm still not used to them. I'm like a kid at a middle school dance. I'm standing there in my kitchen, glancing awkwardly around, unsure what to do with my hands. The dish is cooking, so I'm technically "working," but I can relax, secure in the knowledge that I'm being productive. I have a few minutes to do something else. A rare, unscripted moment.

I can do anything I want.

I head back out into the backyard and sort through the packages of beef. I pull out a bag of bones.

Beef marrow bones are the leg bones of the steer; mine are sliced into about three-inch sections. They aren't especially common in American restaurants, let alone home kitchens, as a dish unto themselves. They are, however, one of the foundational elements used in making stock, as well a key piece of equipment for keeping dogs occupied for long periods of time.

Fergus Henderson is the chef at the groundbreaking London restaurant St. John. He is justifiably famous for creating a nose-to-tail menu at his establishment, offering a culinary wonderland of dishes that diners would be hard-pressed to find almost anywhere else. Pig tails, duck hearts, lamb kidneys—and, yes, beef marrow bones—a cavalcade of weird and wonderful dishes, many uniquely British, all of them prepared with the utmost respect for the animal that gave its life for that meal.

In his excellent book *The Whole Beast: Nose to Tail Eating*, he offers a preparation of Roast Bone Marrow and Parsley Salad that I've been desperate to try. Now is my chance.

The dish is dead simple. Marrow bones, roasted until the fatty, unctuous marrow is wobbly but not rendered. Parsley, roughly chopped. Shallots, sliced thin. A small handful of capers. A vinaigrette of lemon juice and oil. And toasted baguette, sliced thin on the bias and smeared with the bone marrow, to hold it all. Toasted baguette is something I don't really do anymore, but I'm willing to briefly suspend my grain abstinence for the sake of making this dish properly. This baguette isn't some extruded puffed-rice, flavor-dusted concoction. This is made by a baker I trust, toasted at home, and piled high with greenery and fresh bone marrow that I prepared myself. This is a treat—and a rare one.

"Hey. What are you making?" My wife peeks in the door of the kitchen as I'm running a knife through a sea of emerald-green vegetation.

"Sit," I implore, ignoring her question. "I made a salad."

"With the oven?"

"It's a good salad."

She smiles a bit, noticing that I'm being coy. She crosses her hands on the table expectantly.

I array the marrow bones between us, in a ring surrounding the parsley-and-shallot salad. "Bold move, Stone." She looks from the bones to me. "We've always fed these to Basil."

"Let's see what we've been missing." I dig the marrow out of the bones with a butter knife. Then I pick up a slice of toasted baguette, smear the bone marrow across the top, and cap it with a pinch of the parsley salad.

We crunch down into our salad-on-toast. I've never had straight bone marrow before, but now I know this won't be the last time. It's phenomenal. It truly is God's butter. It's well worth briefly violating my prohibition against bread.

"Wow," Summer understates.

"Yeah," I reply. My eloquence knows no bounds.

"Why have you not made this before?"

"Because I'm not very smart." Clearly. "I want to eat this all the time. I want this to always be in my mouth."

She takes another bite. "I'm so happy right now."

"Me too." We chew in silence for a moment, then we each begin to giggle. It's that good. "I'm not giving these to Basil ever again." We laugh like idiots, enjoying the unexpected pleasure of this unplanned culinary adventure.

"How did you make this?"

"I roasted bone marrow and ran a knife through some greenery."

"That's it?"

"That's it."

"It sounds so easy," she notes. She isn't wrong. "You should make this during the week."

"I'd love to. But it just takes a little more time on a Thursday than we actually have, you know?" I crunch down on another bite. "I can barely start cooking by eight. Seven if we're lucky."

"Yeah," she says. "The by-product of a two-income household, I suppose."

"Maybe." I gather up some fallen parsley with a fork. "This is food, though. We should have enough time in the day to adequately feed ourselves."

"We'll work on it," she offers, reaching for another crust of bread. "In the meantime, we aren't starving. Don't be a downer." She grins.

"Fair enough." I laugh. "I'll save up my existential crises for later in the week."

"There ya go."

The fauxxo buco comes out of the braise butter soft and gloriously rich. I pair it with an easy reduction sauce and a quick gremolata—a bright little herb condiment pulled together from some finely chopped garlic, parsley, and lemon zest—and then play the whole drama out over a little pile of long grain and wild rice.

Summer and I laugh and talk—lingering over the meal, enjoying the moment. We pointedly don't talk about the next day or plans or boxes on our to-do list that we need to check off. In other words, we have a completely impractical conversation.

This dance with bones is my first step into offal. And it isn't awful at all.

🐾

For Valentine's Day, I'm giving my wife a heart. Not mine, though.

"Hey, there," she says, sauntering up to me in the kitchen on the evening of February 13. "Are you cooking tomorrow?"

"I am. That okay?"

"Of course!" she says brightly. "Looking forward to it."

I smile back. Were I a colder, crueler person, I'd remain silent. But of course I can't. "I was going to make you a heart."

"What . . . like on a card?"

"Not exactly." My eyes flick to the freezer out the door behind her.

Slowly, recognition creeps across her face. "Oh," she says. "Oh, my."

"It's Valentine's Day!" I offer. "I thought it'd be thematically appropriate."

"Oh, it is," she counters. "I'm just not sure it's romantically appropriate."

"I have it on every authority that it will be delicious."

"And every authority is . . . ?"

"Eben."

"Right." She considers a moment. Finally, grimly, she nods. "Alright, I'm game." She turns to leave the room. "You'll understand if I don't help cook, though."

"Sure." I watch her go, then turn to the fridge and withdraw a large rectangular package, wrapped tightly in butcher paper. I unwrap the heart and lay it on the counter. Examining the centerpiece of the circulatory system, I understand my wife's trepidation. Last time I wrangled a beef heart was in a sixth-grade dissection. Standing in Mrs. Parish's sixth-grade biology unit, a scalpel in one hand and a blood clot freshly excised from a bovine aorta in the other—the air thick with the acrid scent of formaldehyde. Dinner was the last thing any of us were thinking about.

Today, I'm not cooking a whole heart—my butcher has divided it up into sections. To my amateur eye, I'll be cooking the right atrium and ventricle. The piece in front of me is rectangular, a dark ruby in color, overlaid on the outside with irregular layers of hard white fat. On the other side, the interior of the chambers, a spiderweb of very firm, very fibrous tissue of some sort covers the surface. I have no idea what it is, but Zac would later tell me that they're the *trabeculae carneae*, Latin for "meaty ridges." Appropriate.

Heart is a different sort of muscle from what I'm accustomed to. It's cardiac muscle rather than skeletal muscle. As a result, it has a very different texture from the kind of muscle that helps the animal move around. It's much denser and has a much finer grain structure. Per Eben's counsel, I'll have to clean it really well to get off all the fibrous tissue on the interior and exterior of the piece. I'm also told that it has a really pronounced flavor, and I'll be amplifying that flavor with an overnight marinade.

I'm making what in Peru is known as *anticuchos de corazón*, or marinated beef heart on a stick, grilled hot and fast. It's a common street food there, frequently noshed off carts by in-the-know locals or oblivious tourists. I'll admit, I'm a little wary of cooking this particular cut of beef, but I think it's something that I ought to do. I'm taking the responsibility of making the most of this animal that died to feed my family, and this is part of that transaction. And, if it's delicious, all the better.

First things first, though: I have to clean it. I pull a boning knife from my knife block. I need to trim off everything that isn't red and uniform. It takes the better part of a half hour for me to slice off all the fat, valves, and ropy layer of tissue inside the chambers.

Sometimes, when people buy beef at a supermarket, there's a red liquid inside the package, which they quite reasonably assume is blood. It isn't—the blood is all drained during the butchering process. That red liquid is a material called myoglobin—an oxygen-transport protein that's present in meat and is responsible for making red meat red.

Hearts have a *lot* of myoglobin.

My once white cutting board is stained red, as are my hands and part of the counter. There's also some on my shirt (I should have worn an apron), which I'm not especially happy about. A nearby glass bowl holds all the detritus and viscera we won't be eating. Glass was probably a suboptimal choice from a not-freaking-out-the-wife perspective. Because the bowl is clear, the glistening red jiggly bits are visible from any angle. A slasher film could shoot B-roll in my kitchen right now.

Once it's cleaned, I'm left with a few slim steaks that are very lean and very, very red. I knock together a marinade using the *aji amarillo* and *aji panca* pastes that I picked up at the Latin market. These pastes are unfamiliar to me—tiny jars of what could be mustard and ketchup but are made from yellow and red Peruvian chili peppers, respectively. The yellow, *amarillo*, is blatantly spicy, whereas the red, *panca*, is earthier, with a slower burn of capsaicin heat—the stuff that makes hot peppers hot. I add some cumin, pepper, garlic, olive oil, and salt to make a marinade. Finally, I slice the meat into strips, slip them into the marinade, and stash everything in the fridge overnight so the culinary chemistry can work its magic.

Meanwhile, I clean up, offering some of the heart trimmings to my dog. Basil wolfs them down. She's always had a fondness for organ meat, and liver and heart were regular parts of her diet when we fed her raw. Heart is really rich in B vitamins and iron, so I'm happy to be able to supplement her diet.

The next night, I skewer the heart slices on spears of sharpened bamboo, chuckling inwardly at parallels with Cupid's arrow that I don't dare say aloud. I grill the skewers over high heat on a griddle in the kitchen. They don't take long to cook. I pair them with roasted parsnips. I'm getting pretty good with parsnips.

Late in the evening, my wife and I sit down to dinner and glasses of peppery Shiraz. With some trepidation, we slice into our very literal Valentine's Day meal.

Flavor? Good, but intense. Spicy and incredibly rich. I don't have much else to compare it with. I've eaten other organs before, but none like this. None I've met in a scientific context as well as a culinary one. The slices of heart are dense and lean, with an undertone of organ meat. The mouthfeel is quite unlike that of skeletal muscles, which feel almost fluffy by comparison. This is cardiac muscle. This is a very different tissue.

"So?" I ask my wife. "What do you think?"

She puts down her fork. "Thank you for making it."

"That good, huh?"

She smiles, but only politely. "Thank you for making it," she says again.

"You don't like it."

She considers a moment before replying. "I do not."

"I'm sorry."

"It's okay. It's just so . . . rubbery. And it's a heart."

"It *is* Valentine's Day . . ."

"There is such a thing as metaphor, Jared."

I put my own fork down. "I'm sorry. I hope I didn't wreck Valentine's Day."

"It's okay. You didn't." She pats my hand. "I am going to go see what else is in the fridge, though."

No doubt, this meal is intense. And if I'm honest—half that intensity is psychological. It doesn't taste unpleasant per se. It's just that there's a lot more on my plate here besides dinner. Because of the texture and flavor of this meat, there's no question whatsoever that we are eating an animal's heart. Joining us at the table is the unavoidable reality of the sacrifice that puts this meal on the table.

Off-putting? Maybe. That depends on your point of view. Appropriate for a lighthearted and romantic Valentine's Day meal? Perhaps not.

In my opinion, if we take an animal's life for a meal, we owe it to that animal to make the most of the sacrifice. In this case, we're eating a heart. It's one more meal from the carcass, one more dinner where we don't have to look elsewhere—to another cut or another critter—for sustenance. One more moment of recognition that this was once an animal, and we must not—should not, cannot—take it for granted.

It wasn't a great meal. But it was a good meal. And I'm glad we did it.

It has taste buds.

That was my first thought handling the tongue as I patted it dry on my cutting board. Its surface has a very pronounced texture, kind of like a cat's tongue. Bumpy one way, smooth the other. As though nature has designed it to pull food back into the mouth—which in fact it has. When feeding, the steer grabs the blades of grass with his tongue and pulls them back into his mouth to chew. Beef tongues are prehensile.

The tongue is multicolored, white with dark spots, with a blue stamp on the side that means it's been federally inspected for wholesomeness. Tonight, this tongue will be dinner. And since I'm an adopted Angelino, I'm making *lengua* tacos. The tacos that taste you back.

My friend Ben first introduced me to the world of home-style, authentic taqueria tacos here in Los Angeles. I hadn't even moved here yet—I still lived in D.C. but was in town for a shoot for my employer at the time, and Ben was the first guy I called when I crewed up the gig. We grabbed lunch at a tiny hole-in-the-wall taqueria on the wrong end of Hollywood Boulevard. Ben, knowing me all too well, suggested that I might enjoy the *tacos de lengua*, or "beef tongue tacos." He was right.

Tonight, Ben and his fiancée, Roo, will be joining us, a few scant hours from now. Roo is Ben's perfect counterpoint—a tattooed circus performer and film grip with enough moxie to give Ben a run for his money. Los Angeles, because it's a few dozen small towns shoved together and forced to mingle, has a way of atomizing its populace. It's all too easy to maroon yourself on a sociocultural island and lose contact with anyone who isn't a part of your daily routine. I haven't seen Ben and Roo in a while—too long, in my opinion. One of the best aspects of this beef experiment is that it counteracts this atomization—it brings people together over the promise and excuse of a meal and the opportunity to catch up. Something about the ceremony of a special occasion meal demands it be shared with friends.

In the meantime, my house is a maelstrom of activity, as I prep for dinner and Summer turns the piles of laundry and toys scattered around our house into *hidden* piles of laundry and toys stashed in closets and under beds.

The tongue is a big piece of meat, 2.52 pounds and lean. Almost pure muscle, without a lot of fat running through it that I can see— not that I can see very well. It still has an outer layer of taste buds attached. This project has also been a phenomenal anatomy lesson for me. From what I understand, the braising process (because that's essentially what I'm doing) will dissolve the connective tissue holding the outer layer of taste buds onto the muscle itself. Then I can remove the taste buds with a pair of pliers, like a foot from a sock. A meat sock.

For now, however, the tongue is sitting on my counter. Quietly coming up to room temperature. Endlessly pronouncing the letter "L."

Before I cook, I have to prepare. First things first: salsa. Since this should be cool from the fridge when I serve it, it isn't especially time-sensitive. I dehusk and roast some tomatillos under the broiler until gently charred, then drop them in a blender with fresh lime juice, some diced onion, jalapeños, cilantro, and a little sugar.

Thirty seconds of frenzied pulses later, I have *salsa verde*. Into the fridge it goes.

Now to the primary task at hand. This tongue will need to braise for around three hours. The pot I'm using—a twelve-quart behemoth I used to brew beer in—is too big to stash in the oven, so I'll have to do it stovetop and ride shotgun on the temperature to control the simmer.

Generally, I prefer to braise in an oven. There, the heat radiates in from all sides, so that the pot is heated evenly at a determined temperature. In this case, the heat will be coming only up from the bottom and rising up through the column of my cooking vessel. Also, the stovetop doesn't have a thermometer. I'll have to keep an eye on the dial to maintain a gentle simmer; I don't want roiling bubbles, but I don't want a placid surface on the braising liquid, either. I'm looking for gentle bubbles breaking the surface every second or so.

I put eight quarts of water in the pot over the biggest burner I have. I add in two big white onions, quartered; an entire peeled head of garlic—ten cloves or so; nine bay leaves; a fat tablespoon of peppercorns; and two big tablespoons of salt. When the liquid boils, I delicately slip in the tongue and move the whole pot to a smaller burner over low heat.

Somewhere around the fifteen-minute mark, my entire house smells like ground zero of a vampire holocaust. Scents of onions and garlic and many good things fill the air.

"That smells amazing!" my wife comments, dashing through the room with a throw pillow in one hand and a fistful of kid-generated detritus in the other. "What is it?"

"Onions, garlic, and water."

"Well . . . yay, onions, garlic, and water," she says awkwardly.

"Sit tight. I'll give you something to cheer about." If you're cooking, you can be a little cocky. Seriously, friends: Do *not* drop a line like that unless you are standing in a kitchen, in front of a hot stove, holding tongs, and wearing an apron and perhaps a bandanna, as I was. Unless you are cooking, you will come across as a colossal asshole. I don't know why it is, but there is something in the alchemy of good smells and heat that erases all the sins of ego.

Still looking like a bedraggled culinary pirate, I survey my environs. When cooking, and especially when cooking something unfamiliar, I like to be prepared. I'll be serving these with a little radish garnish, so I slice some up. I do likewise with some cilantro and put a fine dice on some gorgeous red onions.

Then, that's it. Nothing more to do. Summer's tidied up the place and sat down to practice the piano. In front of me, I have a wait on a braise and a moment to reflect. I feel the familiar urge to "do something," be productive, make a dent in my day. However, I can't argue with chemistry, and chemistry (hopefully) is what's making this tongue into something lovely over the course of the next few hours. But this tension between productivity and taking a moment to relax is familiar to me by now, so I pick up another book— *Matter* by Iain M. Banks, in this case—and pour a cup of tea. I settle in on the couch for an hour's respite.

Which I really need. Sometimes it's indescribably nice to just sit still for a moment. To decouple from the Machine and productivity and people asking for things. To sit quietly, breathe deeply, and maybe even dare to be just a little bored. Sometimes I feel like the monk who hit himself in the head day and night, because it felt so good to stop. Only frequently, I forget to stop.

Seventy minutes later, refreshed and ready, I run through a quick, last-minute check before my guests arrive. I have all my accoutrements laid out in what—if I do say so myself—is a tight and efficient *mise en place*. I mentally walk through the steps I'll be taking when the tongue comes out. Rest, skin, slice—

Wait. Skin. I need something to skin it with. I fish around in my closet and pull up a pair of pliers. A filthy pair of pliers. Yikes. I'd rather not ruin this beautiful, interesting piece of meat—of which I have only one—by poking it with dirty tools as soon as it pops out of the culinary hot tub.

I can fix this.

I wash the pliers thoroughly, then pour two inches of water into a very small pot over a very large flame. I chuck the pliers in so that the water only covers their steel head. Ten minutes at a rolling boil, and any industrial waste or bacterial creature that could possibly have called those pliers home have definitely crossed the veil and joined the choir invisible.

Ben and Roo arrive and I pour a glass of wine for everyone, while Summer shuffles Declan off to bed before turning to the task at hand. Tortillas.

Summer had the brilliant idea to make homemade tortillas for this little culinary adventure. She picked up some Maseca, a special corn flour that's excellent for making tortillas, from the Latin market near our house. I don't generally eat corn, but I sometimes make exceptions. And if someone makes hand-formed tortillas from scratch in their own kitchen, you can bet I'll descend upon them like a ravenous dog. There's only one acceptable response to someone going to that kind of effort—and that response is "thank you." Real food and earnest effort trump dietary orthodoxy.

Summer begins to build the tortilla dough, and Roo jumps in to lend a hand. Moments later, we are all aboard the express train to Tortillatown, and the dinner preparation is under way.

When the tongue is finished, I fish it out of the braising liquid with two pairs of industrial-sized tongs. Then I snatch up my Pliers of Sanitation and pull off the outer layer of the tongue in two or three enormous, membraney strips, leaving behind a very tender, very aromatic piece of meat.

I thumb the oven to warm and drop my trusty cast-iron skillet onto a burner. I slice the tongue into thin strips and sauté them in a little olive oil. Braises benefit from a sear, but because the tongue was covered in a layer of taste buds, it never got one. I'm rectifying that now.

When all the slices have seared, I dice them up into little tongue bits and stash them in the warm oven. My job here is done.

Ben and I take a seat at the dining room table, outside the kitchen, while Summer and Roo finish tortillas on a hot griddle. The two of them work together like a well-oiled machine, and I'm excited to taste the fruits of their labor.

Suddenly, shrill electronic beeping *screams* from the kitchen. I dash to the door and peer in.

No big deal. There's a little smoke in the air, but nothing out of the ordinary.

"You okay?"

"Yep," Summer answers. "No biggie." She reaches up and pokes the alarm's cancel button with a thumb.

Our smoke alarm goes off all the time. I don't see flames, so I'm not worried. Summer and Roo are probably cooking with olive oil or something and got a little aggressive with the heat. Olive oil smokes if you look at it funny. I nod, relieved, and return to my chair. This wine is delightful.

"So," I say to Ben, swirling wine in my glass. "How's wedding planning coming?"

"Good, man. So much to do."

"I can only imagine," I reply. "Summer and I only had forty people at ours. Roo said you guys are doing a three-hundred-person cavalcade of circus performers and superheroes. You guys must be going nuts."

"Yeah. It's a lot." He sips his wine. "So when you were doing yours, how did you ask your guys to be in your wedding?"

"It was just you and my brother. I just said, 'Hey, you wanna be in my wedding?'"

"Hey, you wanna be in my wedding?" He smiles.

"Of course. Anything you need." I'm touched. I haven't been in many weddings. When I was younger, I never really used to like them—they were just a party with uncomfortable clothes. And then I got married. At last, I understood the magnitude of the event; this thing's for good. And when someone wants you to stand up there with them, to bear witness to the commitment, it's about as grand a gesture as can be made in American life. "I'm honored, man. Thank you." I raise a glass. "To you and Roo." He raises a glass in return.

Then, midtoast, I hear more loud beeping from the kitchen, accompanied by wisps of smoke. "Olive oil can sure be a tricky fat to cook with," I think to myself. I stand and peek into the kitchen—

The kitchen is on fire.

The smoke detector, for once, went off when it was supposed to. The kitchen is a flurry of activity and smoke and fat yellow licks of flame. For a second, I don't know what's happening.

Summer does. She's hitting something. It's right in front of her; a tea towel is on fire. She's beating it mercilessly with the biggest spatula we have.

The smoke alarm, meanwhile, is shrieking to wake the dead.

"Put a lid on it!" I shout. "Not water. Smother it." I still don't know if there is oil involved—water on flaming oil would only spread the fire. I don't enter the tiny kitchen, because the two people inside are already pushing it beyond capacity. Roo deftly reaches for a lid while Summer continues to beat the flames as though they stole from her.

A blur of motion, and Ben pops into the kitchen from a door on the far side, holding a broom. He hoists it over his head and stabs the off button on the smoke alarm.

The shrieking ceases. The fire goes out.

For a moment, all is still. Finally, someone laughs. The rest of us join in.

Summer looks to me, lurking in the doorway. "Don't say it," she warns.

But I can't help myself—when Summer cooks, it's an opaque process. An observer can't deduce how well or poorly the endeavor is going by peeking in. Like the famous paradox of quantum mechanics, the meal is both sublime and catastrophic simultaneously until the process is complete. "Ladies and gentlemen, welcome to Schrödinger's Kitchen."

She swats me with a towel as I move to set the table.

The smoke cleared and the table set, we build tacos from the results of our day's labor. Fresh, homemade corn tortilla. A sprinkling of braised tongue. A streak of homemade salsa verde. A slice of avocado and a sprig of cilantro. I take a trepidatious bite.

Silence around the table.

"Damn," quoth Ben.

"Wow," Roo says. "These are awesome." The meat is aromatic and earthy and rich, and just a little bit spicy. The salsa verde complements it beautifully, adding a touch of acid to the pungency of the meat. A little fat from the avocado. Perfection.

The four of us start to laugh and joke, giddy from how ridiculously good these tacos are. I shouldn't be able to cook something this delicious—I'm basically a chimp in a human suit. The four of us devour the entire two-and-a-half-pound tongue. There are no leftovers.

Ben and Roo stay well into the night. We chat about all the substance and miscellanea of life in the City of Angels—the tremendous joys of biking in the heart of car culture, how sensitive to cold we've become since our Kansas days. The ludicrous productivity of California gardens—Ben and Roo have installed a backyard garden that should be the envy of the county. That time we blew up a car during film school. That time we set the kitchen on fire.

I've been delirious from food before, but always in high-end restaurants. Beautiful plates from career professionals at the top of their game. Never from something I've done myself.

I'm giggly, motor-mouth, grinning-ear-to-ear happy.

I would never have bought a tongue if it didn't come with the cow. I would never have gambled with this meal in front of friends, and in all likelihood, I wouldn't have had the skill to pull this off. It's one thing to understand a process, like a braise—it's quite another to do it over and over, braising countless roasts and stews and obscure, unloved bits of beef that become something wonderful when treated with the respect they deserve, until the process is second nature. Almost a part of you. And then to share that with friends.

This meal—this one night alone—was worth it.

☙

I'm sitting on the couch, leafing through *You Can Farm*, Joel Salatin's treatise on small-scale farming. The steady supply of vegetables from my backyard has me wondering just how much that land could produce. "So I was thinking I'd make dinner tonight. Cool?"

"Ah, *bueno*," Summer replies. She's decided to learn Spanish. And French. At the same time. And she's pretty good and okay at each, respectively. I speak French pretty well, thanks to seven years of schooling. But today, Spanish is nearer the tip of her tongue. "*¿Qué estás cocinando?*"

"Absolutely," I reply, completely devoid of comprehension.

"What are you cooking?" she repeats.

"Oh." I steal a glance out the window. Dec is drawing a maze on the pavement with sidewalk chalk. It's a maze with no exit. "Um . . ." I search the recesses of my brain for scraps of Spanish. "*Corazón*," I stammer, hopeful that she'll think I'm being romantic. "Just for you and me."

"*¿Corazón?*" she asks, looking for clarification.

"*Sí*," I reply. "*Te ama.*" I love you.

Spanish falls away like a veil. "You are not going to cook me another beef heart."

The game is up. "*¿Sí?*" I offer. The other half of the heart is still in the freezer. The time we did it previously, marinated on Valentine's Day, wasn't enough. We need to do it again, give it our best shot, and if we still don't like it—then we gave it the old college try. I am not ready to give up. I won't yet say that I don't like beef heart.

Horror creeps across her features. "No . . . ," she says. "*No quiero . . .*"

I scramble for more Spanish but get nothing. "We can't let it go like this. We have another half a beef heart in that freezer. What are we going to do, throw it out?"

Her answer is a glare. Same in English and Spanish.

"The recipe I found looks fantastic. Lots of garlic, peppers, herbs. *Alla puttanesca.*" That's Italian for "of the whores." Sounds bad—tastes great. According to legend, practitioners of the oldest profession would lure men into their boudoirs with the heady aromas of tomato, garlic, olives, and capers. Summer knows exactly what *puttanesca* is, and it's one of her favorite flavor profiles. Optimistic, I hold up my phone. "Look at the recipe."

She does—and I am immediately regretful. "*Tartare?*" she asks, incredulous. I forgot to mention that part. A French culinary term, now come to signify "raw," perhaps mixed with raw egg. "You want me to eat *raw beef heart*?"

"You don't have to eat it if you don't want to." It's a gastronomic stretch, even for me. "However, I've researched preparations. And this looks the most like something we'd enjoy."

"It's raw beef! It isn't safe!"

I consider for a moment as I wait for Summer's words to cease echoing from the living room rafters. "That isn't really how food-borne illness works," I counter. "The bugs that make you sick live on the surface of the meat—in beef, at least—because it has to be deposited there."

She looks at me sideways but doesn't speak. I continue. "With a beef heart, I'm cutting off all that surface. The rest should be perfectly safe. It's never been exposed to air before. No chance of contamination."

"Raw," she counters.

"But this isn't supermarket beef," says I. "This is our beef. I brought this home."

She considers. But finally, "I'm sorry. I just don't think I can."

"As a compromise, I'll make you anything you want tomorrow. You name it—cut and preparation. I'll tell you what we have, you tell me what to do."

A smile flickers across the corner of her mouth. "I like steaks."

"I've heard."

"I like expensive steaks. Prepared the way I like them. And I don't care if you had another preparation in mind."

"Sky's the limit," I reply.

A long moment passes. Then, "Okay," she says. "Make your raw beef heart."

For a dish that doesn't require cooking, there's an awful lot of prep.

First, I trim the heart. As before, there's an awful (offal?) lot of material that isn't edible or delicious. Unlike last time, however, I'm much quicker with the knife and much more aware of what I'm looking for. A scant ten minutes after tearing open the package, I have three slim, if irregular, steaks laid out on my cutting board.

Also, I use a stainless-steel bowl to catch my trimmings. Opaque. Lesson learned.

Right about now would be a lovely time to have a meat grinder. I don't. What I do have is a good knife and a strong arm. I painstakingly slice the heart steaks into quarter-inch slices. Then into quarter-inch strips. Then, finally, into quarter-inch cubes, which I stash in a glass bowl on the far edge of my counter.

"It looks different," my wife comments as she swings through the kitchen. "Just like beef rather than a crime scene."

I laugh. "I diced it fine, like we did with the tongue. I have a feeling it may quell any texture issues we had."

"It'll still be raw."

"Yes. It'll still be raw."

She glances from the bowl to me, still wary, but I can tell she's warming to the idea. I turn back to my work space. I jettison my cutting board, clean my knife, and wipe down the counter.

Onward to vegetation. I dice some red onion to the same size cubes as the beef and do likewise with some kalamata olives. I slice a couple of serrano chiles into the thinnest little intimations of heat that my knife skills will allow and quarter some cherry tomatoes. All this goes into the bowl with the cubed heart. Then I wander into our backyard, pick a lemon, and zest that into the bowl as well—along with a couple splashes of good olive oil and red wine vinegar, fresh mint and basil sliced into ribbons, some big flakes of sea salt, and a few grinds of pepper. I mix the mass with my own clean hands, turning it slowly without squeezing, letting the meat and the tomatoes and the ribbons of herbs fall gently back into the bowl from my fingers. The bowl will rest in the fridge until dinner.

Finally, I slice a few cloves of garlic into nanometer-thin slices and sauté them in olive oil for ten or so seconds, or until they just begin to color. After they cool, they're crisp and gloriously fragrant.

Two hours later, my wife sits across the table from me. Between us, a red mound of raw beef heart, piled in the center of a large white plate and all the more colorful for the contrast. Crispy garlic flakes strewn atop like fallen leaves. The air between Summer and me is heavy with the smell of good things.

"You sure you aren't interested?" I ask.

"Positive," she replies. "Though it smells wonderful. I'm sure it's delicious."

I gingerly spoon a bit of the mixture onto a slim oval of grain-free almond flour crackers that I made from scratch. I examine the morsel I hold in my hand—it really is a gorgeous dish. Red cubes of meat, the occasional olive or bright green ribbon of herb. A golden shard of garlic.

I take a bite.

"Well?" Summer asks.

I pause a moment. On the one hand, I'm eating a raw beef heart. It's by far the most adventurous thing I've ever cooked—using that term loosely here—and one of the most adventurous things I've ever eaten. On the other hand—

"It's good." And it is. Without a doubt, this is the way to prepare it. When diced small and eaten raw, texture isn't an issue as it was on my previous attempt. Without that textural distraction, the focus is on the taste of the meat—deep and intense. Incredibly robust and heightened by the equally strong flavors surrounding it—garlic and olives, hot pepper and mint, and vinegar. "It's really good."

"Well, great. I'm glad it worked out," she says, eyes darting from me to the bowl between us.

"You'd like this, Summer."

"No, I can't eat it. I'll get sick."

"I don't think you will. That texture issue we had last time? Gone."

"Really?" she asks, still wary.

"Look," I say, placing another dollop. "I'm not trying to guilt you into eating this. If it's too much of a psychological barrier, I get that. But I know you. And I would not tell you this if I didn't believe it was true: You would like this dish."

Looking down at the bowl, she scrunches her mouth up in the

way she always does when she's thinking. Then, slowly, she piles a spoonful onto a cracker and takes a bite.

"Okay, yeah," she says. "That is good." She reaches for a second cracker.

I grin. I'm glad we didn't give up on this one. I'm glad we didn't resign this cut to the list of things we don't like, won't eat, can't eat, won't touch. Making use of every bit of the animal is a sacred act, as well as a practical one. I don't like killing animals—or, in this case, having one killed on my behalf. But it's a very efficient way—if grass-fed—to turn plants into protein without extensive fossil fuel use. Every ecosystem that grows plants has animal participants—and if they don't, the animal's contributions are mimicked: tilling the soil with petroleum-powered tractors and simulating manure with nitrogen fertilizer. Not only do pastured animals not require fossil fuel—they're edible. And what's more, they're good for you. There's a reason why there's never been a fully vegetarian society, outside certain religious communities. It's hard to maintain. It's difficult to get optimal nutrition from a solely vegetarian diet (though I won't say it's impossible), and it would have been even more difficult to be a vegetarian before the development of modern agriculture.

We've evolved to eat animals (and just about anything else that we could get our hands on), but along the way we've also developed a conscience and a sense of regret that we have to take a life to sustain our own. And eating every bit of this animal seems like the right thing to do.

Lengua Tacos

❦

Time: 4 hours, largely unattended

Makes 8 to 10 tacos

It's easy to be scared of tongue, the meat that tastes you back. Don't be. Lengua tacos are a good way to incorporate this unfamiliar cut into a familiar dish. The keys are to cook it for a long time, strip off the taste buds, and slice it thinly.

You may need to convince people to take the first bite. You won't have to convince them to take the second.

This is adapted from a recipe by Elise Bauer.

SALSA VERDE

1½ pounds tomatillos

½ cup chopped white onion

½ cup chopped fresh cilantro

2 jalapeño peppers, stemmed and chopped

1 tablespoon freshly squeezed lime juice

¼ teaspoon sugar

Kosher salt

TONGUE

2 large white onions, peeled and quartered

1 head garlic, separated into cloves, crushed, and peeled

8 bay leaves

1 tablespoon whole black peppercorns

2 tablespoons kosher salt

1 (2- to 3-pound) beef tongue

2 tablespoons olive oil

AT THE TABLE

1 avocado, sliced

1 bunch fresh cilantro, finely chopped

1 red onion, finely diced

Corn tortillas

This meal is improved immeasurably by making the corn tortillas from scratch. They're easy to do: Pick up some Maseca from your local Latin market or supermarket and follow the instructions on the bag.

TOOL

Pliers

1. To make the salsa verde, first preheat the broiler to high and line a sheet pan with aluminum foil. (You can make the salsa verde either in advance or while the tongue is braising.)

2. Remove the husks from the tomatillos and rinse them well. (If they're still sticky, you haven't rinsed enough.) Cut each tomatillo in half horizontally, remove the stem cap, and place on the foil-lined sheet pan.

3. Broil the tomatillos for 8 minutes.

4. Transfer the tomatillos to a blender, and add the onion, cilantro, peppers, lime juice, and sugar. Pulse to liquefy. Add salt to taste, then refrigerate until ready to serve.

5. To prepare the tongue, fill a very large stockpot two-thirds full with water. Add the onions, garlic, bay leaves, peppercorns, and salt. Bring to a boil, add the tongue, and reduce the heat to a simmer.

🐄

At some point during this process, pour 2 inches of water into a small saucepan and place a pair of pliers in the water, head down. Be careful that the level of the water doesn't reach up to the rubberized grips of the pliers, if they have them. Boil the pliers for 10 minutes to sterilize them. Then hold off on assembling that new Ikea bookcase until after dinner.

6. Simmer the tongue, covered, for 3 hours, or until a paring knife slips into it easily.

7. Remove the tongue from the liquid, and let it cool for a few minutes, until it can be easily handled. Using your sterilized pliers, peel off the outer surface of the tongue, removing all the taste buds and pigment. The outer layer of the tongue should come off easily in several large pieces. If it doesn't, you may need to simmer the tongue a little longer. If it comes off in smaller pieces, simply use a paring knife to help the process along, and be persistent.

8. Cut the tongue crosswise into thin slices.

9. Working in batches, sear the tongue slices in the oil in a heavy skillet over high heat.

10. When all the slices are seared, cut each slice into strips, then rotate the strips 90 degrees and cut them into tiny cubes.

11. Serve the diced tongue in a bowl at the table with the salsa verde and the accoutrements listed above.

10

Around the Fire

I am not a morning person.

I deeply wish that I were, but alas, it is not to be. When the morning sun finally just crests the horizon and streams through the partially drawn curtains into my bedroom—I want nothing more than to slumber on, basking in those sunbeams like a Benadryl-addled cat.

My wife is a morning person. This may perhaps explain why on this (presumably) gorgeous morning she is gently nudging me, rousing me from my slumber earlier than is usual. It *may* explain it, but somehow I know it doesn't. Not fully. As I open my eyes, she's sitting on the edge of the bed.

"Good morning, sunshine," she offers.

"Morning," I croak. This is not an hour in which civilized people interact. "Everything okay?"

"Yep. Everything's good." She smiles slightly. "I'm pregnant."

Slowly, I grin. "Are you sure?"

She nods. "I'm sure. I'm very, very sure."

"That's wonderful . . ." I grin wider. "That's fantastic!" I sit up to throw my arms around her and pull her back into bed.

"This looks wrong."

I'm standing in my kitchen. On my counter are a can of cranberry sauce, a sack of Lipton dry onion soup mix, a bottle of ketchup, and a beer. "This looks very, very wrong."

"I'm sure it'll be fine, sweetie," Summer says. "Ellen knows what she's doing."

Ellen is Summer's boss. Together, they negotiate the somewhat treacherous waters of acquiring the rights to use music in movies. What's more, Ellen knows everyone in town. Want to sell a car? "I know a guy." Need to redo your kitchen? "Visit my friend, here. Drop my name." Looking for a way to smuggle endangered monkeys across the border—*any* border? "Call this number, wait for the beep, and say, 'The banana doesn't fall far from the tree.'" We call her the Godmother.

I'm cooking a seder this year, primarily because it seems like such a beautiful ritual. It's an excuse to sit with friends and loved ones and share a meal. How could I resist?

Naturally, when I began the search for brisket recipes, Summer suggested we turn to the Godmother.

"Best brisket on Earth," she promised. "This recipe won a brisket cook-off competition at my temple. There were over a hundred entries, and this one won. Need I say more?"

Looking at the ingredients on my counter—maybe.

I turn my attention to the brisket. I haven't cooked this cut before. Because each steer has only two, I'm very cautious about wrecking them. For a seder, however, I'll take that chance.

The brisket is the breast of the steer, between and in front of the two front legs. It's frequently used in Jewish cuisine because kosher beef in North America is taken only from the front half of the animal. There isn't a lot of oxtail served up in Jewish delis.

Reading this recipe, I see it's essentially a braise. I know braises. I've done more braises than I can count. I'm the Baron of Braises. The Potentate of Pot Roasts. The Magister of Moisture. I can braise a chuck roast with one hand and spin commemorative plates with the other. I got this.

Generally, I would prefer to sear a piece of beef before braising. Searing, contrary to popular belief, does not "seal in juices" or anything of the sort. What searing does is make the surface of the cut golden brown and delicious. And golden brown and delicious tastes good.

"Honey," I note, reading the recipe, "there's no sear in this recipe."

"So?" my wife replies.

"I think there should be a sear," I continue. "And I don't think there's enough liquid. I want to add some beef stock."

"Whatever you want to do, sweetie. Ellen is simply a Jewish matriarch, having grown up in a kosher household cooking this for her own family every Passover for decades. This is only supposed to be the Best Passover Brisket Ever. But I'm sure you know best."

My wife is so dry, she's got vermouth in her veins. But she has a point.

She continues. "You're overthinking it. Listen to the Godmother."

"Okay. Fine."

I prep my *mise en place*. This consists of setting everything on the counter and opening it: beer, ketchup, cranberry sauce, and dry soup mix. Then I dump it all in a big bowl and stir. This is without question the strangest braising liquid I've ever seen. It's fizzy and fruity, with big globular chunks of cranberry floating in it. I must have faith.

I pour the primordial sludge of the braising liquid over the meat and slide the whole morass into the oven. One thing this recipe has going for it is that it suggests cooking the meat the day before serving and just reheating it before service. This is smart; the flavors in the meat and the liquid meld during the time between when they're cooked and when they're eaten. That's part of the reason that, say, chili is always better the next day (if your chili happens to consist of braised meat).

When the brisket is soft but not falling to pieces, I pull it from the oven, slice, and return to the liquid before stashing it in the fridge for the night.

The next day, I skim the fat off the top of the braising liquid and slide the pan back into a warm oven. Ellen suggests pairing the brisket with mashed potatoes and asparagus. So, asparagus and mashed it is.

Mashed potatoes was the first real dish I learned to make.

During the heyday of my misspent youth, I worked as a grip on indie film shoots in the Midwest. That's how Ben and I met; he was my key grip, and I was one of the guys in his crew. If a director with more vision than money needed elegant solutions to ridiculous problems, we were the guys for the job. In film, and especially indie films, crews can get pretty tight. Working with the same bunch of guys on twenty-hour days in rain and sleet and snow, in gorgeous penthouses and grimy industrial parks—doing hard, heavy, yet deeply creative and mentally challenging work—you get to know your guys really well. You become almost like family.

One of the guys in our crew was a gaffer named Ian. He was the human equivalent of those walking stick insects that live in Borneo and look like twigs. He may still be the tallest person I've ever met. When we worked together, he had hair down to his waist and never really stood fully upright during the daytime lest the rest of us try to tell time by charting his shadow.

Ian liked potatoes. A lot. Once, I mentioned that I didn't really know how to make mashed potatoes, and he looked at me like I'd just spontaneously started Tuvan throat singing. Without hesitation, he grabbed a spare scrap of paper and jotted down his recipe for mashed potatoes. "You'll like these," he said. "Don't lose this paper." To this day, I haven't.

Ian's potatoes became the basis of my own mashed potato recipe, which I've tweaked and modified over the years. When pulled fresh from the oven, the dish offers a gently caramelized crust atop garlicky pillows fluffy with dairy. The potatoes aren't difficult to make, but they are labor-intensive. I set to work, while prepping the asparagus to roast.

I should note at this point that we're not actually Jewish—on my better days, perhaps I'm Jewesque—but I enjoy the idea of a seder. A meal, shared with family and friends, lingered over, appreciated. The excuse it offers for us to sit together on a dark night and enjoy one another's company.

More pointedly, however, I have no idea what I'm doing.

I'm in luck, though. Seders have instruction manuals called Haggadahs, which detail the ins and outs of the ritual—mostly a series of specific dishes and a retelling of the story of the liberation of the Jewish people from slavery in Egypt. To cover my cultural ignorance, I'm using Michael Rubiner's *Two-Minute Haggadah*, printed out from Slate.com. I even stapled the printout on the right-hand side for veracity, just like real, nonridiculously abbreviated Haggadahs. I want to make sure Declan has a wide range of cultural experiences, even if imperfectly administered. I've skimmed the document, so I figure I can drive this boat, at least well enough to satisfy a three-year-old.

Once seated around the table, we begin. I look over my Haggadah. "Thanks, God, for creating wine." Amen there. I reach to pour some wine for Summer, to find her hand over her glass.

"Nope," she says.

I smile. "Sorry—habit." I hop up to get her a glass of water.

"No problem," she says. "As soon as this baby arrives, it'll be wine, sushi, and cold cuts for days."

I laugh and continue reading. "Thanks, God, for creating produce." Um, wait. What? I must have missed that part when I skimmed the Haggadah earlier. I see parsley referenced. I don't have parsley. Hmm. I need vegetation. I have pickles. Kosher dills, even. I offer dill pickles to everyone, though pregnant wife turns a delightful shade of nauseated green when the pickles come within five feet of her. I retract her pickle offer and give them instead to Declan. Done.

Summer watches me fumble and smirks. "First Passover?"

"Is it obvious? On to the four questions . . ." Wait, what? "There's a quiz?" I ask. This is unexpected. I read further in the Haggadah. I have no context from which to answer these questions. I know vaguely what they're about, but that's it. At a loss, I improvise. "Dec . . . should you be nice to people?"

"Yes!"

"You sure?"

"Yes!"

"Super sure?"

"Yes!"

"Is this the fourth question?"

A pause, as he counts on his fingers. "Yes!"

"Correct. Quiz passed." Cheering ensues. Once more I check my seder instructions: *Find the matzo*. "Okay, Tiny Man . . . I hid matzo somewhere in the living room. Go!"

Summer laughs.

"What's matzo?" Declan asks.

"It's like a cracker. There's a cracker hidden somewhere over there. Go!"

"That room is filthy," Summer says. "He can't eat the matzo . . ."

"Why can't I eat it?" Dec asks.

"I took care of it," I insist. "Dec. Cracker. Go!"

Declan hops down from his seat and rushes into the living room. He looks all around for the matzo. "I don't see it, Daddy . . ."

"Maybe a dust bunny ate it," Summer opines.

"Hush, you." I turn back to Declan. "Try the coffee table."

He looks for a moment, pawing around under the coffee table. Then his eyes light up. "I found it!" He pulls out a single sheet of matzo, sealed in a Ziploc bag. "Daddy, I found it!"

"Nice work, buddy. Bring that over here."

Summer sees the matzo, wrapped in a plastic Baggie like drugs in a cop show, and starts laughing. After a moment, so do I.

Dec digs into the matzo as I check my seder instructions. It says something about slouching; free people are allowed to slouch at the table, whereas slaves—as the Jews were in Egypt—had to stand. So slouching at seders is a thing. I like slouching. "Let's jump straight to the slouching," I suggest, pouring a little water for everyone and raising a glass. "Here's to bad posture. And to making time to eat together."

"L'chaim," Summer says.

"Cheers!" Dec enthuses.

We each take a sip, savoring the moment and the experience of taking the time to share a meal in one another's company. I serve up fat piles of mashed potatoes, heavy with dairy and onion. Crossed with roasted spears of asparagus and draped with slices of incredibly tender brisket. It's delicious. I'm glad I hewed closely to Ellen's recipe—any added liquid would have wrecked it.

My family and I share a delightful, homey meal made with love. An opportunity to spend a cool spring evening with those closest to me. A moment to count my blessings. We didn't get any of the details of the seder right—or even close to right, really. I'm pretty sure that mixing dairy and meat violated some Jewish dietary laws—but we did our best. And our evening was all the richer for it.

"Daddy, I don't think this cracker is any good," Dec says, his face contorted with disgust.

I laugh. "It tastes funny because it's unleavened. When the Israelites fled Egypt, they didn't have any time to make real bread."

"And that's one of the four questions," Summer notes. "'Why are we eating only matzo?' Good work, Stone."

I check my Haggadah. She's right. The guy leading the seder is supposed to ask the kids present four questions—this is one of them. I've inadvertently stumbled into some semblance of accuracy.

"What's unleavened?" Declan asks.

I explain yeast and how it works. Declan listens, learning a little about the food he eats. A process I'm still continuing myself. We may have missed some of the four questions, but we're getting more answers every day.

It's about three in the afternoon. I'm standing in the hallway of the UCLA Medical Center; bright sunlight streams in through hallway windows. I haven't slept much. I look down at my son, holding my hand. "You ready, buddy?"

"Yes, Daddy."

"Okay. She's super excited to meet you."

"Really?" he asks, raising his eyes to mine. He's clutching a brand-new little girl's backpack, full of blankets, toys, and stuffed animals. A gift.

"Really." I nod. "Let's go in."

We slowly crack open the door to a hospital room. The curtains are drawn, and in the dim light I can see Summer sitting on a couch by the window. Declan and I creep into the room. "Is she asleep?" I ask.

"I don't think so," Summer answers, craning her neck to peek into a plastic crib in the center of the room. "I think she just woke up."

Declan and I take a few more steps into the room. I lift him up into my arms, and we peer into the crib. There, blinking up at us with enormous blue eyes, is my new daughter. Nora.

"Hi, Nora. This is your big brother, Declan." My son only stares, transfixed. I lean into his ear and whisper, "Dec, this is your sister, Nora."

"Hi, Nora," he whispers, his voice creaky. She coos and blinks. Slowly, Declan smiles.

I set Declan gently on the ground. "Would you like to hold her?"

He thinks a moment, then his whole face lights up. He nods.

Declan takes to Nora immediately. As soon as we bring her home, they're inseparable. He wants to hold her all the time, and he's incredibly gentle. He nudges our hundred-pound dog out of the way when she gets too close and keeps trying to offer her wildly inappropriate toys and joys that he likes—on the logic that if he likes them, she'll like them, too. "Nora, do you want to hold my lightsaber?" "Nora, I built a robot for you." "Nora, look! I found Daddy's skateboard!"

Family floods into our Los Angeles home from far and farther away—Texas, Kansas, Georgia. We rarely get to see our parents; Summer and I are the sole outposts of our families on the West Coast. Our nearest relatives live two thousand miles away, so it's wonderful to have them darken our doorway to welcome the newest addition to our family.

To celebrate Nora's birth and the all-too-rare visits of far-flung relatives, we do what people always do to mark events and milestones. We cook. As the next few weeks blur together into a disjointed mental slide show of diapers and laughs and late-night feedings—we all cook together. And we eat like kings.

I braise a chuck roast as a welcome when Summer's mother, Tricia, comes to town.

And then Tricia does the same for us, when we're too tired to think straight or make consonant sounds with our mouths.

I grill rib eyes to mark the first time my parents have been able to visit the Left Coast in years.

And then I turn leftovers into a hash for us all to eat for breakfast; I haven't gone shopping in a couple of weeks, and we're down to eating sauerkraut and canned sardines.

It's easy to cook whole foods and glorious meals when time is cheap and there's nothing more pressing clamoring for attention. It's something else entirely with a houseful of guests and only a few hours of sleep a night, with a brand-new life in the world that needs what she needs when she needs it.

In those times, cooking becomes again what it always was, back before we forgot the value of preparing a meal. Before we became accustomed to food extruded and sprinkled with flavor dust and sold two for $1.99. Cooking is a solace. A little corner of the world where I store my peace of mind. While everything's blowing up and nothing's going right, and what is the dog into? And why is my daughter still crying, I just changed her! In the middle of all this calamity, I will have a pot roast. In my often futile daily rush to get ahead and get things done—this actually *is* done. This is finished. I can find something in the freezer and it will be nutritious and satisfying and wholesome, as long as I don't wreck it. And then we can sit down together, take a deep breath, and enjoy it. There will be dinner. We will not starve.

And it will be an event. A moment, probably timed for after the kids fall asleep, where we can sit. Exhale. And for just that fleeting moment—clean no floors. Change no diapers. Answer no e-mails. And be people again. An opportunity to tell a tale between bites of a meal hard fought for and toiled over. To relate an anecdote— something cute or terrifying that happened when everybody else was turned away or trying to prevent Armageddon from a different angle. To raise a glass and take a breath before our eyes slip shut into slumber and we do it all again, only another day older.

When people talk about the good life—what do they mean if not this?

Anthropologist Claude Lévi-Strauss, in *The Raw and the Cooked*, proposed cooking as one of the handful of delineators between humans and all the other beasts of the earth. He saw it as a physical example of human control over the natural world. In the act of cooking, he argued, we transform organic matter from a natural to a cultural object. Cooking, then, marks the very edge of what it is to be human.

Others have taken the primacy of cooking even further— anthropologist Richard Wrangham, in his book *Catching Fire: How Cooking Made Us Human*, posits that beyond being a marker for humanity, the act of cooking actually enabled the human species. By cooking food, and specifically meat, our hominid forebears could extract more energy from that food. Per this cooking hypothesis, the ability to cook food meant that we could, in essence, begin the digestive process outside the body, rather than performing that task solely in the gastrointestinal tract as the other apes do. This ability changed us irrevocably; we could afford to have smaller molars, adapted to softer cooked foods. Shorter intestinal length, as those intestines didn't have to do as much work. The caloric surplus that ensued allowed early hominids to develop larger brains and to use those larger brains to fully master fire, come down from the trees, and take the first tentative steps toward *Homo sapiens*.

In any case, without cooking, we'd be something other than human. We'd likely be less aware. Less capable of wonder. Less able to react to the demands of our circumstance—to revel in our triumphs and mourn our inevitable defeats. We'd be on the other side of the nature/culture divide, instead of the glorious, ridiculous, exasperating, beautiful, petty, anomalous hairless apes we've somehow managed to become.

These meals are magic.

Slumped in a hard-backed chair, surrounded by people I love, the remains of a steak and salad splayed across the table in front of me as my children slumber peacefully in their rooms, I smile. I lay a hand on the back of my wife's neck and squeeze it right where I know she always carries her tension.

If anyone wants to know why cooking is important to me, this is why.

A couple of weeks later, the in-laws are gone. The kids are sleeping. The house is clean and the phones are silent. The sun has set long ago.

I slip into the kitchen, where I've thawed two slim ovals of beef from the tenderloin. Filet mignons. Dinner for two.

Filet is the most tender cut on the entire animal, with a silken texture and almost no connective tissue. Cooking hot and fast is key—and no more than medium rare. They won't take long to cook, which I appreciate today. Summer and I haven't slept a whole lot lately, and we've been entertaining visitors to boot. The hubbub is a treat, but so is the respite after.

In my ancient mortar and pestle, I crush some peppercorns. Just fine enough that we won't eat gravel, but not wholly into dust. There are easier ways to do this, but I like my mortar and pestle. I can control the process as precisely as I'd like and know that I crushed the peppercorns exactly as I wanted. With my own two hands and a chunk of rock. One Step Back once more, I suppose. No electrical intermediaries. No extra gewgaws to wash. There's something of a meditative quality to it. I turn the crushed peppercorns out onto a plate and press both steaks into the rubble, coating both sides, then turn my attention elsewhere.

Butter into a hot pan with a splash of olive oil, to heat just until the drama bubbles and fades. Gently, I lay the steaks into the pan. They announce their arrival with a satisfying hiss. A couple of minutes on each side for a hard mahogany sear, then I set them aside under foil.

Quickly, I kill the heat and add a little brandy to the pan. The alcohol vaporizes immediately. I slip a lit match into the open air above the liquid, and a pyramid of blue fire erupts from the pan. Had I been able to do this for my Christmas dessert, I would have been ecstatic. I couldn't figure it out then, but it's easy now. I swirl the liquid until the fire goes out, then bring back the heat to deglaze the pan.

When the burned-on fond is dissolved from the bottom of the pan, I pour in heavy cream. Aromas of pepper and liquor and seared meat flood the room, drawing my wife to the kitchen.

"What are you doing?" she asks.

"Cooking." I hand her a glass of red wine I had waiting.

In minutes, some of the water has boiled out of the liquid in the pan, and the cream looks very much like a sauce. I splash in another touch of brandy and a pinch of salt. Then kill the heat. Nestle the steaks back into the pan and cover them with the cream sauce. Finally, when they're just warm, I place each steak in the center of a plate, pour over the sauce, and sit down to dinner with my wife.

We sit for a long, languid moment, silently eating our meals. Candles light the scene, and Duke Ellington wafts in from another room. We're tired. But happy. And, for me, at least, feeling disproportionately blessed.

Summer's the first to speak. "This is really, really good."

"Yeah," I say. "It really is."

"Was it hard to make?" she asks.

"No," I say. "Not especially."

"Thanks for making it," she says.

I consider. The steak is perfect. But I know full well that any technique I brought to the cooking process was just window dressing. The meat is the star here. I didn't do anything special. I just shut up, kept my head down, and let a really good thing be really good.

"Thanks for letting me buy a whole damn cow," I reply. Summer looks up at me, and her hair frames her face exactly as it did when we first met, on a rainy night in Kansas, when she was a promising young pianist and I was a shaggy underachiever. I don't think many people would let their spouse run off and buy a quarter ton of beef just to appease his curiosity or prove a point. It was an insane proposal, at least for us, and she didn't even hesitate. She just asked when and how much. She faced the latest in a string of ludicrous adventures, and once more, she said yes.

At that moment, wreathed in the light of late night candles, I remember very vividly one of the billion and one reasons I love this woman.

"You're welcome," she says.

Steak au Poivre

Time: About 30 minutes

Serves 2

Perfect for a special occasion. Like a Wednesday.

2 tablespoons whole black peppercorns

2 filets mignons, at room temperature

Kosher salt

1 tablespoon unsalted butter

1 tablespoon olive oil

⅓ cup plus a dash of brandy

1 cup heavy cream

1. With a mortar and pestle, crush the peppercorns until they're cracked but still gravelly. You're looking for rustic charm, not black dust.

2. Spread the peppercorns on a plate. Sprinkle the steaks with salt, then press the filets firmly into the peppercorns so that they stick to the meat. Flip the steaks to coat the other side.

Ever go barefoot at the beach? The peppercorns should stick to the meat like sand to your bare feet.

3. Place a stainless-steel skillet over medium heat and melt the butter with the oil until the mixture just begins to brown.

4. Add the steaks (carefully!) and cook for 3½ to 4 minutes, un-til the bottom is nicely seared. Flip and sear the other side for another 3½ to 4 minutes.

5. Turn off the heat, but leave the pan on the burner. This is important. If you pull the pan off the burner, it'll cool faster. Cool pan means no flambé.

6. Remove the steaks to a plate and loosely tent with aluminum foil.

7. Quickly pour off the excess fat from the pan. Add the ⅓ cup brandy—it should heat instantly from the still-hot pan. Ignite the brandy with a long match and wait until the flames die.

8. Kick the burner back up to medium. Add the cream and bring it to a boil, whisking furiously, and cook until the liquid thick-ens enough to coat the back of a spoon, 5 to 10 minutes. Add another small dash of brandy and salt to taste.

If your steaks are being held together with a string, remove it now. String is not delicious.

9. Return the steaks to the pan, spoon the sauce over them, and gently warm through.

10. Place a steak in the center of each of two plates and spoon sauce over them. Serve.

11

I Am an Animal

A few months after Nora's birth, I learn of a new position opening up at a studio I've done some work for. The people in the department seem like good people, and the work seems challenging and fun. I make a few phone calls, throw my name in the hat, and—after a rather exhaustive interview process during which I apparently didn't sound like an ass nearly as much as I thought I did—I get the job. I'm now present in those meetings that used to decide the fate of my day. Having been on the other side of the equation, I resolve to do it better. I want to be the client I wish I'd had. I want to do the best work I can in the best way I know how.

Hard as it may be to believe, I'm now the weird guy at the new office. I skip the pasta salad at lunch meetings because I don't eat wheat. I decline the cupcakes at company birthday parties because

I don't eat refined sugar. But I put heavy cream in my coffee, and I make my own butter. I can speak knowledgeably about the best way to strip taste buds off a beef tongue and trim fat from a heart without shredding the ventricle wall.

At the same time, I feel fantastic. My energy level is insane. I don't get hypoglycemic and grumbly when I miss a meal anymore because my metabolism isn't anticipating a periodic sugar/starch boost. I run barefoot in the mornings and whenever the mood strikes me. I also walk more than anyone I know.

I've had this beef in my freezer for a little over two years now. It hasn't gone bad, and God and the power company willing, it never will. When meat freezes, ice crystals form inside the muscle cells. If meat is frozen slowly, those ice crystals become huge and shred the cell membranes, ruining the steak once it's defrosted. If meat is frozen quickly, the ice crystals are tiny.

Meat frozen at home takes forever to freeze. My steer was frozen in a matter of seconds. As long as I never let it thaw and re-freeze, it will functionally last forever.

Freezer burn is the other main concern for meat stored for a long time. It's usually a result of poorly wrapped food—if there's air in the packaging, water at the surface of the food can sublimate from solid to gas, dehydrating the meat and causing tissue damage. My packages all remain tightly wrapped, and my freezer dial is set to Arctic Midnight (another cool band name, by the way—or perhaps a scintillating color option for a new Buick). Knock on wood, but I haven't had any problem with freezer burn, either.

I cook beef once a week or so. Not as much as I could, but I'm constantly trying to push myself harder, to do more with each beef cut. To use each steak and roast and organ in a way I haven't before. If I'm going to cook beef, I'm going to do it right.

In a week, the guys and I will attempt to summit Mount Whitney again. Like last time, I will be making jerky out of top round for protein on the mountain. Unlike last time, I will be actually smoking the meat, rather than strapping it to a box fan for twelve hours. This is partly because I simply want to try something different and partly because drying meat with a box fan, I've learned, makes my entire house, yard, garage, attic, or outhouse smell like a meat locker. To wit, if I happen to be in any of those places, it makes me smell like a meat locker. I don't mind it so much, but Summer told me I will be sleeping in the yard if I wind up smelling like a Slim Jim again.

This change in my jerky prep is an easy one—since I'll be smoking the meat instead, I drop the liquid smoke from the marinade I make late on Friday night, resulting in an aromatic witches' brew of only Worcestershire, soy sauce, black pepper, onion, garlic, red pepper, and honey. I add my thinly sliced round steak to the liquid and stash it overnight in my fridge.

The next morning—after closer to eight hours in the marinade rather than the six of the last time I made it—I drain the meat and pick up some hickory wood chunks from the friendly neighborhood grill shop. I'm going to be using a gas grill for precision—I need the heat to be as low as possible because I'm trying to dry the meat, not cook it. As grillheads everywhere know, gas grills are generally less finicky than their charcoal cousins. They have a temperature control dial, for Pete's sake. I set my grill for indirect heat, turn just one of the three burners to low, and prop the lid open slightly with a wadded-up piece of aluminum foil just to make sure the temperature doesn't inadvertently creep upward. I drop a foil packet with a half dozen chunks of hickory on the active burner and hang my jerky strips everywhere but directly above it. The smoke swirls out toward the cracked lid, inculcating the meat with savory goodness, and a strategically placed oven thermometer tells me that the thermal environs are just north of 120 degrees. That's not cooking—that's hanging out in a hot room. Perfect.

Two hours later, instead of twelve—as with my previous attempt—I text Zac to let him know that I have 13.5 ounces of hickory-smoked jerky waiting for him. And then I text him again that no, that is not a weird metaphor for something untoward.

I try the jerky. As before, it's smoky and savory. It's perhaps a bit more brittle than my last endeavor, probably from the added time in the marinade. The smoke is noticeably more pronounced—in a good way. Real wood smoke is a glorious thing. It's not better than my last jerky attempt, just different. It's still a flavor that will pair well with the scent of pines and high country.

While removing the meat, I hear a tiny voice. "Daddy, are you cooking?"

I glance down. Declan's wandered out to the backyard to see what I'm doing. "Yeah, buddy. I'm making jerky."

"Oh," he says, not really understanding what that is. "Daddy, is the mountain you're going to climb the tallest in the whole world?"

"No," I answer. "It's pretty tall, but not that tall."

"Oh," he says again. "What's up there? Is it just, like, you're in the sky and stuff?"

I sit on the ground beside him. "Well, there's a book up there. And when you get there, you write your name in the book as proof that you made it all the way to the top."

"Can I see it?" he asks.

"Well, no. It's on top of the mountain," I explain. "You have to go up there to see it."

"Oh," he says, a bit crestfallen.

"Tell you what . . . when you're bigger, you can come with me. Would you like that?"

He brightens. "Yeah." He thinks a minute. "If I climbed the mountain, would I have to carry my tent and sleeping bag and stuff?"

"Yes, you would. That's part of the deal."

He considers, then nods. "That's okay. I can build a robot to do that for me."

I laugh. "Perfect. I can't wait to see it."

He runs off, and I return to mountain prep. Jerky is my lean protein source for the trip, but I also need a source of good old saturated fat. Fat is one hell of an energy source and doesn't cause blood sugar fluctuations like sugary granola or glucose gels—the very materials that powered my first attempt up the Old Man. Sausage would be an ideal source of both protein and fat, but my grass-fed beef isn't ideal sausage stuff. To supplement my jerky, I'm adding organic, hormone-free cured salami to my pack. No need for refrigeration—and a decent source of protein in and of itself. Other than that, I'm taking some toasted sweet-potato chips that I made for a nearly weightless carbohydrate and some single-serving packages of honey and almond butter, just in case I need them for quick energy. Zac, the logistical genius of our previous Whitney ascent, will provide a hot meal for each night on the hill. He's made the same dietary changes that I have, so he'll put together something amenable to our new habits.

We're going up the Mountaineer's Route again. Same trip, same crew (minus Natalie, who has to sit this one out due to a knee injury), but hopefully a very different result. I haven't trained as much, but I'm in much better shape. We're leaner; I've dropped fifteen pounds and now perform random physical challenges for giggles. (Zac has dropped ten pounds or so but has always been military-fit.) We're keener; I know more about mountaineering than I did previously and have considerably more backcountry skill than I did the first time out. And we know what kept us off the summit the first time—weather; bad planning; and delicious, delicious breakfast foods. We're determined to not let it happen again.

The morning I'm to leave, Declan runs up to me with a sheet of paper. On it, he's drawn a large humanoid figure composed primarily of squares. "This is the robot I'm going to make when I climb the mountain," he explains.

"Perfect. He looks very tough."

"He is," Dec explains matter-of-factly. "He can carry anything."

I kiss Dec on the head, then do likewise with Nora. My daughter's getting so big already, the line between baby and little girl already blurring. Her blond hair is starting to curl up in back, though her eyes are as blue as the day she was born. "See you soon, honey." Silently, she waves bye-bye.

I turn to Summer. "I'll miss you."

"I know," she says with a sparkle in her eye. "See you when you get back."

By the time the guys and I are breathing the pine-scented air at Whitney Portal, a sense of adventure is almost palpable. The scene is familiar from our last attempt, here in this place where the road ends and the trail begins. Granite cliffs and pine trees tower hundreds of feet above us. For now, we have the small, rustic backpacker's campground all to ourselves. It feels like a different world from the landscape I inhabit at sea level. Grander. More epic—a place plucked straight from the tale America tells of itself.

We can't wait to get moving. But that's for tomorrow. Today, we should relax, take stock of our gear, and try to move slowly. We've just driven from sea level to elevation 8,500 feet—it's easy to get winded. But fairly typical for me now, I am a ball of energy. I try to rest, but I keep trying to rest *aggressively*, as if that were possible. Finally, I give up and decide to put that excess energy to use. I prep my pack, disassemble it, and prep it again. I manage to get its weight down to just over thirty-three pounds, which is good for me. I don't want to carry anything I don't need, and I don't need much. I do, however, sacrifice precious ounces for my beat-up Vibram FiveFingers—"shoes" I picked up to protect my feet while running essentially barefoot. They're more like minimalist foot gloves. Hard rubber, very thin, and precisely foot-shaped. Like a Batman suit for feet. They don't weigh much, and they could come in handy at elevation.

Tomorrow, we will drink from streams and eat sausage off of dirty knives, but tonight we feast. I brought rib eyes. I season them simply with kosher salt—which I brought this time, lesson learned—then place the steaks on a grate over our small campfire. The scent of seared meat wafts through the mountain air as the sun slips beneath the horizon.

At 8,500 feet, beneath a canopy of stars and towering pines, this rib eye is the centerpiece of our ascent-team reunion. The guys and I banter about the miscellanea of our lives, filling one another in on the two years of trials and triumphs between our last ascent and this one. The moves, the kids, our injuries and recoveries. Finally, after we clean up, we nurse some beers and try to decide just how early we're going to set out in the morning. The verdict, informed by the lessons of last time: as early as we can.

As the night winds down, Zac and Rich wander off to stash a few things in the car. Uriah and I hang back to watch the fire slowly die. Over by the tents, I hear my dog, Basil, rummaging through some grocery bags, looking for scraps. "Dammit, Basil."

Then I realize: Basil is at home.

I flip on my headlamp and swivel it to our tents. I see a huge black head, whuffing through an empty paper grocery bag that must smell ever so faintly of rib eyes or almond butter. It's an adult black bear, standing maybe thirty feet away. Bears must like steak, too.

The huge black head turns to look at me, green eyes glinting in the darkness.

I leap to my feet. "Uriah!"

"Yeah?" He is staring down at the fire.

"Bear."

"Bullshit."

"No. He has a grocery bag."

Uriah leaps to his feet and flicks on his headlamp as well.

"Wow," he understates.

"What do we do?"

"Nothing. It's his now."

"Not about the grocery bag. About not dying."

"Oh. Right."

"Do we hold still? Make some noise? Play dead?"

"I vote noise."

In unison, we both shout at the top of our lungs. The bear starts at the sudden ruckus, then throws the grocery bag up in the air like a beagle caught with a slipper. He catches it and races off across a nearby creek into the woods.

Uriah and I immediately sprint to the site the bear left behind, expecting campsite carnage. Thankfully, my pack is untouched. I'm pretty diligent about not leaving anything with any scent at all in my bag. Uriah's pack is also untouched. We seem to be good.

Then, I notice some litter. A single powder electrolyte-drink pack, torn in half, lying about four feet from our gear site.

We don't litter.

I pick it up. "Uriah . . ."

He looks over at me. Then asks, "Where's Rich's pack?" A moment later we find it. It's wet and sticky and absolutely covered in sugar and bear spit and generalized biotic slime. The bear must have investigated it after he ate the dry drink mix. However, this is not Rich's first rodeo, and he doesn't keep food in his pack. Thankfully, it's otherwise undamaged.

Just as Uriah and I are examining the pack, two big green eyes blink in the darkness about twenty feet away.

I grab Uriah's arm and point. Both of us freeze, standing over Rich's sticky, nasty pack.

The bear begins to walk toward us.

"Noise now," I suggest.

"Yes."

Both of us train our headlamps on the bear's eyes. We throw our hands over our heads. We shout the vilest insults we can think of. I yell stuff about that bear's mother that'd make Don Rickles blush. We roar. We curse. We bang things. We don't hurl anything, because that'd involve taking our eyes off the bear to grab something. At this distance, the bear could charge and be on us in a second or two. We need to convince him that'd be a bad idea. Thankfully, after an impossibly long moment, we succeed. The bear lopes off into the woods.

A few minutes later, Zac and Rich return. They don't believe our story until they see Rich's pack, which presents a new problem.

Though mercifully undamaged, the pack is unusable. It has to be cleaned and dried for tomorrow's ascent. That rules out a bear box—the large, steel boxes the campsite provides for overnight food storage—where it wouldn't be able to dry. It also rules out our cars, which the bear could easily break into.

Our plan: We wash the pack in the creek, run a bear line between two trees, and hang the pack to dry overnight. In other words, we wash the pack in the creek that we *just saw the bear retreat across*, thus taunting him with it, and hang the known bear target near our tents. Then lie down and go to sleep.

Still, Operation Bear Bait is the best plan we have. Rich empties his pack and washes it thoroughly in the stream, while I cover him at high volume with some of my best low-rent, midnight-set-at-the-Ha-Ha-Hole insult comic material. Uriah, possessing actual practical skills, runs the bear line between two trees. Finally, we hang Rich's pack to dry.

Before turning in, I patrol our campsite, sweeping the ground with my headlamp. I want to make sure there's absolutely no food detritus on the ground that could lure our large nocturnal friend back. Frankly, I can't say I blame him for nosing around here—this campground must be the biggest single source of calories he has available. However, those calories could cost him his life. Bears that become accustomed to eating human food can become more aggressive around people, causing a public health risk. Bears in that situation are usually shot. It's another example of an ancient impulse in conflict with a modern world. Bears are supposed to crave sweet things. So are we. Once it led both bears and humans to berries. Now, this sweet-seeking instinct leads humans to too much candy, and bears to Kool-Aid packs and a bullet. Unlike bears, we humans can become aware of these urges and channel them to healthier outcomes. Though all too often, we don't.

One thing is certain: If that bear charged, I was absolutely, positively going to beat the hell out of it for the few short seconds before my highly probable death. The adrenaline surging through my veins demanded it with a deeply primal urgency. My demise would not have been pretty, or perhaps even especially meaning-ful, but I would have died brave. For those brief seconds, I was a warrior. I felt alive. I'm not encouraging anyone to pick fights with black bears, but it's heartening to know that the instincts and bio-logical responses our species developed for humans One Step Back are still there and still ready for action.

The encounter was a reminder that out here, I'm not necessar-ily at the top of the food chain anymore. I bought my steer because I felt that the death of one animal to feed another—namely, me—was too important to take for granted. Now, I'm potentially on the other side of that equation. To some extent, the tables have turned, and nature plays for keeps.

The next morning, we start our ascent. We head up the main Mount Whitney trail before veering off to follow the north fork of Lone Pine Creek. The trail is narrow here, slipping along and across and through the creek while gaining steadily in elevation. Overhead, willows lean over to offer shade, their roots trying to claw the path back to wilderness. In my opinion, this part of the Whitney ascent is the hardest. The packs are still unfamiliar burdens on our backs, and our bodies still haven't quite acclimatized to the elevation. I focus on putting one foot in front of the other. Next step. Next breath. We rest every minute or so. Today is an easy day—we're only climbing about two thousand vertical feet—but right now it doesn't feel especially easy.

Midmorning, we take our first real break in front of a waterfall just below the Ebersbacher Ledges. I look up at the cliffs high above, excited for the views I know they offer of the valley far below us. I nosh on some jerky. A ranger on his way back down squats in the shade next to us and fills us in on conditions higher up. No snow this time, which is exactly what we've been hoping. That's one of the hurdles from our last attempt eliminated.

I offer the ranger some jerky. He accepts. Up here, we have only the supplies we can carry, the skills of our group, and the kindness of strangers. A little more jerky in the first category helps make up any deficits in the latter two. I brought enough to share freely, but hopefully not enough to become a burden again.

When it's time to move, we start the scramble up to the beginning of the ledges. This is when it hits home: I am in far better shape than I was on our previous attempt. This scramble was awkward and clumsy then. Now it's easy. Even fun.

We pass through the ledges. There's a several-hundred-foot plunge to certain death a few feet away, but it's easily avoided— notably, by not falling off. We keep putting one foot in front of the other, slowly and surely making our way up the cliff face. At this point we have one job: walking. And we're pretty good at it.

An hour or so past the ledges, we reach our next campsite at Lower Boy Scout Lake. We're camping here at elevation 10,500 feet to acclimatize as much as possible to our elevation before exploring the high peaks farther up the range. We also don't want to miss the forest for the trees, literally. It's beautiful here, and we want to take our time.

We pitch our tents, refill our depleted water supplies from the stream, and then—sit. There's nothing more to do and, without the artificial time pressures of a day in the city, no reason to hurry. I eat a small lunch of sausage and sweet-potato chips and watch dragonflies court above the waters of the lake. There is no phone to check—I purposely left it behind. No e-mails to answer. No appointments to keep. Right now, my job is to let my body adjust to the lower oxygen level in the air and let my muscles recover from the climb in anticipation of the next one. I can't rush that process. I have to wait for it to happen in its own time. And unlike last night, now that the adventure has begun, I'm able to let that process happen.

By late afternoon, we're rested. And we're ready for fun. I ditch my boots in favor of my now well-used and much-loved Five-Fingers. They aren't barefoot, but they're about as minimalist as one can get.

The four of us head out for no particular destination, scrambling over fields of talus as the rocks gradually grow from table-sized to car-sized to house-sized. Without heavy boots, I feel like a gazelle. Atop a boulder, with the choice of a long scramble back down its face and up another boulder, I simply leap across the small gap between them. It's utterly exhilarating. It may be dangerous, though I wouldn't say overly so. But then again, what isn't dangerous? Without distraction, I focus on the next move. Look. Prepare. Jump.

Zac and I vault from boulder to boulder, carefully lining up our trajectories. Two years ago, I would never have done this. On our previous Whitney ascent, I trudged. I had heavy boots and a heavier pack, and I moved with purpose. This time, after two years of eating differently and starting to think differently, I carry as little as possible and move ecstatically. I'm not thinking about where I need to reach, I'm thinking about where I want to go.

Finally, we reach a large expanse of rock on a cliff overlooking the valley seven thousand feet below us. The four of us take a seat and watch the shadows of the High Sierras spread slowly toward the horizon. I breathe deep. The air is cold and clean.

The next morning we rise with the sun. Nobody planned it—hell, none of us have alarm clocks. But we pop up like roosters at the crack of dawn. This is especially unusual, because ordinarily I'd rather volunteer for a Justin Bieber tramp stamp than wake up before nine. My philosophy for a good chunk of my life was that no one should be conscious at sunrise for any reason. Yet here I am.

For breakfast, I eat five slices of my jerky. Here on the mountain, I am once again intensely aware of how much food I have left. There is no grocery store at elevation. There is no other way to replenish lost calories unless I fashion a spear and hunt marmots or something. In a way, it's refreshing. I just have to worry about this food, this gear, these people. They're what's important. Everything else falls away or is literally left behind.

We begin to hike. Two hours later, even trees fall away, leaving us in a world of granite and sky. We hike ever upward as the mountains transform from distant scenic vistas to sheer stone walls. The day passes too quickly in camaraderie and stupid jokes and gazing awestruck at the vistas around us. After several hours hiking upward, we build our high camp, the last we will make on the mountain. There, the guys and I chat about everything and nothing for a couple of hours until the sun goes down. Then, as a now familiar nighttime silence creeps across the high peaks, we turn in.

The next morning, we wake just as the sun begins to crest over the granite cliffs. I'm not sure how much sleep I'm getting, but it's a lot. Ten hours, maybe? All I know is that I sleep when it's dark and rise when it isn't. I can't remember the last time I got this much sleep at sea level. But here at elevation, I can't remember the last time I yawned. I don't feel tired in the slightest. Not groggy, fuzzy, or weary. Simply calm and refreshed—a deep rejuvenation I can feel in my bones. I feel like a million bucks.

Today is Mount Whitney summit. Last time, we enjoyed a long, heavy breakfast filled with carbs and sugar and chatted well into the morning. Today, we are four hard men eating dried meat in the morning twilight. The conviviality is still there, but so is a grim determination that we will summit today. We must summit today. What happened last time will not happen again. For breakfast, I eat two-thirds of my daily food allotment in one sitting and pack my jerky in my daypack. I'm taking my steer to the top.

I'm in fine form for our hike to Iceberg Lake at 12,800 feet. This place is a scene that should be airbrushed onto the side of a van. The lake is circular and an impossible iridescent blue. Above is Mount Whitney itself, shooting straight up two thousand feet, with the rest of the range slouching behind it like backup singers—a wall of gray peaks, each higher than the last. On the other side of the lake are Mounts Russell and Carillon, two other California fourteeners (i.e., peaks higher than fourteen thousand feet). I am a man in the land of giants.

We head for the couloir we'll be following to the top, a fifteen-hundred-foot scramble up a forty-five-degree incline. Last time, this is where we turned back. This time is wholly different. The snow from our last ascent is absent now, revealing enormous boulders and yards of scree. The boulders are spaced in such a way that one can avoid the scree if one wants to, and I definitely want to. I clamber over the boulders, inch across cracks, and lever up onto ledges and higher paths to avoid trudging through the gravel. It's like playing a long game of The Floor Is Lava—only instead of lava, the floor is covered with barbed, pea-sized caltrops sprinkled a dozen feet deep.

Fifteen hundred feet above Iceberg Lake, we find what is called "the Notch." Now, the hiking is done, and the climbing begins. We stare up at five hundred vertical feet of bouldering. Ledge after ledge, handhold after handhold, straight up.

This is where it really becomes apparent that we're at the top of the country. We're above everything. In all directions but one, granite cliffs fall away to glacier-carved lakes far below.

"Careful here," Rich advises. "That's a twenty-five-hundred-foot drop."

"Copy that," I say. "That's a long way down."

We turn away from the view and face the wall. It's the only thing left at eye level that isn't sky, Zac, Rich, or Uriah. We begin to climb. No particular maneuver is especially difficult. We put our hands on a waist-level ledge and mantle up onto it. Stand on the foot or two of horizontal space available, look around, and do it again. Easy.

After climbing onto a dozen or so ledges, we're four stories above the Notch. A fall would likely mean death—a bouncing, skidding death, perhaps, but still death. And that assumes we'd stop before we hit the 2,500-foot drop.

As at the Ebersbacher Ledges, death is one wrong step away. The trick is to just not take that step. It's good to recognize this, but bad to dwell on it. Death is always a step away, really. The trick is to focus on the next move, the next mantle up, the next ledge. I could stare into the abyss, but then I wouldn't be climbing. I'd be focusing on what could—maybe—be, instead of what definitely is. And what is definitely, incontrovertibly, happening is that I'm perched on the side of a cliff in a heartbreakingly gorgeous mountain range on a beautiful day, surrounded by dear friends. I don't want to get lost in the miasma of potential futures—I'd miss all this. I'd miss now. Next step. Next ledge.

"This is amazing," Uriah opines, pausing to admire the view.

Zac nods. "Yeah. It really is." He gestures to the vista around us. "It almost seems like a painting."

I laugh, giddy. "I'm glad we did this again. I couldn't leave it like last time."

Nods all around. A moment of silence.

Then, Uriah speaks. "Ready?"

Rich nods. "Let's do it."

The four of us turn to look at the wall ahead of us. Here, so close to the top, we fan out, each of us picking our own line. Rich heads toward some fat boulders below a ledge and an uncertain ascent from there. Zac slips to the other side of the wall toward a notch at what he believes is the top. Uriah and I clamber straight up toward a stone balcony that looks like the descent point for groups headed back down from above.

We all clamber over the top of the ledge at about the same time. We step away from the cliff and walk in the only direction available to us: up. Across a broad landscape of granite boulders, toward a rough stone hut in the distance. Summit.

We did it.

We stand on the highest point in the continental United States and look down on the world. Everything we've ever known and everywhere we've ever been is below us now. Though my view is enormous, up here, my world is much smaller. I have only what I need in the moment.

Last time I attempted Mount Whitney, I enjoyed myself immensely even though I didn't summit. Then, I wished that my life could always be like this: simpler. Manageable—but exhilarating. Now, on top of the world, I recognize that life is always like this. Beneath the veneer of commerce and productivity and constant competition, there are the fundamental truths of what one really needs. What's really important. Family. Friends. Health. Appreciation of the small moments that build our lives the way trees build a forest. There is no fundamental difference between my time on the mountain and my time off it.

To "wish it could always be like this" is a nonsensical statement. *It always is like this.* The world is a magical place, abundant and full of opportunities for happiness. Moments of joy abound in the simplest of things and the smallest of moments. I just forget, sometimes. I get distracted.

I walk over to the registry book in front of the emergency hut at the top of America. I sign my name and dedicate my trip to my wife, Summer, my son, Declan, and my daughter, Nora.

Silently, I resolve to focus on what matters. And to hell with the rest of it.

Steak Frites

Time: About 90 minutes

Serves 4

Coming down from the mountain, I wanted nothing more than a big steak—and a little bit of comfort. Steak frites is both.

The traditional cut for this bistro dish is the hanger steak. It's tender and wildly flavorful, perfect for standing up to rich frites and a gorgeous pan sauce. The frites—French for "French fries"—are fried twice in duck fat. These will ruin your taste for all other fries.

1 (1- to 1½-pound) hanger steak

1 russet potato

2 cups rendered duck fat (many fine supermarkets carry it in their deli sections)

4 tablespoons unsalted butter

Sea salt and freshly ground black pepper

2 shallots, thinly sliced

1 cup red wine (Cabernet Sauvignon and Merlot are good choices)

1. Trim your hanger steak and set aside. The steak has a lot of connective tissue that has to go away. First, trim the fat band of elastin that runs down the center (if your butcher hasn't already

done so), to separate the cut into two pieces that look something like tenderloins. Then, carefully trim the silverskin off the outside of the cut as necessary.

2. Slice the potato into spears about ⅜ inch thick using either a mandoline or mad knife skills. Soak the cut potato in cold water until you're ready to cook. The water bath washes starch off the surface of the spuds, keeping them from browning too quickly. You are frying them twice, after all.

3. Melt the duck fat in a large skillet and heat it to 325°F on a deep-fry thermometer.

4. As the fat comes to temp, remove the potatoes from the water and pat them dry to remove any excess moisture. Don't skip this step! If the fries are wet when they hit the hot oil, the water will evaporate instantly, throwing oil everywhere: on your counter, on you, and possibly onto the flames of your burner, starting a fire. Dry those fries.

5. Working in batches so as not to overcrowd the pan, fry the potato spears until they just begin to color. (The point of this first fry is to cook the fries through—not to crisp them. The fries should be soft and slightly blond when you pull them from the heat.) Set aside on a plate or baking sheet lined with paper towels.

6. Slide the skillet to a back burner, but don't empty it—you'll be using it again shortly.

7. In a new skillet, melt 2 tablespoons of the butter over medium-high heat. Season the meat with salt and pepper, then gently lay it in the pan. Sear the first side of the meat for about 2 minutes, until the surface is appropriately brown. Flip and cook for an additional 2 minutes, or until the internal temperature reaches 125 to 130°F. (Do *not* overcook. Check the internal temp

with an instant-read probe thermometer.) Remove the meat and set aside to rest, uncovered, on a cutting board.

8. Working quickly, add the shallots to the meat pan and cook until crisp—1 minute at most. Add the wine to deglaze, scraping up the browned bits stuck to the bottom of the pan. When the sauce has reduced by about two-thirds, after 3 to 5 minutes, remove from the heat and whisk in the remaining butter.

9. At the same time, reheat the duck fat to 375°F. When the duck fat is at temp, fry the frites a second time, just until they reach the appropriate level of golden brown and crisp. The frites are already cooked through; this is just to make them pretty and delicious. Remove them to a fresh plate or baking sheet lined with paper towels and sprinkle them with salt.

10. Now, slice the steak very thinly against the grain. Fan across a plate and pile a stack of frites alongside. Drizzle a stripe of the pan sauce across the meat.

11. Enjoy. Pair it with a big pale ale and a shower.

12

Bones

OFF THE MOUNTAIN. ALL GOOD. *Send.*

I sit in my car at Whitney Portal, thumbs poised over the virtual keyboard of my phone. Slowly, I crack a grin.

MADE SUMMIT. CHASED OFF A BEAR. SEE YOU SOON. *Send.*

A second later, my phone chirps and displays a message: WHAT?!

I chuckle and toss the phone into my glove box. I don't touch it for several days.

Back at home, I put my feet up on the coffee table. Unlike last time, I'm not sore in the slightest. But I don't smell any better. Odors rustic and unassuming in the high wild places acquire a distinct and noteworthy pungency in a suburban living room. My wife is a woman of endless patience.

"I'm so glad you're home. . . . We missed you," she says.

I smile, remembering her parting words. "Yeah, likewise. I'd like to take you and the kids to the mountain sometime. You'd love it."

"Maybe," she replies, before changing subjects. "So, I was thinking about what we talked about."

Summer cranes her neck to look out the window to our kids, playing in the backyard. Then back to me. "And?"

As a result of my new job, my schedule has become more manageable and I'm less subject to the whims of remote meetings and anonymous edicts. Now, however, Summer and I are considering a more dramatic change. "I think I want to do it," she says.

"It's completely your call," I say. "It'll present some challenges. But if you want to try it, I'm on board."

She nods, considering. "We'll have to stick to a budget."

"Sure. I'm not a bad cook now. I think I can keep us fed."

"We could grow more vegetables, if you want."

"Makes sense."

We both sit for a moment, silent. "It's a big change," Summer says.

"Yeah," I say. "If we do it, I just don't want you to regret it. To feel like you got left behind in your career, or whatever. I'm fine with anything you decide." I pause a beat. "It's your job. Only leave if you want to. I don't want you to feel like you missed out."

She smiles a little. "I appreciate that."

Just then, the door bursts open and Declan leaps into the room. "I need string!" he shouts, before disappearing back down the hallway to his room. In his wake, moving as fast as she can toddle, is Nora. She's nearly a year old now, and walking is a very new, very exciting experience for her. She beams at us as she passes.

Summer laughs and turns back to me. "I don't think I'll miss out."

❦

Together, Summer and I resolve to make our lives more livable. After she leaves her job, the kids come out of day care and stay home with her. This arrangement presents its own challenges, but we work through them. We're losing her income, but we're also losing the expense of two kids in day care. And in this case, less is more.

We're gaining immeasurably in time with the wee ones. Summer is with them both all day, and I'm around as much as I can be. My new position, in addition to being more family-friendly in general, is a chance to start fresh—a moment where everything is mutable, and we can step back and decide which routines we really want to keep and which we can let fall away.

Back at sea level, I do my best to retain the lessons I've been learning for the past few years that suddenly became abundantly clear on the mountain. The aspects of life that are actually important aren't necessarily the ones cultivated by the workaday experience of career and commute and grind and striving to get through another day. Even that phrasing—*to get through another day*—is asinine. Who wants to *get through* another day? Who wants to trudge another twenty-four hours toward decrepitude and the grave without taking a little time to drink in the glory and wonder of another few hours on planet Earth?

I want to go play for a while.

"Dec," I say one morning as he's coloring in his room. "Let's go for a hike." Nora is with Summer, out running errands.

"Can we find a waterfall?" he asks. He really likes waterfalls.

"Absolutely." Basil lopes in and sees her leash in my hand. She dances back and forth excitedly. I grab some water and a few supplies, and the three of us set out.

I've heard of a stream in the Santa Monica Mountains on the edge of town that eventually cascades off a cliff of volcanic rock. And I almost know how to get to it. We spend the better part of an afternoon—hell, the best part—wandering through the mountains in search of it. Eventually we find that waterfall and stop to rest beside a pool at its base.

I reach into my pack. "Dec, would you like a piece of jerky?"

"What is it?" he asks. Despite seeing me make it, he's never actually had it before.

"It's outdoor food." I reach into the bag and offer him a tiny piece. And one for Basil as well.

Declan slips it into his mouth. "It's chewy," he notes. "But I like it."

"Me, too." Together the three of us sit in the fine mist erupting from the base of the waterfall and watch the droplets glitter like jewels in the afternoon sun.

As months roll on, I reclaim my commute. Rather than creeping in lockstep ten feet at a time along a concrete ribbon, I get loose. Leave early. Grab a book on tape and a back road and point my automobile vaguely workward, but see where the path less taken takes me. I make it a goal to discover something new on each trip between home and the office. A just opened Himalayan restaurant. A store that specializes only in fly-fishing. An ancient velodrome and a park with a cricket pitch where teams from the far reaches of the commonwealth battle ferociously according to rules I find incomprehensible. But I want to learn. Los Angeles is a varied and glorious place if one has the temerity to explore.

I mean, there's a Thai joint staffed with Elvis impersonators, for Pete's sake. Our morgue has a gift shop. Come on.

On the weekends, we eschew cars altogether. Odds are that a Saturday without a car ride is a pretty darn lovely Saturday. Instead, we load up my enormous longtail cargo bike, pile the kids on the back, and turn mundane errands into adventures. On a bike, a trip to the grocery store becomes a story out of myth—The Saga of the Broken Streetlight. The Bicyclist Who Brought Home Ice Cream in August. The Stone Clan Versus the Market of Doom. And like myths, they turn our days into manageable tribulations—and a chance to grow stronger together in their negotiation. Bereft of a tank full of burning dinosaur bones, bikes trawl the world at a more human pace. In the world, rather than barreling, isolated, through it. Much as it must have been done before cars, One Step Back.

The beef in our backyard has forced us to slow down a little. And in doing so, I've had a chance to see what I'd been missing. I'm not completely able to disengage from my particular productivity compulsions, but I'm getting better. Breathing deeper. And I like it.

I try to take an hour a day to do absolutely nothing.

Finally, I make a fresh appointment with my doctor. It's been a few years since my last one, and without putting my health in order, every other change is moot. When my blood work comes back, my fasting blood glucose level is completely normal. For now, at least, inclination toward diabetes has receded. That isn't to say it won't ever come back. But for today, at least, all is well. And that's enough.

When the Machine starts to tug at my mental sleeves, I try to remember that I am in all likelihood becoming stressed out over nothing, really. I'm not going to starve. I'm not going to die. There are no bears here. I am in absolutely no existential danger whatsoever. The problems I'm facing are not by any stretch of the imagination actual dangers. In fact, by historical standards, Americans live in a world of almost unfathomable abundance. So I tell myself to shut the hell up and breathe. An inhalation. An exhalation. A realization that odds are very good that everything's going to be just fine. And then, often as not, I head into the kitchen.

It is on one of those days that I find myself standing at my counter, staring at a four-pound package wrapped in white butcher paper. The label indicates "knuckle bones."

My first thought: Hey, cows have knuckles! Something I did not know.

Second thought: What can I do with it?

I amble over to my cookbooks. My collection has grown from a stack to a shelf to an entire section of a bookcase, heavy with enormous tomes of tiny text. Knuckle bones, it seems, are primarily used in stock. I haven't yet made a stand-alone stock in this project, though I did use these bones to make that pretty killer pho. I have no idea why stock has evaded me, but it's time to rectify that situation.

Stock should be the easiest thing in the world. It used to be a much more common preparation in home kitchens than it is now. It is a process born of frugality; when you're trying to make the most of every molecule of food from a given animal, stock is an excellent way to wring some utility from a skeleton and sinew and bits otherwise inedible. A person boils some bones. Perhaps a few veggies. Then leaves time and chemistry to do the work.

Generally speaking, there are a couple of ways to approach stock—white and brown. For white stocks, you blanch the bones, boiling them in water to remove impurities, and then discard the water of the initial boil. For brown stocks you instead roast the bones, adding a layer of toasty flavors from the Maillard reaction to the finished product and coagulating the proteins so they don't cloud the final result.

After consulting with *Nourishing Traditions*, the *Larousse Gastronomique*, the Internet, the CIA (the Culinary Institute of America, not the spy agency), and a half dozen other cookbooks great and small, I decide on a brown stock. I enjoy those Maillard flavors. I toss some bones, both knuckle and marrow, into a roasting pan with a mirepoix and some garlic and shove them into a hot oven to roast.

Familiar now with the rhythms of the kitchen, I take a seat just outside the door with a book. Faced with a time frame too long to loiter but too short to shoo away, I take a position where I can keep an eye on the application without obsessing. If something goes wrong, I'll see it. Or smell it. It'll be fine.

Basil, not as content to pass the time with a book, walks over to me and nuzzles my hand, whining in the way she does when she's hungry. I know this behavior—it will not end until Basil puts something in her stomach, be it kibble or banana or stick of butter or nearly anything else that will hold still long enough for her to wolf down. Knowing this, I amble over to the fridge and pull out a raw chicken quarter, drop it into her bowl, and place it in the backyard. She grabs the poultry in her jaws, settles down, and gets to work as I return to my book.

A half hour later, I stash the bones and veggies in my trusty twelve-quart stockpot. I splash some water into the hot roasting pan and scrape to deglaze it, adding the resultant liquid to the stockpot as well. There's gold in that water—the bits stuck at the bottom of the pan, when scraped and dissolved into the liquid, are glorious stuff—and if I omitted them, my stock would be much the poorer for it.

I stab a finger into my phone and Mike Doughty's "I Hear the Bells" pours out of speakers hanging on the wall of my kitchen as I grab my knife. I chop some parsley and add it to the pot. A little fresh thyme. Bay leaves. Some whole peppercorns. I head out into my backyard for a fresh lemon. Dear God, it's beautiful out today.

Back inside, I juice the lemon into the pot and cover the bones with cold water, bring the pot to a boil, knock the heat back to something in the neighborhood of low, and let the pot simmer, bubbling once every second or so.

And that's it. There's no time limit. I need to simmer this for as long as I can stand to. In this case, I'll probably let it bubble along on the back of my stove for six hours or so. I can't ignore it, though. I'll swing by every fifteen minutes or so with the biggest, flattest spoon in the house to skim off the scum that rises to the surface of the simmering liquid.

Late in the evening, I strain the stock through a fine-meshed strainer lined with cheesecloth and stash the pot in a sink filled with ice to cool to room temperature. Finally, I pour the stock into ice cube trays to divide it into easily used portions.

Now I have stock for months.

And I use it. In braises. Sauces. Soups and stews. In almost any preparation that calls for water, I can substitute my homemade beef stock for superior results. It may be the single greatest improvement to my culinary game that I've made as a result of this experiment. Why haven't I done this sooner? Correction: *How* haven't I done this sooner? It couldn't be simpler. Water. Heat. Bones. Time.

And the wherewithal to look closely at the process, concentrate all the good things that go into it, and discard all the crap that would otherwise make it less than wonderful.

I'm trying to perform the same feat of concentration and eradication with life outside the kitchen. This journey started out with some basic questions about the food I eat: How do I make the most out of the very stuff that becomes "me"? But that question has led me to a slightly different one: How do I make the most of what that food actually becomes—how do I make the most out of the life this beef enables?

The elements of my life that I'd like to concentrate and enhance aren't novel and aren't complicated. Time spent with family and friends. Pleasant meals and good conversations. Time to appreciate beauty, wherever I happen to find it—interspersed with bursts of unstructured, adrenaline-fueled mayhem and mad fits of laughter. These don't fit especially well with the Machine, because the Machine runs on a ticking clock and a fear of the future. It runs on the anxiety that, somehow, we aren't doing enough. We aren't preparing adequately for some half-glimpsed future that we're told could turn out to be very, very bad. We aren't ready for what lies ahead, and time is rapidly running out.

That ticking clock, used forever to sell convenience foods and brushless shaving cream and countless time-saving industrial widgets, is largely fiction. There's only one clock that matters.

The white-hot singularity at the core of the Machine is— ultimately—a fear of death. It's the inevitability of journey's end and the threat of a question nobody can honestly answer: What does it mean to make the most of a life? How can you tell that you've spent your time well? There is no metric, no answer key at the back of the book. It's a question that I think everyone has to answer for themselves and hold tight to that answer with both hands. But that's hard.

Through the proxy of this steer, in some tiny way, I've interviewed death. I wanted to make the most of a life that died to support my own. In doing so, I've had to ask what it even means to make the most of a life. And although I haven't yet found a definitive answer to this ultimate question, it's led to other, smaller ones, dealing with how I spend my days and what I hope to gain from them. I've learned, above all, that it's okay to slow down. It's okay to remain taskless for a time. It's okay to not want something—to not have a plan. Sometimes, it's okay to just sit. To inhabit the moment, smile, and let the future be whatever the hell it's going to be. As a result, I'm no longer completely willing to sacrifice the present to an imagined future. I want to live in present tense.

Some years ago, a steer from a small herd in Northern California walked into a nondescript building and, in an instant, lost consciousness, never to regain it. As a direct result, my family gained years of quality meals, lovingly prepared, shared, laughed over, celebrated, and deeply appreciated. We gained better health, new skills, and myriad opportunities to come together as a family and enjoy the simple pleasures of one another's company.

In making the most of this steer's death, I've accidentally made more of my own life. And I'm indescribably grateful for it.

It's a bright summer day. I'm sitting in my backyard, reading a book and smoking a pastrami in my kettle grill. Like people do.

"Daddy . . ." A tiny voice calls out from behind me. I turn, to find my daughter, Nora, standing barefoot holding one of her dolls. Gold ringlets frame her face, just like they sometimes frame Summer's after a long day in the sun.

"What's up, sweetie?"

"Daddy. Can we go on an adventure?"

Yes, my dear. Yes, we can.

Stock

❦

Time: 7 to 8 hours

Makes about 3 quarts

Stock makes every good thing better. It's kitchen alchemy, a simple, borderline-magical way to turn humble ingredients and culinary detritus into something approaching the divine.

This isn't the only way to make stock, but it's a good one.

3 to 4 pounds beef knuckle bones
3 to 4 pounds beef marrow bones (or some combination thereof)
Olive oil
4 carrots, peeled and chopped
4 ribs celery, chopped
1 head garlic, separated into cloves and lightly smashed but unpeeled
2 white or yellow onions, peeled and quartered
½ bunch fresh flat-leaf parsley
4 sprigs fresh thyme
2 bay leaves
¼ teaspoon whole black peppercorns
Juice of 1 lemon

1. Preheat the oven to 400°F.
2. Rub the bones with oil, put on a sheet pan, and roast for 30 minutes.
3. Toss the carrots, celery, garlic, and onion in oil and place on another sheet pan. Roast along with the bones for another 20 to 30 minutes, until the bones are appropriately golden brown and lovely.
4. Transfer the bones and vegetables to a large stockpot in the 12-quart-capacity range. Deglaze the roasting pan with ½ cup water, scraping to dislodge the bits stuck to the bottom, and add this water to the pot as well.
5. Add the parsley, thyme, bay leaves, peppercorns, and lemon juice to the pot, along with enough cold water to cover the bones by several inches. Don't add salt! Stock is not a stand-alone food; it's prefood. You'll salt whatever dish you eventually use it in.
6. Bring to a boil, then lower the heat and simmer for 6 hours. Don't let the liquid remain at a rolling boil or it will result in a cloudy stock. If the water evaporates too quickly, partially cover the pot to slow evaporation. Add water, if necessary, to keep the bones covered.
7. As the liquid simmers, use a wide spoon to skim off any frothy impurities that rise to the top of the stock. Don't stir, or you'll disperse these impurities back into the liquid.
8. Strain the stock through a fine-mesh sieve lined with several layers of cheesecloth, then place the pot in a sink filled with ice to cool to room temperature.
9. Once cooled, stash the stock in the fridge, and remove any fat that rises to the top. Working in batches if necessary, pour into ice cube trays and freeze, then transfer the cubes to a freezer

bag for long-term storage. It'll keep for about six months—longer if stored in an airtight package in a deep freeze. Freezing stock in ice cube trays will allow you to control how much you thaw for use at any given time. Each cube is about 1 tablespoon.

Epilogue

I s that what I think it is?" Summer asks.

"That depends what you think it is." She is referring to a tapering tube of meat about the length of my arm. It's roughly segmented, notches made more pronounced by a butcher's knife.

"It looks like a tail."

"Then, yes. It is what you think it is."

"Gross." She moves toward the door.

"It's just a tail! You ate raw beef heart, for Pete's sake. This is no scarier than short ribs."

"Okay. Call me when you've cooked it."

"I'm gonna braise it in red wine and stock."

"Our stock?"

I nod. "With herbs and celery root."

"Have I had celery root?"

"Maybe. It's like celery. But . . . more so."

Her eyes narrow, considering. Finally, she speaks. "Whatever.

I know it'll be good." She resumes her trajectory out of the kitchen. "Just let me know when dinner's ready."

"I'll call you when the tail is on the table."

The oxtail is the tail of the beef critter. As far as function is concerned, it swishes. It does not move the beast. It does not perform any structural purpose other than swatting the occasional fly. It does have a lot of fat and connective tissue, necessitating a braise. But otherwise, it just hangs at the end of the animal. And swishes.

Similarly, I've reached the tail end of my beef project. My freezer, once full nearly to overflowing with beef and countless promises of adventurous meals, is now filled mostly with water, in case the Big One comes and California slides off into the ocean.

So that's it. It's finished. An entire grass-fed steer provided nutrition and sustenance for my family for years. During that time, my son has grown from a baby to a boy. My daughter was born. My wife left her job to stay home with the kids, and I took a new position as well. I tried to climb the highest mountain in the Lower 48 twice, succeeded once. Got in possibly the best shape of my life. Cooked dishes from England to Vietnam to France to Argentina to Peru to Italy to Germany to the good old United States. Shared those meals with friends and loved ones on holidays and weeknights, quickly and slowly, for the most spectacular and mundane of reasons.

I slice the tail and drop the pieces into my Dutch oven to sear, and the meat hits the enamel with a satisfying hiss. New at the beginning of this project, the pot now looks as if it's been to war. Blackened by licks of flame and the scorches of meals gone wrong. Scratched by metal implements and momentary bouts of stupidity. The project and the meals it's engendered have changed it.

Similarly, I think of how this project has changed me. I once contemplated *terroir* and a life lived at a slower pace. Well, a slower pace is a relative thing. I am, however, considerably calmer. If I, like a grass-fed steer, have come to more perfectly reflect my surroundings, I take some comfort in the changes this project has wrought. Every night, I set aside my phone, kick off my shoes, and get down on the floor with my kids. It's an ongoing process, but I let go of whatever's going on in the wider world and focus on what's in front of me. Kids. Food. My lovely wife. And beautiful weather. Next step, next breath.

This project has also made me consider the cataclysmic change that occurred in the middle of the last century—the heyday of my grandparents' generation. Society as we think of it today, with all its abundance of food and comfort and information and demands, is a relatively recent development. We tend to think of however the world is *right now* as how it's always been—or we romanticize an invented, idealized past that never really existed—but the fact remains that our current moment in history is a blink in the entirety of human experience. A lot of good has come out of the mechanization and innovation of the middle of last century, and I don't mean to denigrate it. But those innovations have come at a high price, in the form of greater fossil fuel dependence and the resulting pollution. But it's very easy to consider how things happen to be right now, the accidents of history and the efforts of people who've come before us, as an eternal normal. It's the default option.

Cooking with this steer has taught me, if nothing else, not to accept the default option. In cooking, in eating, in running, in working, in playing—other options exist and have their own benefits and shortcomings. And in some cases, I've found them preferable to their more recently developed defaults.

The slices of oxtail in my Dutch oven are a deep golden brown. I add sliced shallots, along with diced carrots and celery root. Soon the air is filled with the smell of good things. I add wine and stock to the pot, along with some herbs plucked fresh from my backyard garden. Then I lid the pot and slide it into the oven.

Summer slips back in from the other room, drawn by the scent of my handiwork. She peeks into the oven. "So that's it? The last of the beef?"

"That's it."

"Wow." She thinks. "This is the first time in years we haven't had an ungodly amount of beef in the freezer. It's weird."

"I know."

"I've gotten used to just having it on hand. It's been so convenient."

"It has."

"Huh," she says. Then, acknowledging the end of an era, she nods. "Well. Good job, Stone." She rubs my back briefly, then turns to leave. Over her shoulder, she calls out, "So what's next?"

I smile. "I need to see a man about a buffalo."